Evernote® FOR DUMMIES®

A Wiley Brand

2nd Edition

by David E. Y. Sarna

Evernote® For Dummies® 2nd Edition

Published by: **John Wiley & Sons, Inc.,** 111 River St., Hoboken, NJ 07030-5774, www.wiley.com

Copyright © 2014 by John Wiley & Sons, Inc., Hoboken, New Jersey

Published simultaneously in Canada

For general information on our other products and services, please contact our Customer Care Department within the U.S. at 877-762-2974, outside the U.S. at 317-572-3993, or fax 317-572-4002. For technical support, please visit www.wiley.com/techsupport.

Wiley publishes in a variety of print and electronic formats and by print-on-demand. Some material included with standard print versions of this book may not be included in e-books or in print-on-demand. If this book refers to media such as a CD or DVD that is not included in the version you purchased, you may download this material at http://booksupport.wiley.com. For more information about Wiley products, visit www.wiley.com.

Library of Congress Control Number: 2013956851

ISBN: 978-1-118-85594-2 (pbk); ISBN 978-1-118-85775-5 (ebk); ISBN 978-1-118-85759-5 (ebk)

Manufactured in the United States of America

10 9 8 7 6 5 4 3 2 1

Contents at a Glance

Table of Contents

Introduction

Welcome to *Evernote For Dummies,* 2nd Edition. I asked to write it because Evernote has changed my life. My hope is that Evernote improves your life just as much.

Before I found Evernote, I was a typical messy-desk person and a pack rat. Piles were everywhere. File cabinets were overflowing. When I found something of interest, I printed it and piled it. I never had time to file it. And if I did file it, I could never remember where I'd put it. When I did remember which stack something was in, I'd have to determine how deep I needed to excavate based on the item's presumed age. Then I'd dig in. This system — if you can call it that — worked as badly as you can imagine. I never lost anything because I didn't throw things out. On the other hand, actually retrieving things was frustrating and time-consuming. Getting older didn't help any. Many times, I would initiate an Internet search to locate something I'd already found. My messy surroundings and frequent archaeological excavations made me the butt of jokes at home and in the office.

Then, in January 2010, I saw a review of Evernote, then 2 years old, by my fellow Brandeis alum Walt Mossberg. He described a wondrous "Digital File Cabinet You Can Bring with You Anywhere" in AllThingsD (now at http:// online.wsj.com/news/technology), a highly regarded website devoted to news, analysis, and opinion on technology, the Internet, and media.

Even at that point, Evernote already had 2 million downloads. (It's now registered more than 100 million users.) It was free to try, so try I did. Evernote immediately grabbed me. It was the product I'd been dreaming about. The more I used Evernote, the more addicted I became and the more valuable it became for me.

I was hooked. Goodbye, messy desk. Hello, Evernote, with access to everything everywhere.

About This Book

Evernote For Dummies, 2nd Edition, is a reference book, which means that it isn't meant to be read from front to back. Each chapter is divided into sections, each of which includes self-contained information about a specific task in Evernote.

Just as in Evernote, you don't have to remember anything in this book because you can look up what interests you in the table of contents or index and immediately find what you need to know — and nothing more.

Within this book, you may note that some web addresses break across two lines of text. If you're reading this book in print and want to visit one of these web pages, simply key in the web address exactly as it's noted in the text, pretending that the line break doesn't exist. If you're reading this as an e-book, you've got it easy; just click or tap the web address to be taken directly to the web page.

Foolish Assumptions

If you're not an engineer with an advanced degree in cognitive engineering (there aren't many people like this), you don't need to worry! Here's a reasonably complete list of what's *not* required to use this book:

- ✔ I make no assumptions about your previous knowledge of Evernote.
- ✔ I make only the most basic assumptions about your use of the Internet or any devices that Evernote supports.
- ✔ I don't assume any knowledge of the many products that Evernote works with.

So what *is* required? A supported device, a connection to the Internet, and a desire to clear your clutter and actually find things when you want them. Evernote is a unique product that helps you wherever you are, and it supports almost all devices. I cover Evernote on Windows PCs, Macs, iOS devices, Android devices, Windows Phones, and BlackBerry smartphones and tablets.

Icons Used in This Book

To make your experience with the book easier, I use various icons in the margins of the book to indicate particular points of interest.

Whenever I give you a hint or a tip that makes an aspect of Evernote easier to use, I mark it with this little icon. It's my way of sharing what I've figured out the hard way so that you don't have to.

This icon is a friendly reminder or a marker for something that you want to make sure that you keep in mind.

Ouch! This icon is the equivalent of an exclamation point. Warnings give you important directions to keep you from experiencing any nightmares.

As a reformed geek, I sometimes feel obligated to give you some technical information, although it doesn't really affect how you use Evernote. I mark that stuff with this geeky fellow so that you know it's just background information. You can just ignore me. I won't get offended, and you won't miss out on anything important.

Beyond the Book

I've created a public Evernote notebook, accessible at `https://www.evernote.com/pub/dsarna/davidsarnasevernotefordummiesnotebook`, to keep readers up to date about Evernote and about new tips and tricks that I learn. It's my way of thanking you for purchasing a copy of this book. In addition, you can visit `www.dummies.com/extras/evernote` to find unique bonus material about Evernote.

Where to Go from Here

If you're looking for information on a specific Evernote topic, check the headings in the table of contents or skim the index. By design, this book enables you to get as much (or as little) information as you need at any particular moment. (Need to know how Evernote works with Facebook, for example? See Chapter 10.) If you want to focus on the specific ways that Evernote works with a device, jump right in to Part IV.

Part I

Getting Started with Evernote

In this part . . .

- ✔ Seeing what Evernote can do for you
- ✔ Choosing and creating the account you need
- ✔ Downloading Evernote for the platforms you use
- ✔ Creating your first notebook and notes

Chapter 1

What Can Evernote Do for You?

In This Chapter

▶ Using Evernote no matter where you are

▶ Saving all types of data

▶ Keeping track of your notes

Is Evernote right for you? That depends. Evernote is for the following types of people:

✔ It's for geeks who peck or tap away at their smartphones, tablets, phablets, and other devices for hours a day, often using two devices simultaneously. (I'm guilty as charged.)

✔ It's for road warriors who are vying with John Kerry and Hilary Clinton for the "most traveled" award.

✔ It's for homebodies who want to keep track of their favorite TV shows and recipes.

✔ It's for occasional users who are satisfied with one or two devices.

✔ It's for every device owner who needs to remember and find things.

In short, Evernote is for nearly everyone, including you. You can use it in your job and your personal life, on mobile devices and on desktop or laptop computers anywhere you have Internet access. Best of all, it's easy to use.

As an Evernote user, you'll be far from alone. At this writing, Evernote has more than 80 million users around the world (20 percent in the United States) and is adding tens of thousands of new users each day. Evernote reports that 25 percent of users use it on a single device, 46 percent on two devices, 18 percent on three, 7 percent on four, and 4 percent on five or more (just imagine).

Using Evernote Everywhere

I've been playing with computers since I was growing up with Abraham Lincoln, more or less (1964, to be more exact), and I tend to think I've seen it all. Remarkably, Evernote is the first piece of software I've ever seen, much less used, that pulls off a credible balance among contradictory attributes:

✔ It runs nearly the same way on very different devices, each of which has its own user interface and natural ways of working.

✔ It manages to look native on each device and takes advantage of the unique features of each, letting you use it on each device to the best advantage.

✔ It keeps everything securely in one place.

✔ It lets you clip things from the web and find them easily.

✔ It has powerful search capability.

✔ It lets you easily save worthwhile information from social media and send things to social media, too.

✔ It lets you work locally (offline).

That's a tall order, and Evernote pulls it off with aplomb.

Evernote supports PCs and Macs; the Google Chrome, Apple Safari, Dolphin, Mozilla Firefox, and Internet Explorer web browsers; iPads, Android devices, and Chrome OS tablets; iPhones and iPod touches; BlackBerry phones and tablets; Palm Pre and Pixi devices; and Windows Phone smartphones. Whew! The good news is that you need one — and only one — Evernote account to access all your information from any of your devices.

When you work with Evernote on a laptop or desktop computer or on a mobile device, you can have your cake and eat it too. You have all the benefits of fast, local storage for your notes and the comfort that comes from knowing you always have an up-to-date backup in the cloud. You can use the backed-up version everywhere you have connectivity.

Like anything else, Evernote also has a down side:

✔ There are some inconsistencies among versions, and a few of your favorite features on one device may not work exactly the same way — or even be implemented at all — on another.

✔ Not all devices are created equal, not all web browsers are created equal, and not all Evernote versions are equally polished. Not surprisingly, the most popular, hottest devices and browsers sport the best Evernote implementations, but even the weakest is completely serviceable. (I don't pull punches, and I give kudos and point out the benefits and flaws of each platform in Part IV.)

Seeing What You Can Save with Evernote

With Evernote, you can save, or *capture,* just about anything: your ideas, things you like, things you hear, and things you see. You can save web pages or portions of them, photographs, scanned documents, and music almost without limit. You can also set up machines (such as electronic cameras and scanners) so that the information on them (such as photos and faxes) is transferred like magic directly to Evernote, where it's stored forever (or until you erase it) and is accessible from all your devices. Perhaps by the time you read this book, you'll be able to capture video, too.

Notes and research

Evernote is ideal for taking notes and for doing research. Whenever you want to remember something, don't write it down anymore. Papers create clutter and are easy to misplace. Just make a note of it with Evernote.

If you're incurably addicted to paper, however, Evernote has a solution for that, too. Partnerships with Moleskine and 3M give paper and Post it Notes a digital life and a whole new set of tricks.

Notes, notebooks, and stacks

A *note* is a thing of some sort. It's the atomic unit of Evernote. A *notebook* is a collection of notes — a giant molecule. You can group notebooks into collections called *stacks.* If you want to keep the chemistry analogy going, think of stacks as being organisms. (Part I provides the basics on working with notes and notebooks. Notebook stacks are a little more advanced and are covered in detail in Chapter 14.)

It's not necessary to get overly involved in the taxonomy, though. A lot of how you use and organize Evernote depends on how you like to work. A shopping list can be a note, for example. A collection of stuff related to shopping may be grouped in a notebook. You may have one notebook for bills and another to keep track of tax deductions. All your notebooks related to home stuff can be grouped into a stack.

If you like. . .or not. It's up to you.

Web-page clips

When I surf the web, I often find interesting things that I'd like to refer to again. My grandfather, of blessed memory, used to cut them out of newspapers, bind them, and keep them in his library. I save clips too, but I use Evernote.

Bookmarks in browsers just don't cut it, especially because webmasters don't need to consult you when they update their web pages. Content disappears from websites all of the time, and many times we are none the wiser!

Here's a nifty solution: Clip what you want to save, and create a note. Then you can easily find the clip again. Even better, you can search the web-page information at the same time you search all your other interesting stuff, no matter how you collected it.

The web-clipping feature is one of the most convenient features of Evernote, allowing easy clipping of sections, images, or entire web pages. Part II provides some web-clipping basics. This technology has evolved a lot recently and is a lot smarter and easier to use, so be sure to read the details.

Notes from whiteboards and blackboards

Maybe you're wondering why I'm singling out whiteboards and blackboards. Aren't they just pictures? They are, but here's the magic part: Evernote uses its handwriting-recognition feature to try to interpret what it sees, and what it sees, it indexes automatically. So if you write "Einstein's Equation: $e=mc^2$," and that text is at all legible, you can search for either *"Einstein's Equation"* or *"$e=mc^2$"* so that Evernote can find the note quickly, as well as all the others in your notebooks that contain the same reference. (This handy feature is incorporated with the other visual notes in Parts II and V.)

Saving notes from whiteboard or blackboard sessions is especially useful when you've been working collaboratively and want to quickly share the results with attendees or others who didn't make the meeting.

Task and to-do lists

A popular use of Evernote is to maintain task and to-do lists. Sure, lots of dedicated tools are available to do these jobs, but who needs another tool when you already have Evernote?

Part III covers many of the basics on synchronizing and working across many platforms and devices to make your information more portable. Part VII offers ideas on how to effectively use task and to-do lists in your everyday interaction with Evernote.

Snapshots and photographs

There's more to life than text. Most people want to keep and find their favorite photographic memories. Once again, myriad programs and websites offer this service. Evernote, however, does them all one better — and maybe two or three better.

You can go directly from a suitably equipped scanner, digital camera, webcam, or other capturing device directly into Evernote — passing Go not required. You can save your photographs right alongside clipped pages, audio, notes, and all your other related memories. Finally, as you can with any note, you can access the photos from all your devices.

Part II shows you how to create notes that help you remember everything of importance to you in your world. Chapter 15 gives you a detailed look at the plethora of devices on which you can make and save notes. Part V takes you to the limit, expanding your skills to maximize your visual notes.

Audio capture

Many popular devices, such as smartphones, make recording sound a snap. Evernote supports these features and turns them into notes. Then, if you use one of the add-ons described in Part V, you can convert your voice notes to searchable, taggable text.

Amazing.

Printed and handwritten text

Evernote includes a powerful image-recognition engine. It tries to understand the information in images and to turn what it has read into searchable text that you can use to find things later. Evernote looks at things like a photograph of Times Square and sees text that it tries to use to index the note. An especially nifty feature intelligently photographs and interprets business cards. I discuss all this in Chapter 17.

For the most part, handwritten notes are included with the other visual media because you'll often scan notes after jotting them down. For a closer look, check out Parts II and V.

You can use Evernote to do things like manage your business card collection and share content on LinkedIn. Check out Chapter 17 for more information on how to implement and utilize these features.

Retrieving Your Stored Information

To be useful, information needs to be accessible. Evernote lets you keep what you find interesting so you can find it again later. It's your own searchable scrapbook of everything you've found and liked and want to be able to find again.

A complete copy of everything you've saved on Evernote's servers is kept up to date (synchronized) on each of your desktop or laptop machines (Windows and Mac). With iOS, Android, and BlackBerry devices, you have the option to store files locally as well.

 Titling and tagging notes can make the information in them easier to find later. I cover titling and tagging in Chapter 3. Chapter 8 also provides some tips on keeping tags under control.

Your data is yours

Trust me on this one: You're going to create a valuable collection of useful information in Evernote. Accordingly, you're right to ask "Am I locked in?" or "What happens if [fill in the contingency you're concerned about]?"

No. There's no data lock-in at Evernote. The Evernote folks want you to stay forever, of course, but they think you're more likely to do so if you know that you're free to leave at any time. You can also export your data at will. Read Chapter 11 for more information on how to export your notes.

Chapter 2

Opening an Evernote Account

. . . .

. . . .

*B*efore you can harness the power of Evernote for your personal and business needs, you have to choose which type of account you want to use — and then, of course, sign up for it. In this chapter, I show you how to get your own Evernote account, choose the right account type for you, and get the Evernote products you need for all the devices you use.

You can always start with a free account and later trade up to a Premium or Business account, but after reading this chapter, you may find some features of the paid accounts so compelling that you're willing to pony up for them from the get-go.

Choosing an Evernote Account

Evernote offers free, Premium, and Business accounts, all of which have their own benefits.

Table 2-1 lists the differences between free and paid account types, which I describe in more detail in the following sections. *Note:* All account types provide access to all versions of Evernote, allow synchronization across platforms, offer text recognition inside images, and provide Secure Sockets Layer (SSL) encryption.

Table 2-1	Free and Paid Evernote Accounts		
	Free	*Premium*	*Business*
Note allowance	Upload 60MB/month, 250 notebooks, 100,000 tags per account, and 100,000 notes	Upload 1GB/month, 250 notebooks, 100,000 tags per account, and 100,000 notes	Upload 2GB/month, 250 personal notebooks and 5,000 business notebooks, 100,000 tags per account, and 500,000 notes
File limits	Any file type	Any file type	Any file type
Search within PDFs, Microsoft Office, and iWork documents	No	Yes	Yes
Access to note history	No	Yes	Yes
Offline notebooks (iOS and Android devices)	No	Yes	Yes
Notebook sharing via Evernote Web	Read only	Read and edit	Read and edit
Maximum single note size	25MB	100MB	100MB
Support	Standard support	Premium support	Dedicated support team
Cost	Free	$5/month or $45/year	$10/month or $120/year per user

Free accounts

A basic Evernote account is free, and Evernote promises that it always will be. The free account has some limitations, including the following:

✔ **Capacity limitations:** Free accounts have a ceiling of 60MB of uploads per month. The individual file-size restriction is 25MB.

✔ **Feature restrictions:** Both Premium and Business users can move notebooks to offline access. Premium users can also search inside PDFs and documents created using Microsoft Office and iWork.

More details on free Evernote accounts are available at `http://evernote.com/evernote`.

Paid accounts

Evernote offers three types of paid accounts: Premium, Evernote Business, and Evernote Business for Salesforce.

Premium

A Premium account is priced at $5 per month or $45 annually (at this writing). Premium users can create a single note up to 100MB and can upload up to 1GB of new content each month. (Additional monthly storage is available for purchase.) Premium users can allow friends and colleagues who are also Premium or Business subscribers to view and edit shared notes.

Presentation mode (Mac only) is available only to Premium users. Educational and not-for-profit institutions are eligible for a 75 percent discount on the standard monthly Business subscription price for five seats or more. See `https://evernote.com/schools/` for details.

For details on Premium accounts, see `http://evernote.com/premium`.

Evernote Business and Evernote Business for Salesforce

Business users now have Evernote Business, which is ideal for collaborative work. A monthly subscription is $10 per user (five user minimum). Business users get 2GB monthly upload capacity for personal notes and business notes. In a Business account, the organization owns any business notebook and its contents. All personal notebooks and their contents remain completely private and controlled by the user who created them. Learn more about Evernote business accounts at `http://evernote.com/business/`.

Evernote for Salesforce lets your sales team manage customer relationships and share knowledge, leaving more time for cultivating relationships and following up on leads. Evernote leverages records in the Salesforce program to automatically suggest notes that may be useful. See `http://blog.evernote.com/blog/2013/09/27/introducing-evernote-for-salesforce/` for more information on how this integration can work for your sales team.

Registering for a Free Evernote Account

It's a good idea to start with a free account so that you can see just how powerful Evernote is at even the most basic level.

Follow these steps to sign up for a free Evernote account:

1. **Navigate to** `http://evernote.com`.

   The Evernote home screen appears (see Figure 2-1).

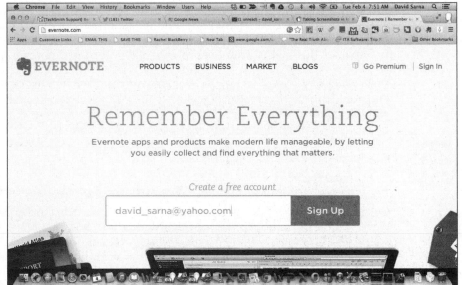

Figure 2-1:
The
Evernote
home
screen.

2. **Enter your e-mail address in the text box, and click Sign Up.**

   A new screen invites you to register.

3. **If you don't want to use your e-mail address as your account name, click Change, and follow the onscreen instructions.**

   Evernote checks username availability as you type. If the username is available, the word *Available* appears below the Username field.

   Usernames are not case-sensitive.

   Finally, you're taken to the Almost There password-entry screen (see Figure 2-2).

Figure 2-2:
The
Evernote
password-
entry
screen.

4. **Type a password.**

Your password must be between 6 and 64 characters long and may contain letters, numbers, and punctuation but not other symbols. Spaces
are not permitted.

I recommend choosing a strong password. You will — I promise — end
up keeping lots of useful information in Evernote, and you'll want to protect it with a password that's not easy for someone else to guess.

After you enter your password, the license agreement appears.

5. **Click Agree.**

6. **Do one of the following, depending on your computer platform:**

   • *Mac:* Drag the Evernote icon to the Applications folder, and click
     Open when you see a message warning that the application has
     downloaded from the Internet.

   • *Windows PC:* If the Evernote executable file doesn't start installing
     itself after download, click it to begin installation.

7. **Click Run to run the installation.**

8. **Click Create Account.**

   A confirmation screen appears (see Figure 2-3), listing your Evernote
   e-mail address and asking you to confirm that you want to create the
   account.

   If you don't already have the Evernote software, you can click Download
   Evernote in this screen to download the software.

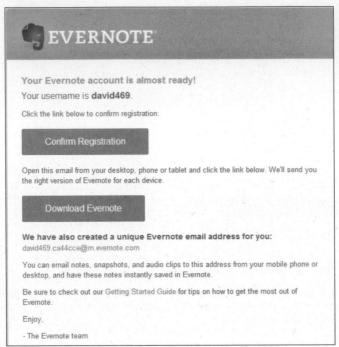

Figure 2-3:
Confirm your
registration
in this
screen.

9. **Click Confirm Registration.**

   Evernote sends an e-mail to the address you supplied in Step 2.

   Save the e-mail in a permanent folder in your e-mail program so you can conveniently open it in all your web browsers and on all your devices.

10. **Click the link in the confirmation e-mail to confirm your identity.**

    When you click the link, you see the welcome screen shown in Figure 2-4. Your registration is complete, and you can continue to use Evernote on the web or download an app to use (see the next section).

    When activation is complete, you can click the link shown in Figure 2-4 to go online, or you can go to the Evernote software on your computer. In either event, you need to log in.

11. **Enter your username and password.**

12. **(Optional) Check the Remember Me for a Week box if you don't want to reenter your password on this computer.**

    Never check this box when you're working on a public computer.

13. **Click Sign In.**

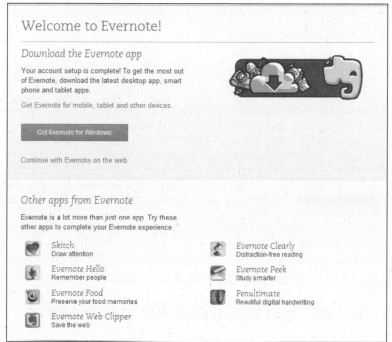

Welcome to Evernote!

Download the Evernote app

Your account setup is complete! To get the most out of Evernote, download the latest desktop app, smart phone and tablet apps.

Get Evernote for mobile, tablet and other devices.

Get Evernote for Windows

Continue with Evernote on the web

Other apps from Evernote

Evernote is a lot more than just one app. Try these other apps to complete your Evernote experience.

Skitch
Draw attention

Evernote Hello
Remember people

Evernote Food
Preserve your food memories

Evernote Web Clipper
Save the web

Evernote Clearly
Distraction-free reading

Evernote Peek
Study smarter

Penultimate
Beautiful digital handwriting

Figure 2-4:
The
Welcome
to Evernote
screen.

When you complete the registration process, you're immediately taken to Evernote. A welcome note appears in your notebook, inviting you to get Evernote for mobile devices or to continue with Evernote Web.

Getting the Correct Software for Your Devices

You can download Evernote for your mobile devices at `http://evernote.com`. Evernote is free of charge for all supported devices, and you can download all the versions you need for all your devices.

After you create your Evernote account (see the preceding section), you can choose the version for the platform or device you need. Simply click the link in the Welcome to Evernote e-mail (refer to Figure 2-4, earlier in this chapter). Evernote recognizes the device you used to open the e-mail and proposes the right software. If you open the e-mail in a different device, click the link titled Get Evernote for Mobile, Tablet and Other Devices.

Evernote has versions available for these products:

- ✔ Desktop and laptop computers
- ✔ Mobile devices
- ✔ Web browsers

It's worthwhile to install Evernote on all your devices. The process takes only a few minutes, and there's no cost. Downloading Evernote on all your devices is also the best way to make sure that you have access from anywhere you roam at any time. Finally, it means that no matter where you are, so long as you have your mobile device, even if you don't have Internet access, you can still create and view your notes. (Chapter 3 guides you through basic note creation; Part IV provides more detailed instructions for the various devices.)

On most devices, for Premium and Business users, offline access is supported from the local copy of your notebooks when a network connection isn't available; notebooks are synchronized when you get back online.

Installing Evernote for computers

You can install Evernote on Windows and Macintosh desktop and laptop computers, as I show you in this section.

Windows computers

Evernote supports all versions of Windows 7, Vista, and Windows XP, and they all install from the same download.

To install Evernote on a Windows PC, follow these steps:

1. **If you haven't already done so, navigate to** `http://evernote.com/evernote` **and click Download for Windows (see Figure 2-5).**

   You're taken to `http://evernote.com/download`, and the download should start automatically (see Figure 2-6). If it doesn't, click the Click Here link.

2. **When the download is complete, and you're prompted to do so, click Run.**

   When the download has completed, Windows will ask if you want to run the installation program. You may see a message telling you to close some open applications.

3. **Click OK to close open applications.**

   If you don't, installation will proceed, but a reboot may be required.

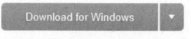

Figure 2-5:
Click to
download
Evernote for
Windows.

Figure 2-6:
Down-
loading
Evernote.

4. **If you're asked whether to permit the Windows Installer to install Evernote, click Yes.**

5. **Click Next in the next screen.**

6. **Click Finish in the next screen.**

7. **Click Start to start Evernote for Windows.**

   Drag the Evernote icon to your taskbar to pin it so that you can start Evernote easily without any fumbling around.

8. **Close Evernote.**

   Evernote for Windows is installed on your PC. The Getting Started with Evernote page usually opens in your browser. If not, navigate to `http://evernote.com/getting_started`.

Macintosh computers

To install Evernote on a Mac, follow these steps:

1. **Click the Mac link in your welcome note from Evernote (refer to Figure 2-4 earlier in this chapter) or navigate to** `http://evernote.com/evernote`.

   Evernote recognizes your computer platform and offers you Evernote for Mac (see Figure 2-7).

Figure 2-7: Download Evernote for Mac.

2. **Click Download for Mac.**

   The Mac download page appears (`http://evernote.com/download`), and the application downloads automatically. If a problem occurs, click the Click Here link. The license agreement appears.

3. **Click Agree.**

4. **Drag the Evernote icon into the** `Applications` **folder.**

5. **Close the Installation window.**

6. **In the** `Applications` **folder, double-click the Evernote icon.**

   A message warns you that Evernote was downloaded from the Internet and asks whether you're sure you want to open it.

7. **Click Open.**

   Evernote opens.

8. **If you see the Welcome to Evernote screen, type your username and password.**

9. **(Optional) If you like, select the Stay Signed In check box.**

10. **Click Sign In.**

    You've installed Evernote on your Mac.

Installing Evernote for mobile devices

Every mobile device that Evernote supports has a web browser. The easiest way to install Evernote on a mobile device is to click the link in the welcome e-mail you received after signup (refer to Figure 2-4 earlier in this chapter). You can also fire up the app store for your device, such as Apple's App Store, Google Play, BlackBerry World, or Windows Marketplace.

Android devices

To install Evernote on an Android device, follow these steps:

1. **Tap the Google Play icon on the Home screen.**
2. **Tap Apps.**
3. **Tap the magnifying glass in the top-right corner, enter** Evernote **in the Search box, and then tap the magnifying glass in the bottom-right corner.**
4. **Tap Evernote.**
5. **Tap Install.**
6. **Tap Accept & Download.**

   Evernote downloads.
7. **Tap Open.**
8. **Tap Sign In.**
9. **Type your username and password, and then tap Sign In.**

   Evernote is installed on your Android device.

iOS devices

To install Evernote on an iPhone, iPod touch, or iPad, follow these steps:

1. **Tap App Store on the Home screen.**
2. **Tap the search box, type** Evernote, **and execute the search.**
3. **Tap Evernote.**
4. **Tap Install.**
5. **Type your Apple ID and password, and tap Return.**

   The Download Now message appears.

6. **Exit the App Store.**

   Evernote downloads, although it may take a while. You can continue to use the device for other things during downloading.

7. **Tap the Evernote icon to launch Evernote.**

8. **Type your username and password, and tap Sign In.**

   Evernote may take a few moments to load; then it synchronizes, downloading snippets of all notes. Patience — this delay happens only once.

   Evernote is installed on your iOS device.

BlackBerry devices

To install Evernote on a BlackBerry, follow these steps:

1. **Navigate to** `http://evernote.com/evernote`, **and tap Download for BlackBerry.**

   You're taken to `http://appworld.blackberry.com/webstore/content/1700`.

2. **Tap the Download button.**

3. **Log in with your BlackBerry ID, and tap Login.**

   Evernote downloads.

4. **Tap Run.**

5. **Type your Evernote username and password; then tap Sign In.**

   Evernote is installed on your BlackBerry.

Windows Phone

Windows Phone is the most recent addition to Evernote, and in mid-2011, Evernote for Windows Phone got a serious boost. It went from an extremely basic version for Windows Mobile to a robust, very capable application, which Evernote says is its most powerful version.

To install Evernote for Windows Phone, follow these steps:

1. **Go to** `www.windowsphone.com/en-US/marketplace`.

2. **Search for Evernote.**

3. **Tap the Evernote app.**

   Evernote may take a few moments to load the first time. Then it synchronizes, downloading snippets of all notes.

   You've installed Evernote on your Windows Phone.

Installing Web Clipper for web browsers

Evernote Web Clipper is a browser extension that saves all or parts of web pages and creates notes for them in Evernote. With just one click you can "clip" anything you see in your web browser, whether it's an entire web page or just a small part of it, mark it up with comments or other annotations, share it with friends, or just store it for future reference.

When you clip something, all text, images, and links are captured and automatically sent to your Evernote account, so even if the content on the web disappears, you will always have your clipping saved. As of this writing, the only supported browsers are Google Chrome, Apple Safari, Firefox, Internet Explorer, and Opera.

Clipping on iOS devices is discussed in detail in Chapter 15.

You can install Web Clipper in your web browser by navigating to `http://evernote.com/webclipper`. Evernote detects your browser type and offers to download the right one.

The download and installation procedures vary among browsers. If, like me, you work with multiple browsers on one computer, you need to access the link from each browser on your computer to install the corresponding clipper. (The process is easier than it sounds.)

If you're using Internet Explorer, that browser installs Web Clipper as part of the Evernote for Windows installation. For Safari 5 or later, get it from the Safari Extensions Gallery in the productivity category.

I recommend that you use Chrome, because it's the first browser that Evernote updates, so you'll have greater capability with it than with the other browsers. My second browser choice is Firefox because it's updated relatively quickly following Chrome updates. Recently, the Safari browser has been much enhanced, too.

Chrome

If you don't have Chrome, download it at `https://www.google.com/intl/en/chrome/browser`.

When you have Chrome, you're ready to install Web Clipper. Follow these steps:

1. **In Chrome, navigate to** `http://evernote.com/webclipper`.
2. **Click the green Download for Chrome button in the center of the page.**

   The page shown in Figure 2-8 invites you to download Web Clipper.

Evernote Web Clipper

From interests to research, save anything you see online—
including text, links and images—into your Evernote account
with a single click.

Download for Chrome   ▼

See what's new ▸

Figure 2-8:
Download
Web Clipper
for Chrome.

3. **Click the Add button in the dialog box that descends from the top of your web browser.**

   As the message box says, clicking this button allows Evernote to access your data on all websites, your tabs, and browsing activity.

    The message "Evernote Web Clipper has been added to Chrome" appears at the right end of Chrome's navigation bar, along with a new icon that shows the Evernote elephant.

Safari

Safari comes preinstalled on your Mac, so you need only download Web Clipper. Follow these steps:

1. **Click the Evernote Web Clipper link in the welcome note you received from Evernote (refer to Figure 2-4 earlier in this chapter) or navigate to** http://evernote.com/webclipper.

2. **Click the down arrow on the right of the green Download for Chrome box and select Safari from the drop-down menu.**

3. **When the file downloads, do one of the following:**

   • Drag Web Clipper to your Safari browser, if you have that option.

   • If you don't have the option of dragging Web Clipper to the browser, the Evernote Safari Clipper Plug-in package downloads, and the dialog box shown in Figure 2-9 appears. Click Open. Then, in the confirmation dialog box, click Install.

   The Safari browser now has the Evernote Web Clipper button installed at the left end of the address bar.

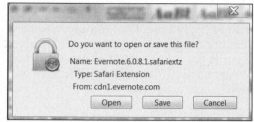

Figure 2-9:
Click Open
in this dialog
box.

Safari doesn't support extensions in iOS 7, Apple's new operating system
for mobile devices. You have to use bookmarklets. Therefore, Evernote had
to develop a work-around. So for me, the Web Clipper worked fine on my
Macbook Pro but did not work on my iPhone 5s under iOS 7; I use the Dolphin
browser on my iPhone. Other work-arounds, including several bookmarklets
that I succeeded in getting to work, are described in Chapter 15.

Firefox

If you don't have Firefox, download it from www.mozilla.org. Then follow
these steps to install Web Clipper:

1. **Click the Evernote Web Clipper link in your Evernote welcome
   note (refer to Figure 2-4 earlier in this chapter) or navigate to**
   `https://addons.mozilla.org/en-US/firefox/addon/`
   `evernote-web-clipper`.

2. **Click Add to Firefox (see Figure 2-10).**

   An install window descends from the top of your browser window. Click
   Install.

   You see the message `Evernote Web Clipper will be installed`
   `after you restart Firefox`.

Figure 2-10:
Add
Evernote
Clipper to
Firefox.

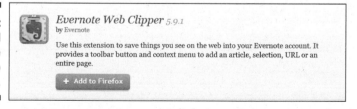

Evernote Web Clipper 5.9.1
by Evernote

Use this extension to save things you see on the web into your Evernote account. It
provides a toolbar button and context menu to add an article, selection, URL or an
entire page.

+ Add to Firefox

3. **Click Restart Now.**

   The Firefox browser restarts, with the Web Clipper bar on the right side
   of the screen. A new tab may open, showing the document "How to Use
   Evernote Web Clipper," and the Evernote elephant icon shown in the
   margin appears on the Firefox toolbar.

Internet Explorer

Web Clipper doesn't appear in the Internet Explorer browser bar because Internet Explorer doesn't support add-ons like Evernote. The good news, however, is that Web Clipper is part of the native Evernote installation for Windows. You just have to get used to a slightly different way of accessing it (and accept reduced options).

If Evernote detects Internet Explorer, it installs Web Clipper along with Evernote. Although Web Clipper doesn't work the same way in Internet Explorer as it does in other browsers, you can still work with most of the Web Clipper options by right-clicking on any part of the website you're currently on and selecting either Clip This Page, Clip URL, or New Note.

Chapter 3

Creating Text Notes

*N*o longer do you need to have random thoughts scattered around your brain or colorful sticky notes all over your monitor and desk. To better manage your life, you can take advantage of Evernote's electronic notebooks and notes.

You can create your own notes by typing or recording. You can also have notes created automatically, using event-triggered rules, by having them e-mailed to your account, by scanning, or by web clipping.

In this chapter, I start at the beginning, showing you how to create your first notebooks and notes.

Signing In to Evernote

Before you can do anything in Evernote, you need to create an account and sign in. (If you haven't already created an account, see Chapter 2.)

To sign in to your Evernote account, follow these steps:

1. **Navigate to** `http://evernote.com`.

   If you haven't signed in to Evernote on this computer and asked Evernote to keep you signed in, the Evernote home screen appears (see Figure 3-1).

Figure 3-1:
The
Evernote
home
screen.

2. **In the top-right corner, click Sign In.**

   You're invited to sign in to Evernote (see Figure 3-2).

Figure 3-2:
Sign in to
Evernote.

3. **Type your username and password for your Evernote account (if they aren't filled in), and then click Sign In.**

   Optionally, you can check Remember Me for a Week, and then click Sign In.

After you sign in to Evernote, you see your first note and notebook in the top-left corner of the screen (see Figure 3-3). These are there by default; they are a great place to start so let's jump right in!

I recommend starting by renaming the default notebook. To rename the notebook, follow these steps:

1. **Right-click the notebook's name and choose Rename from the contextual menu.**

   The Rename Notebook dialog box appears.

2. **Type the new notebook name (see Figure 3-4).**

   In this example, I renamed the notebook Michelle's Recipes.

3. **Click Save.**

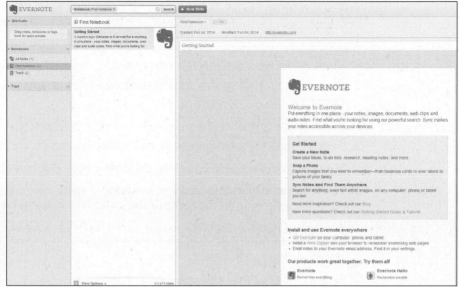

Figure 3-3:
Your
Evernote
notebooks.

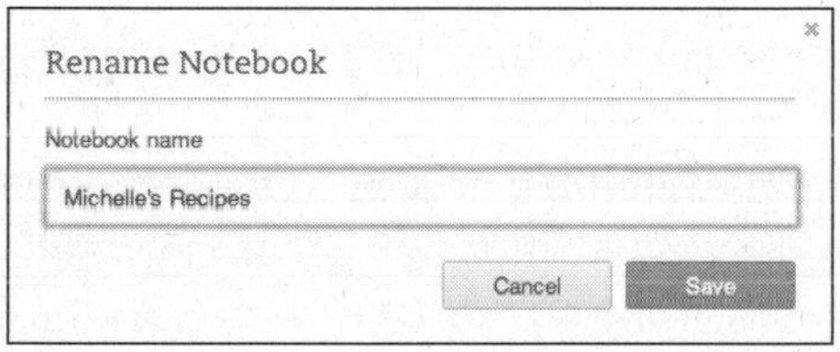

Figure 3-4:
Renaming
your
notebook.

Working with Notebooks

An organized Evernote user is a happy Evernote user. The main building block for organization in Evernote is the notebook. For both Premium and free accounts, you can collect up to 250 notebooks, which should be plenty for the everyday user. For Business Evernote users, you can have as many as 5,000. Let's get started on building your notebook collection!

Creating a notebook

Although Evernote creates a notebook for you when you create an account (see Chapter 2), and although you can join an increasingly large collection of public notebooks or those shared by your friends (see "Working with shared and linked notebooks" later in this chapter), chances are that you'll want to create notebooks other than the initial one that Evernote supplies. Creating a new notebook is a simple task. Follow these steps:

1. **Click Notebooks in the left menu bar.**

2. **Click the +New Notebook button on the top left of your screen, directly under the top menu bar.**

   A box appears with a space for you to name your notebook.

3. **Type a name for your notebook and press Enter.**

   For this example, call the notebook Evernote For Dummies Practice.

4. **Hover your mouse over the box containing your new notebook, and click the gear icon to the right of the notebook name (see Figure 3-5).**

   A box with more notebook settings appears. Here you can choose to rename your notebook, make it your default notebook, and select the notebook type.

5. **Specify whether to synchronize the notebook.**

   By default, a notebook is synchronized across all your devices. To create it only for local use on this computer, click the Local Notebook radio button. For the Evernote For Dummies Practice notebook, though, leave Synchronized Notebook selected.

6. **If you want to make this notebook appear automatically whenever you open Evernote, select the check box titled Make this my default notebook.**

   You're using the Evernote For Dummies Practice notebook just for practice, so don't check this box.

7. **Click Save.**

   The new notebook appears in the list of your notebooks (see Figure 3-6). To the right of each notebook name, you see the number of notes stored in that notebook.

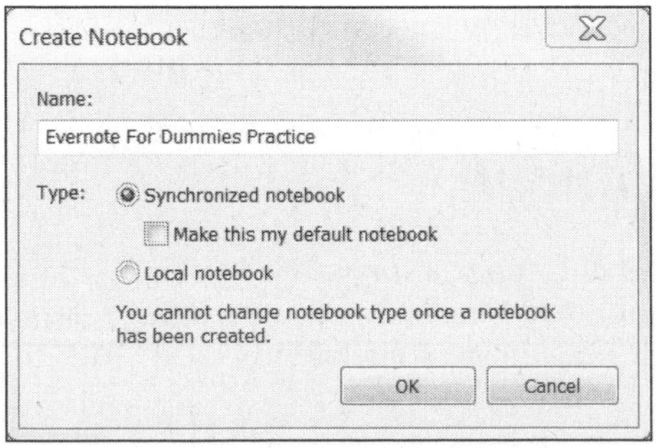

Figure 3-5:
The
Notebook
settings
dialog box.

> Create Notebook
>
> Name:
>
> Evernote For Dummies Practice
>
> Type: ⦿ Synchronized notebook
>   ☐ Make this my default notebook
>   ○ Local notebook
>
> You cannot change notebook type once a notebook
> has been created.
>
> [OK]   [Cancel]

You can have up to 250 personal notebooks on free and Premium accounts plus an additional 100 joined notebooks that are shared with others. An Evernote Business account can have up to 5,000 notebooks and 250 joined notebooks.

Working with shared and linked notebooks

A *shared notebook* is a notebook that you're sharing with others and that you can always update because it's yours. A *linked notebook* is one created by another user that you can link to your Evernote account. If the user who created the notebook is a Premium member, you can — if given rights to do so by the notebook owner — update information in the linked notebook. Otherwise, you have read-only access to the linked notebook.

Sharing a notebook

When you hover over the name of a notebook, you see two icons: a gear icon, which allows you to rename a notebook (as described earlier in this chapter), and the Share icon, which looks like a box with an arrow coming out of it. You have the option to share a notebook with only certain individuals or you can create a public link to share it with everyone.

To continue sharing a notebook with individuals, follow these steps:

1. **Click the Share icon.**

   You will get a dialog box where you can select whether you want to share the notebook with individuals or share it with everyone by creating a public link.

2. **Clicking the Share with Individuals button takes you to the screen shown in Figure 3-7.**

   Enter the e-mail addresses of the people you want to share the notebook with in the box. If you are entering multiple e-mail addresses, they must be separated by a comma.

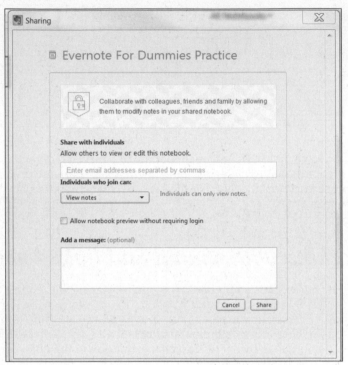

Figure 3-7:
Sharing a
notebook.

3. **Select permission level for the invitees.**

Under the heading *Individuals who join can*, click the drop down menu to select one of the following permission levels:

- *View notes:* Invitees can only see the notes in the notebook.

- *View notes and activity:* Invitees can see the notes in the notebook as well as any activity on the notebook such as updates or deletions.

- *Modify notes:* Invitees can view, create, delete, and edit existing notes as well as see the activity on the notebook.

- *Modify and invite others:* Invitees have the same privileges as the notebook creator: view, edit, delete and create notes, see the activity stream, add new people to the invite list as well as update the permissions of those people who already have access to the notebook.

4. **Select whether or not to make invitees log into the notebook.**

   By checking the *Allow notebook preview without requiring login* box, you are giving the recipients the opportunity to see your notebook without having logged into their own Evernote account. Unchecking the box will require them to be logged into their account to view the information.

5. **(Optional) Add a message.**

   Add a message to the e-mail invitation telling the recipients why you are sharing this notebook with them.

6. **Click the Share button.**

   Enter the e-mail addresses of the people you want to share the notebook with in the box. If you are entering multiple e-mail addresses, they must be separated by a comma.

7. **(Optional) Perform additional sharing activities.**

   A dialog box appears giving you the opportunity to share the document again via the Public link URL or by inviting more people via e-mail. You can also manage the notebook access permissions of the people you have already invited to access the notebook.

8. **Click the Dismiss button.**

   The dialog box disappears and you are returned to your Evernote account page.

A notebook that you make public can be accessed by anyone who has the link. Links you share with contacts can be accessed only by them.

To create a public link URL to share your notebook, follow these steps:

1. **Click the Share icon.**

   You will get a dialog box where you can select whether you want to share the notebook with individuals or share it with everyone by creating a public link.

2. **Select the Create a Public Link URL option.**

   You are given a dialog box with a URL that you can share with others by copying and pasting it into e-mails, chat windows, or anywhere else you want to share the notebook (see Figure 3-8).

3. **Copy the URL by selecting it with your mouse and pressing Ctrl + C on your keyboard for PCs and ⌘ + C for Macs.**

   Once you have copied the link URL to your clipboard, you can go ahead and share it wherever you want such as in a chat message or on Twitter.

Figure 3-8:
Creating a
public link.

4. **Click the Dismiss button.**

   Click Dismiss to complete the notebook-sharing process and be taken back to your Evernote account page, or, if you have changed your mind about creating a Public URL link, click the Delete Public Link.

   You will then be taken back to the original Share this Notebook dialog box in case you want to start the share process over again and choose the other option. Click the Dismiss button to close this box.

Accessing a notebook shared with a Public link URL

To access a notebook shared with a Public link URL, follow these steps:

1. **Navigate to the notebook you'd like to join.**

   For this example, I created a public Evernote notebook that you can link to by going to `https://www.evernote.com/pub/dsarna/david sarnasevernotefordummiesnotebook`. (Please note that the link is case-sensitive.)

2. **Click the Join Notebook button to view everything in the shared notebook on any of your devices.**

   You have access to the notebook at the level that the sender had set your permissions. See the section "Sharing a notebook" earlier in the chapter for more information on setting permissions for notebook sharing. If you don't want to sign into or sign up for an Evernote account just yet, skip this step and move to Step 3.

3. (Optional) Click the View Notebook button.

Click the View Notebook button instead if you don't want to sign into your Evernote account and would rather just see the contents of the notebook. You don't accept any permissions associated with the notebook that you were granted by the notebook sharer. This would be the case if you don't have an Evernote account and don't want to create one at this time.

Once you have joined the notebook, you can access it at any time from your own Evernote account. Simply click the Join Notebook link in the left sidebar (see Figure 3-9).

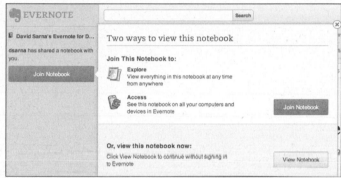

Figure 3-9:
Click Join
Notebook to
see shared
notebooks.

 On web browsers, a notebook that was shared with a Public link URL appears in the left sidebar under a separate heading called Joined Notebooks. On the desktop implementation, an icon that looks like three people appears to the left of any notebook that is shared.

Creating Your First Note

You started off with a default notebook when you created your Evernote account so it only stands to reason that you would start off with a default first note as shown in Figure 3-10. I recommend you read through that note as it gives some helpful hints on how to get the most out of your Evernote account.

Once you are finished with the welcome note, you are ready to get started creating notes of your own. Anything you want to add is fair game; after all, it's your notebook! If you like to make lists, you can create a grocery list or a to-do list. Or perhaps you want to redecorate your kitchen; simply add photos of looks you like, along with links to decorating ideas. You can organize everything in the form of notes in your notebooks.

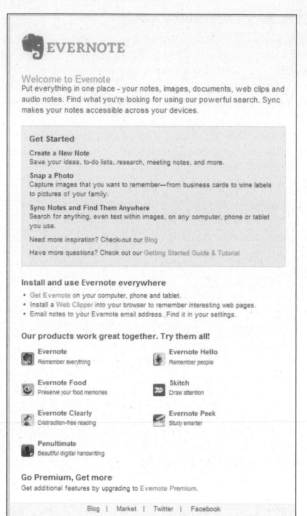

Figure 3-10:
The
Welcome
to Evernote
note.

To create your note that contains typed text, follow these steps:

1. **Click the +New Note button on the top menu bar.**

   An untitled note is created (see Figure 3-11).

Enter note title here.

![A new note screenshot]

Figure 3-11:
A new note.

2. **Give your note a title.**

   Click the box that says Untitled as shown in Figure 3-11 and enter your title.

3. **Tag your note by clicking the +Tag button right above the text formatting bar (see Figure 3-12) and typing the tag.**

   I entered the tags *desserts* and *chocolate cake* (see Figure 3-13).

   Evernote uses words in the title and tags to search for information, so assign a descriptive title and a tag to the note. (Read more about tags and searches in Chapter 8.)

Click and enter tags.

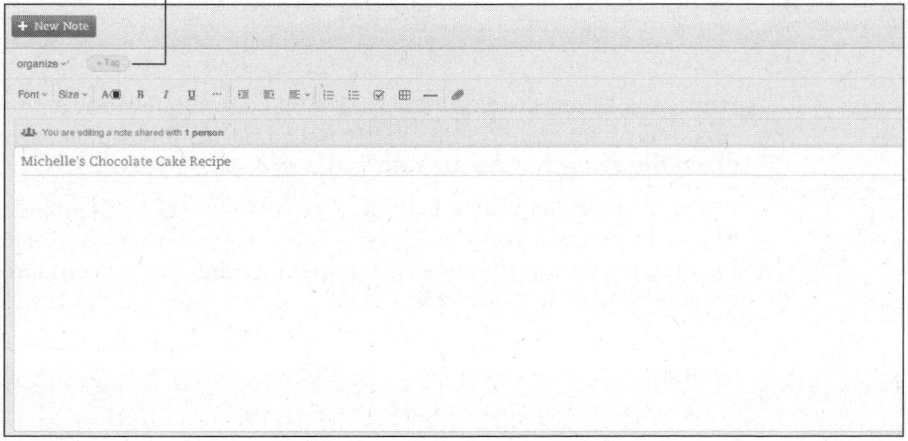

![New Note screenshot with Michelle's Chocolate Cake Recipe]

Figure 3-12:
Click here to add a tag.

Figure 3-13:
Use
descriptive
words.

4. **To add a Reminder, click the Reminder button, which looks like an alarm clock, on the right side of the screen (see Figure 3-14).**

Figure 3-14:
Adding a
reminder.

5. **(Optional) Click the calendar icon next to the Reminder Added dialog box and pick a date on the Notify Me calendar that opens, and then press the Enter button on your keyboard (see Figure 3-15).**

If you do not select a specific date by clicking on the calendar icon, Evernote just lists your reminder in the left side bar under the Reminders heading. If you select a date and time for a reminder, a notice will appear on your screen at the selected time.

When you are in the Notify Me drop-down menu, you have several options:

- Click the Tomorrow button to be notified tomorrow.

- Click the In a Week button to be reminded in one week.

- Type a specific date and time.

- Navigate the calendar and click a date.

Figure 3-15:
Setting a
reminder
date and
time.

After you set a reminder, it is added to the left sidebar under the Reminders heading. You can also receive an e-mail reminder on the date you specified.

After you set the first reminder on your new Evernote account, a dialog box appears in the left sidebar asking whether or not you want to receive an e-mail on the day you chose for your reminder. Click Yes if you want to get e-mailed reminders or No if you don't.

Clicking the shield icon gives you more control over what reminders you see and how you want them to be sorted.

6. **Click the body of the note to enter the note's contents.**

   The formatting toolbar becomes visible.

7. **To assign a URL, set a location, or see other useful descriptive information about a note (including revision history), click the Info button to open the metadata dialog box (see Figure 3-16).**

8. **In the dialog box that appears, type a URL.**

   Assigning a URL makes sense, for example, if you're abstracting an article and want to refer to the source.

9. **Clicking anywhere outside of the dialog box closes it.**

   Your note is saved automatically as you go along. All your notes are listed in the left pane. Clicking a note makes it active (indicated by the shading) and opens it in the right pane.

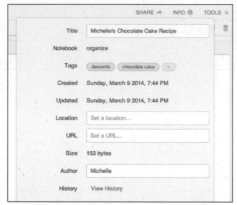

Figure 3-16:
View and update descriptive information (metadata) about a note.

A note isn't a dump. The purpose of saving notes is to allow retrieval as needed. Although Evernote can find whatever you save, you'll find that intelligently titling notes, organizing them in logical collections (notebooks), and tagging them judiciously will dramatically reduce retrieval times without slowing you down while you're capturing other information. See Chapter 8 for more information on organizing your notes.

Changing the note's look

Depending on the browser or Evernote platform you're using, you may be able to change the note's font, font size, and other formatting by using the formatting toolbar.

To change the formatting of an existing note, simply open the note, click anywhere in the note body, and use the formatting toolbar to make changes. This toolbar works like the formatting toolbar in nearly every word processor. You can set the font and type size, and control underscoring, bullets, justification (left, right, or centered), indenting, and check boxes to use for to-do lists. The toolbar even has an option to add hyperlinks to a note. You have a lot of flexibility — the formatting toolbar is a powerful feature — so it's best to experiment with it on a practice note.

Most, but not all, devices and browsers support the formatting features. The toolbar is missing if you use Evernote in a device or browser on which formatting isn't supported. You can always revisit a note on a different device if you want to add fancier formatting.

Adding an attachment

Suppose that you are planning a dinner party, and you created a note in Evernote showing everything that you're going to serve and the ingredients you need to purchase. You recently downloaded a recipe file from a cooking website but you haven't had a chance to add the information to your menu note yet. Evernote makes it easy to attach the recipe file to your menu note so you can access it later from the supermarket.

Even in the free version of Evernote, you can attach an audio clip, picture, PDF file, Microsoft Word document, or spreadsheet up to 25MB. (Premium and Business subscribers can attach up to 100MB.)

Here's how to attach an item to a note:

1. **Click the paper-clip icon on the formatting toolbar.**

   The Attach Files dialog box appears (see Figure 3-17).

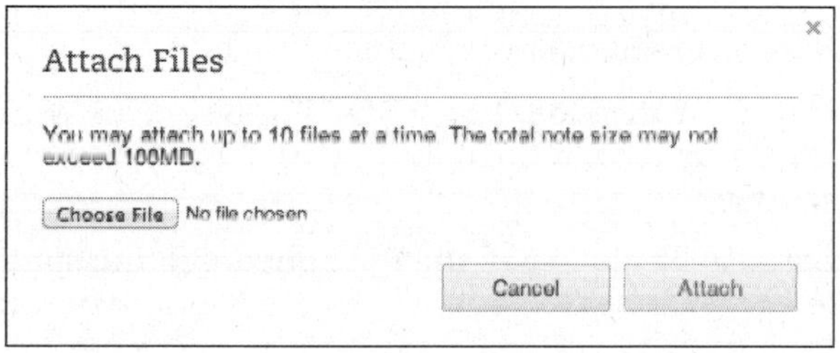

Figure 3-17:
Select files
to attach.

> **Attach Files**   ✕
>
> You may attach up to 10 files at a time. The total note size may not
> exceed 100MB.
>
> [Choose File] No file chosen
>
>   Cancel   Attach

2. **Click the Choose File button and select the file(s) you want to attach.**

3. **Click Open.**

   You are taken back to the Attach Files dialog box.

4. **Click the green Attach button.**

   The attachment appears in your note.

Is the item you attached not as great as you thought it would be? No problem. You can remove it by highlighting the attachment in the note and pressing the Delete or backspace button on your keyboard.

Dragging and dropping files into notes

Creating a note from scratch is easy, but what if you already have all the information you need in a file, or what if that file is a graphic? Those situations are where dragging and dropping come in.

If you've ever moved files and folders around in the Mac Finder or Windows Explorer, you're already familiar with how dragging and dropping works.

You can drag and drop all files, no matter what their extensions are. If you're a Premium member, Evernote can show you previews only of the supported extensions for which the platform has a built-in viewer or of PDF files in Windows.

Evernote processes PDFs and other supported files for Premium users before it processes them for free users. Scanned PDFs are made searchable for both free and Premium users, though.

Here's how to create a note by dragging and dropping files:

1. **Click New Note to create a new note.**

2. **Click a file (on your desktop, in the Mac Finder, or in Windows Explorer), and drag it onto the note in your Evernote account in your web browser.**

3. **Release the mouse button when the file appears in the spot where you want it to be.**

    Seriously, it's that simple. Like magic, your file is saved as a note.

The process is virtually the same in all of the desktop versions of Evernote.

By default, in Windows, the name of the file is used as the title of the note; on a Mac, the default filename is `Untitled Note`. To change the title, click it and then type the name you want.

Deleting notes

You can delete any note by clicking the trash-can icon in the upper-right corner of the note's toolbar or right-clicking on the note and selecting Delete from the menu. That's so easy that you might think it's really easy to delete things accidentally. No worries. This deletion is just a virtual deletion. Deleted notes go to a special notebook called Trash that is at the bottom of the left sidebar. To undelete, simply click the note and then click the Restore Note button in the top-right corner of the Trash notebook. To permanently delete a note, click it, and then click the Delete Note button.

Creating Shared Notes

Note links are links to individual notes that you can place anywhere you can add in a URL. Using note links, you can always share the latest version of a note, no matter what device you used to update it. Anyone who clicks the link or types its URL can see the latest version of the note, delivered directly from Evernote's servers.

No one has access to any of your other notes. Other people can access just the shared link.

Creating a note link

Here's how to create a note link that other people can open:

1. **Right-click the note you want to share, and choose Share⇨Link⇨Copy to Clipboard from the contextual menu.**

   The link appears in your clipboard.

2. **Paste the note into another document.**

   You can paste that link into just about anything: other notes, calendars, to-do lists, third-party apps, and so on. The link is a URL. Whenever you click the link, the note opens.

Shift-clicking (Windows) or ⌘-clicking (Mac) opens the linked note in its own window.

Creating multiple note links

You can also create a list of links. To do so, select multiple notes; then right-click what you selected and choose Copy Note Links from the contextual menu. When you paste the notes, you see a list of links.

These links are local links; they don't work as links when they're shared.

A list of links is a great tool for building bibliographies, tables of contents, and citations when you're doing research.

Changing Your View

Snippets view is the default view of your newly created notes, but you can use the commands on the View menu to change your view. How you control your view is different on a Mac and in Windows. Table 3-1 shows which shortcut key does what in each platform.

Table 3-1		Evernote Views	
View	*Mac Command*	*Windows Command*	*What It Does*
List view	⌘+1	Ctrl+F5	Gives you a compact, flat view, minus the icons, with just the titles, tags, and summary history (see Figure 3-18).
Snippets view	⌘+2	Ctrl+F6	Gives you a snippet of the note, plus a small image, if there is one.
Thumbnail view	⌘+3	Ctrl+F7	Shows an icon of the note.

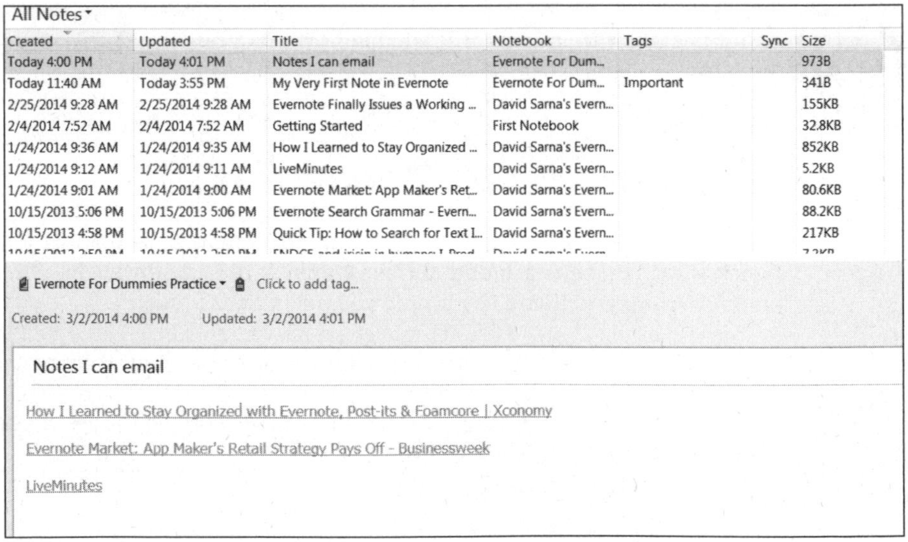

All Notes ▾

Created	Updated	Title	Notebook	Tags	Sync	Size
Today 4:00 PM	Today 4:01 PM	Notes I can email	Evernote For Dum...			973B
Today 11:40 PM	Today 3:55 PM	My Very First Note in Evernote	Evernote For Dum...	Important		341B
2/25/2014 9:28 AM	2/25/2014 9:28 AM	Evernote Finally Issues a Working ...	David Sarna's Evern...			155KB
2/4/2014 7:52 AM	2/4/2014 7:52 AM	Getting Started	First Notebook			32.8KB
1/24/2014 9:36 AM	1/24/2014 9:35 AM	How I Learned to Stay Organized ...	David Sarna's Evern...			852KB
1/24/2014 9:12 AM	1/24/2014 9:11 AM	LiveMinutes	David Sarna's Evern...			5.2KB
1/24/2014 9:01 AM	1/24/2014 9:00 AM	Evernote Market: App Maker's Ret...	David Sarna's Evern...			80.6KB
10/15/2013 5:06 PM	10/15/2013 5:06 PM	Evernote Search Grammar - Evern...	David Sarna's Evern...			88.2KB
10/15/2013 4:58 PM	10/15/2013 4:58 PM	Quick Tip: How to Search for Text I...	David Sarna's Evern...			217KB
10/15/2013 2:50 PM	10/15/2013 2:50 PM	ENDCE and irisin in humans: I Prod...	David Sarna's Evern...			7.2KB

🖹 Evernote For Dummies Practice ▾ 🖉 Click to add tag...

Created: 3/2/2014 4:00 PM   Updated: 3/2/2014 4:01 PM

Notes I can email

How I Learned to Stay Organized with Evernote, Post-its & Foamcore | Xconomy

Evernote Market: App Maker's Retail Strategy Pays Off - Businessweek

LiveMinutes

Figure 3-18:
List view.

Part II
Harnessing the Power of Notes

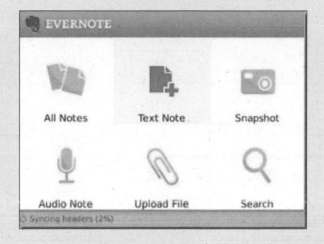

In this part . . .

- ✔ Clipping content from the web
- ✔ Storing photos and other content
- ✔ Adding audio and video recordings to notes
- ✔ Creating and forwarding notes via e-mail and Twitter
- ✔ Scanning into Evernote

Chapter 4

Web Clipping

*I*n this chapter, I show you a quick and easy way to get content that you find on the Internet into your Evernote account for safe keeping. After you single out a particular article or web page, crop it, highlight some lines of text, or add an arrow to point something out, all by using the Evernote Web Clipper tool.

Web Clipping: Capturing Screens and Web Pages

When you find something on a web page that you want to keep as a note, you may not want to save everything you see. As often as not, all you need is a portion of a site, such as a picture on the page. Evernote makes it easy to pull in as much or as little of a web page as you like. Evernote calls this process *clipping.* The Evernote software that does the magic is *Web Clipper* — an extension for your web browser that makes it easy to store, mark up, and share just about anything you find on the web, including selected text, articles, and even entire web pages.

At the time this book was written, the newest clipping features of Web Clipper were available for the Google Chrome, Apple Safari, Mozilla Firefox, Internet Explorer, and Opera browsers. Navigate to http://blog.evernote.com to check for rollout to your favorite devices.

I discuss web clipping for some of these platforms in the following sections, and I cover web clipping for smartphones in Chapter 15.

For up-to-date information on using the Evernote Web Clipper, you can also visit `http://evernote.com/webclipper/guide`.

Web Clipping on a Mac

Clipping on a Mac is the same whether you're clipping from Internet Explorer Safari, Chrome, or Firefox. In Opera, clipping is the same as for Windows (see the next section).

Chapter 2 gives you instructions for downloading Chrome, Firefox, Safari, and their respective Web Clipper extensions. You can also use the Opera browser, available at `www.opera.com`. You must have the browser on your computer to use its Web Clipper extension. The Web Clipper extension for Internet Explorer is included in Evernote for Windows, so there's nothing left for you to do.

To clip on a Mac, follow these steps:

1. **Ensure that you've installed the clipper for your browser, as described in Chapter 2.**

   If you don't see it (that is, you don't see the elephant icon on the toolbar), go to `http://evernote.com/webclipper` to install it.

2. **To initiate capturing all or part of a screen to create a note, click the Web Clipper icon (the Evernote elephant) on the toolbar in your browser.**

   Figure 4-1 shows the screen that appears.

3. **Choose one of the following clipping options:**

   - *Article:* Click this link to capture the entire page you're viewing, minus things like the website header and footer.

   - *Simplified Article:* Click this link to capture just the article you're viewing, including photos. Other parts of the page — such as the header, footer, sidebars, and even lines delineating sections — are excluded.

   - *Full Page:* Click this link to capture everything you see on your screen: the article, header, footer, images, sidebars, ads, and any social media features (such as tickets or comment boxes).

   - *Bookmark:* Click the Bookmark link to copy a snippet of the article in addition to the article's URL. Clicking the snippet in your Evernote note takes you to the full article.

   - *Screenshot:* Click this link to copy the entire web page; then you can use the Markup tools to crop out the precise sections that you want to showcase (see Step 4).

Figure 4-1:
Capturing
web content
in Evernote.

Irrespective of the web clipping type you originally selected, if you subsequently choose to use the Markup tools, your web clipping is changed to a screen shot; then you can crop out the portion you want to use.

4. **(Optional) When you're done clipping your web content, you can modify it by using one of the Markup tools (some of which are visible in Figure 4-2):**

   - *Highlighter:* Use this tool to highlight portions of text or images. ***Note:*** This markup tool is the only markup one that works with all the clipping types.

   - *Marker:* Use this tool to draw or write freehand on your screen shot.

   - *Shape:* You should use this tool when you want to draw shapes on your clipping. The options available are arrow, line, circle, oval, and square.

   - *Type:* When you want to add typed content to your clipping, use this tool.

   - *Stamp:* This tool adds colorful little "stamps" to your clipping to help call attention to whatever you're showcasing. The options are a heart, X, exclamation point, and check mark. See Figure 4-3 for an example of web clipping that uses stamps.

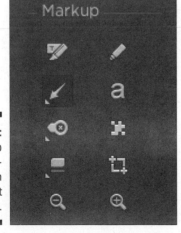

Figure 4-2:
Marking up
your clip-
ping with
different
tools.

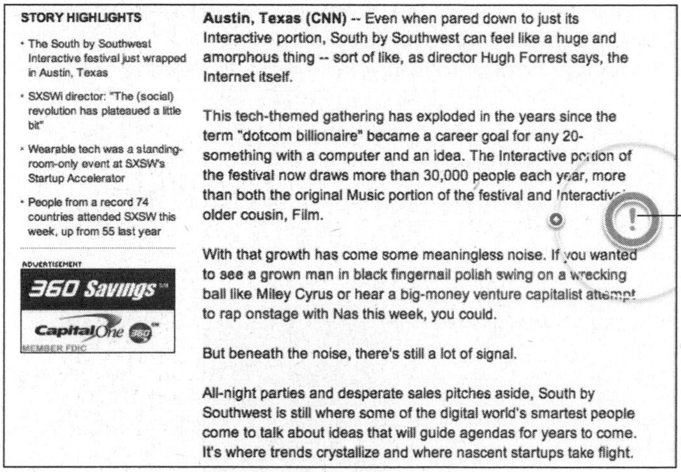

STORY HIGHLIGHTS

• The South by Southwest Interactive festival just wrapped in Austin, Texas

• SXSWi director: "The (social) revolution has plateaued a little bit"

• Wearable tech was a standing-room-only event at SXSW's Startup Accelerator

• People from a record 74 countries attended SXSW this week, up from 55 last year

ADVERTISEMENT

360 Savings℠

CapitalOne 360℠

MEMBER FDIC

Austin, Texas (CNN) -- Even when pared down to just its Interactive portion, South by Southwest can feel like a huge and amorphous thing -- sort of like, as director Hugh Forrest says, the Internet itself.

This tech-themed gathering has exploded in the years since the term "dotcom billionaire" became a career goal for any 20-something with a computer and an idea. The Interactive portion of the festival now draws more than 30,000 people each year, more than both the original Music portion of the festival and Interactive's older cousin, Film.

With that growth has come some meaningless noise. If you wanted to see a grown man in black fingernail polish swing on a wrecking ball like Miley Cyrus or hear a big-money venture capitalist attempt to rap onstage with Nas this week, you could.

But beneath the noise, there's still a lot of signal.

All-night parties and desperate sales pitches aside, South by Southwest is still where some of the digital world's smartest people come to talk about ideas that will guide agendas for years to come. It's where trends crystallize and where nascent startups take flight.

A stamp in a web clipping

Figure 4-3:
Fun with the
Stamp tool.

• *Pixelator:* This tool blurs anything you want to hide, such as names, faces, or account numbers.

• *Colors:* Yellow is the only color option for the Highlighter tool, but you can select the color you want to use for the Marker tool. Your options are red, orange, yellow, green, blue, pink, black, and white.

• *Crop:* Maybe you just want to clip a small part of the screen but you also want to draw some shapes and lines on it. Because your clipping was automatically converted to a screen shot when you chose a Markup tool, you can use the Crop tool to single out the original portion that you had your eye on.

• *Zoom Out and Zoom In:* Get a closer look at your screen shot by clicking the magnifying glass with the plus (+) inside it, and get back to the normal view by clicking the magnifying glass with the minus (–) inside it.

5. **Click the notebook icon below the File heading (refer to Figure 4-1) to select the notebook where you want to save your web clipping.**

   The Notebook selector box opens, listing your default Evernote notebook.

6. **(Optional) Select a different notebook, if you don't want to use the default.**

7. **(Optional) Add any desired tags and comments to your web clipping.**

   You can read more about adding tags in Chapter 8.

8. **Click the blue Share button or the green Save button (refer to Figure 4-1).**

If you click Share, your web clipping is automatically saved to Evernote as a note, and the dialog box shown in Figure 4-4 opens. The URL is automatically copied to your clipboard for sharing purposes, but you can also choose to share the note on Facebook, Twitter, or LinkedIn, or via e-mail. Click Update when you finish sharing the note, and the note syncs with Evernote.

If you don't want to share the note, click Save. The note syncs with Evernote.

Figure 4-4:
Sharing
your web
clipping.

Web Clipping in Windows

Clipping on a PC is the same whether you're clipping from Safari, Chrome, Firefox, or Opera. Web clipping using Internet Explorer is covered in the next section.

To clip a web selection in Windows, follow these steps:

1. **Ensure that you've installed the clipper for your browser, as described in Chapter 2.**

   If you don't see it (that is, you don't see the elephant icon on the toolbar), go to `http://evernote.com/webclipper` to install it.

2. **To initiate capturing all or part of a screen to create a note, click the Web Clipper icon (the Evernote elephant) on the toolbar in your browser.**

   Figure 4-1, earlier in this chapter, shows the resulting window.

3. **Select one of the following clipping options:**

   • *Article:* This option automatically detects the main text of a blog, news article, or web page. To modify the area of the web page captured, click the + or – buttons onscreen or press the arrow keys on your keyboard.

- *Simplified Article:* This option clears all ads, sidebars, headers, and footers from the article.

- *Full Page:* This option saves a static copy of the entire page, with all navigation, headers, footers, and images. This option is a good one to choose if you want to save the exact appearance of the web page.

- *Bookmark:* Choose this option to bookmark a URL, one image, and a snippet of text.

- *Screenshot:* This option takes a static snapshot of your browser screen.

4. **If you chose Screenshot in Step 3, use the markup tools in the sidebar that appears (refer to Figure 4-2) to crop the image and add text, shapes, stamps, and more.**

   - *Highlighter:* Use this tool to highlight portions of text or images. **Note:** This markup tool is the only markup one that works with all the clipping types.

   - *Marker:* Use this tool to draw or write freehand on your screen shot.

   - *Shape:* You should use this tool when you want to draw shapes on your clipping. The options available are arrow, line, circle, oval, and square.

   - *Type:* When you want to add typed content to your clipping, use this tool.

   - *Stamp:* This tool adds colorful little "stamps" to your clipping to help call attention to whatever you're showcasing. The options are a heart, X, exclamation point, and check mark. Refer to Figure 4-3 for an example of web clipping that uses stamps.

   - *Pixelator:* This tool blurs anything you want to hide, such as names, faces, or account numbers.

   - *Colors:* Yellow is the only color option for the Highlighter tool, but you can select the color you want to use for the Marker tool. Your options are red, orange, yellow, green, blue, pink, black, and white.

   - *Crop:* Maybe you just want to clip a small part of the screen but you also want to draw some shapes and lines on it. Because your clipping was automatically converted to a screen shot when you chose a Markup tool, you can use the Crop tool to single out the original portion that you had your eye on.

   - *Zoom Out and Zoom In:* Get a closer look at your screen shot by clicking the magnifying glass with the plus (+) inside it, and get back to the normal view by clicking the magnifying glass with the minus (–) inside it.

5. **Click the notebook icon below the File heading (refer to Figure 4-1) to select the notebook where you want to save your web clipping.**

   The Notebook selector box opens, listing your default Evernote notebook.

6. **(Optional) Select a different notebook, if you don't want to use the default.**

7. **(Optional) Add any desired tags and comments to your web clipping.**

   You can read more about adding tags in Chapter 8.

8. **Click the blue Share button or the green Save button (refer to Figure 4-1).**

   If you click Share, your web clipping is automatically saved to Evernote as a note (refer to Figure 4-4). The URL is automatically copied to your clipboard for sharing purposes, but you can also choose to share the note on Facebook, Twitter, or LinkedIn, or via e-mail. Click Update when you finish sharing the note, and the note syncs with Evernote.

   If you don't want to share the note, click Save. The note syncs with Evernote.

You can click links in the note to open the web clipping in your default web browser as long as you can connect to the Internet.

Web Clipping in Internet Explorer

Internet Explorer is the odd browser out when it comes to web clipping. You just have to follow some slightly modified instructions.

To use Web Clipper in Internet Explorer, follow these steps:

1. **Highlight the text you want to clip or (if you're clipping an entire article or screen), skip to Step 2.**

   If you're clipping just a portion of an article, you must highlight the content before clicking the Web Clipper icon.

 2. **Click the Web Clipper icon (the Evernote elephant) on the browser's address bar.**

   If you don't see the Web Clipper icon, make sure that your Command toolbar is enabled. (Right-click your toolbar and make sure that you see a check mark next to Command Bar in the contextual menu.)

3. **Click the down arrow to the right of the Save button to select the portion of the screen you want to clip.**

   Figure 4-5 shows the options on the contextual menu that appears:

- *Save Article* saves just the article and omits any other content on the page, such as ads or links to other pages.

- *Save Full Page* saves the entire web page to your notebook. Links on the page still work, but the content is saved so that you can edit it.

- *Save URL* saves just the link of the article or blog. Although this option may not give you as much information as Save Full Page, it saves space.

4. **(Optional) Update the fields as desired.**

   You can change the title of the web clipping, select the notebook to save it to, add tags, or add comments.

5. **(Optional) Click the green Options link in the bottom-left corner of Web Clipper to open the Web Clipper default dialog box.**

   You can set the default web-clipping action to Save Article, Save Full Page, or Save URL.

6. **(Optional) Use the drop-down menu to enable or disable the Article Selection tool.**

   This tool enables you to modify the size of the selection before creating the web clipping. If you disable it, you can't change the clipping area, so I recommend that you *not* disable this tool.

7. **Click the Close button when you finish making any adjustments.**

   You return to your web-clipping selection.

8. Click the Save button to open the clipping in an Evernote note.

This button is attached to the down arrow you clicked in Step 3.

Your new web clipping opens in a new note. You can edit this note as you would any other by changing the font, adding attachments, adding tags, or sharing it. The note saves and syncs just like any other note.

 If you have more than a single web page to capture, I suggest capturing each page as a separate note. If you like, you can combine these notes into a single note later. To combine notes in Windows, select the notes to be combined (by pressing the Ctrl or Shift keys) and then right-click the selection and choose Merge Notes from the contextual menu. On a Mac, ⌘-click to select the notes you want to combine; and then Option-click and choose Merge Notes from the contextual menu.

Chapter 5

Working with Audio and Video

*I*n this chapter, you work with some of the most exciting file types: audio recordings, images, and video. Saving memories of more important stuff, like visuals and vocals, is how you'll get really attached to Evernote (if you aren't already). Capturing events and conversations for later review and reminiscing have never been this easy.

Answering machines and camcorders got most people over the novelty of recording themselves. But everything was segregated to different devices or files, which meant that locating the right recording was as difficult as locating your tax return from five years ago. Now, Evernote makes it possible for you to centralize all your recordings and images, which is especially important when it comes to meetings or family vacations. Evernote is also awesome for working with files like PDFs and other images containing text because it's capable of "reading" them and then making them searchable.

Recording a Voice Note

Sometimes, you're on the go and don't have time to type or tap and fix notes, particularly with the "help" of autocorrection. You spend more time fighting your keyboard than getting stuff done. If you're hurrying to your next location, recording voice notes is the perfect way to catch your thoughts before they flit off into oblivion.

The way to record a voice note in Evernote is similar for all devices. The following instructions point out the minor differences.

TIP

If you want to add notes or text to any of your recordings, you can do that, too. After you create your recording, just click in the note area and begin typing. Best of all, you can add the text from any device, not just desktop computers or laptops.

Mac desktop or laptop

To record on a Mac desktop or laptop, follow these steps:

1. **Choose File⇨New Audio Note.**

   An untitled audio note opens in your default notebook, but you can change the notebook at any time.

2. **Add a title and text (optional)**

   You should always add a title to your audio recording to identify it, but adding text to the note is optional.

3. **Click the Record button when you're ready to start recording your first voice note (see Figure 5-1).**

   While the recording is taking place, the blue Record button turns into a red Save button.

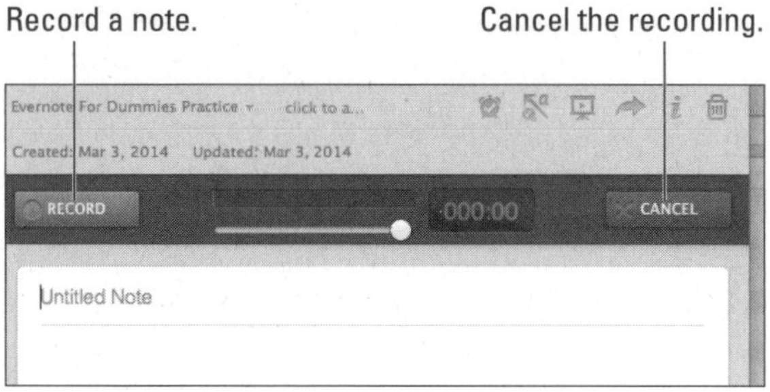

Record a note.   Cancel the recording.

> Evernote For Dummies Practice ▾   click to a...
>
> Created: Mar 3, 2014   Updated: Mar 3, 2014
>
> ⊙ RECORD ─────────●────── -000:00   ✕ CANCEL
>
> |Untitled Note

Figure 5-1:
Recording a
voice note.

4. **When you finish, click Save.**

   The recording is inserted as an audio note. Click Play to play it back. Click Done to save the note.

5. **Click Play to determine whether your recording is a keeper.**

   Take the time to review your recording (see Figure 5-2). If you like what you hear, you're done. If you want to take another crack at it, go to the next couple of steps.

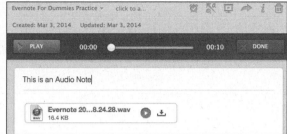

Figure 5-2:
Playing
back your
audio note.

6. **(Optional) Press Delete.**

    After you have saved a recording, the audio file is added to the note (see Figure 5-2). You can click anywhere inside the note and press the Delete or backspace button on your keyboard to delete the audio file. The note remains, however.

7. **To rerecord your note, click the Record Audio icon, which looks like a microphone.**

    The icon is on the toolbar just above the notes.

Windows desktop or laptop

To work with voice notes in Windows, do this:

1. **Choose File⇨New Note or use the Ctrl+N keyboard shortcut.**

    An empty note is created.

2. **Click anywhere in the note to make the formatting bar visible (see Figure 5-3).**

Figure 5-3:
The format-
ting bar in a
note.

3. **Click the microphone icon.**

    The recording controls open above the note (see Figure 5-4).

Figure 5-4:
Evernote's
recording
controls.

4. **Click Record.**

Recording begins (see Figure 5-5).

Figure 5-5:
Recording a
note.

5. **Click Save to save recording or Cancel to stop recording and start over.**

A saved recording is added to the note (see Figure 5-6).

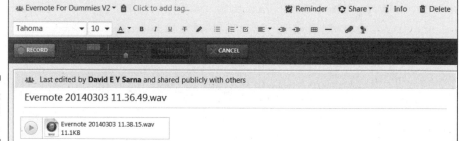

Figure 5-6:
A saved
voice note.

If you want to add another voice note, click Record again in an open note. The additional recording is inserted into the same note.

iOS devices

To record on an iPhone, iPad, or iPod touch, follow these steps:

1. **Launch your Evernote app and tap the Text note icon.**

2. **Tap the microphone icon on the home screen.**

A new voice note is created (see Figure 5-7).

The app starts recording right after you tap the microphone icon, so be ready to talk.

Figure 5-7: Recording an audio note on the iPhone.

Microphone icon

3. **Begin speaking.**

4. **Tap Done when you're finished.**

   Your recording is automatically saved to the note (see Figure 5-8).

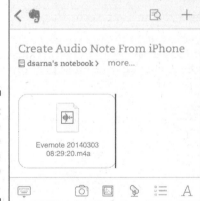

Figure 5-8: iPhone voice recording inserted into note.

Android devices

Here's what you need to do to record on an Android device:

1. **Tap the microphone icon on the home screen (see Figure 5-9).**

   The editor appears, with the formatting bar visible (see Figure 5-10).

Figure 5-9:
Getting
ready to
record
a voice
note on an
Android
device.

Figure 5-10:
The format-
ting bar in
the voice
note editor.

2. **Tap the microphone icon, and start speaking.**

   Recording starts as soon as you tap the microphone icon, so make sure that you're ready.

3. **Tap the Checkmark icon when you're done recording.**

   On an Android device, when you touch the Checkmark icon to stop the recording, the audio automatically attaches to the note (see Figure 5-11). If you want to listen to your recording, tap the audio portion of the note.

Figure 5-11:
Audio added
to note on
an Android
device.

BlackBerry

To record on a BlackBerry, follow these steps:

1. **Tap Audio Note on the Evernote home screen (see Figure 5-12).**

   A new note is created.

Tap to create a voice note.

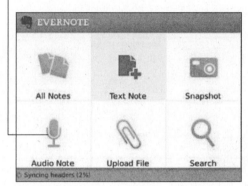

Figure 5-12:
Creating an
audio note.

2. **Tap the Voice Note icon to begin recording (see Figure 5-13).**

   The recording starts as soon as you tap the button, so make sure that you're ready.

Figure 5-13:
Tap Voice
Note to
begin
recording.

3. **Tap Stop when you're done recording.**

   You can play the audio back by tapping the audio portion of the note. Then you can decide whether to rerecord or save what you have.

4. **When you're satisfied with your recording, tap the BlackBerry button.**

   The recording is saved to the new note (see Figure 5-14).

Figure 5-14:
Saved audio
note on a
BlackBerry.

Creating Notes from Images

Saving images is similar to saving notes with audio files attached (see the earlier section "Recording a Voice Note,"); you can save multiple images in a single note. You can work with images on a website, which you can clip into a note, or you can work with individual image files.

The best way to add an image file is to drag and drop it into a note, but this method has limitations. As with audio notes, you can save as many files as you want to a note, but each note has a size limit based on your account type, so make sure that you're aware of that limit when you start to add images. (Check out Chapter 2 for details on your account-type limitations.)

Here's how you get your cool images saved to Evernote:

1. **Click New Note to create a new note.**

2. **In the Finder (Mac) or Windows Explorer, go to the location where you store your images, and drag one or more images to your Evernote account in your web browser.**

   The default location on a Mac is the Pictures folder inside your user folder. The default location on a PC is the My Pictures folder on your C drive.

   When you complete this step, your image is in Evernote.

Saving photos in Windows

When Evernote for Windows detects that a webcam is installed, a new command appears on the File menu, allowing you to capture photos in notes. In this section, I show you how to use this feature.

To save a photo to a note in Evernote for Windows, follow these steps:

1. **Choose New Note⇨New Webcam Note or press Ctrl+Shift+W.**

   The New Webcam Note window opens, displaying the video image captured by the webcam.

2. **Do one of the following:**

   • Click Take Snapshot to capture the image.

   • Click Cancel to close the capture window. Evernote creates a blank note, which you need to delete manually.

3. **Do one of the following:**

   • Click Retake Snapshot if you're not happy with the image.

   • Click Save to Evernote to load the snapshot into a note.

   • Click Cancel to abandon the task. Evernote doesn't create a blank note.

Saving photos on a Mac

FaceTime also enables you to save a photograph or screen shot to a note on a Mac running OS X version 10.6 or later. Follow these steps:

1. **Choose File⇨New⇨New FaceTime Camera Note.**

   The camera opens.

2. **When you're ready to take the picture, click Take Snapshot.**

   If you're not happy with the picture, click the Try Again button to retake it as many times as you like.

3. **When you're satisfied with the picture, click Use to save it to your default notebook as an untitled note.**

Saving Pictures from a Mobile Device

Mobile platforms are discussed in more detail later in the book (Chapter 15), but here I show you how to take and save pictures from your mobile device or — if you have Eye-Fi Pro X2 — any digital camera that supports a memory card that's compatible with Secure Digital High-Capacity (SDHC) format cards (see Chapter 18).

Taking pictures on an iOS device

To take and save pictures on an iPhone, iPod touch, or iPad, follow these steps:

1. **Launch the Evernote app.**

2. **Create a new note, and select the Camera icon.**

   This opens up your device's built-in camera.

3. **Take the picture when you're ready.**

   This feature operates the same way as simply taking a picture.

4. **Tap Retake or Save, depending on whether you're happy with the picture.**

   Retake allows you to try again. If you're satisfied with the picture, save it to the note by tapping Save.

Taking pictures on an Android device

To take and save pictures on an Android device, follow these steps:

1. **Launch the Evernote app.**

2. **Tap New Note on the main screen.**

3. **Tap the camera icon in the top-right corner to take a picture.**

4. **Tap Save when you're satisfied with the picture.**

   The picture automatically attaches to the note.

Taking pictures on Windows phones

To take and save pictures on a Windows phone, follow these steps:

1. **Launch the Evernote app.**

2. **Tap the Camera quick note button on the Home screen.**

   This opens up your device's built-in camera.

3. **Take the picture when you're ready.**

   This feature operates the same way as simply taking a picture.

4. **Tap the device's back button to save the note and return to the Home screen.**

   The picture automatically attaches to the note.

Taking pictures on a BlackBerry phone

To take and save pictures on a BlackBerry phone, follow these steps:

1. **Launch the Evernote app.**

2. **Tap the Snapshot button on the top right of the Home screen.**

   This opens up your device's built-in camera.

3. **Take the picture when you're ready.**

   This feature operates the same way as simply taking a picture.

4. **Tap Done to save the note and return to the Home screen.**

   The picture automatically attaches to the note.

Adding screen-shot images to a note

You probably have a million pictures that you want to save to Evernote. If you'd like to save an image from a screen capture, the steps are short and sweet, but (of course) they vary based on whether you use a Mac or a Windows PC.

Mac method

To create a screen shot for a new note on a Mac, follow these steps:

1. **Open the image or application you want to take a screenshot of to add to Evernote.**

2. **Press ⌘+Control+C to create a new note with the image you want to save.**

3. **Drag the crosshair pointer to select the portion of the screen you want to save, and click to create the note.**

   Whatever is inside the selection rectangle is captured in the new note.

4. **Click the note area, and add text.**

   Go wild. Add whatever text you need to help you remember what the note means and why it's important.

5. **Save the note.**

   You have a screen shot in your new note.

Windows method

To create a screen shot for a new note in Windows, open Evernote and follow these steps:

1. **Open the image or application you want to take a screenshot of to add to Evernote.**

2. **Press Win+PrtSc on your keyboard.**

   You get a screen shot of everything on your monitor (or monitors), and it is automatically copied to your Clipboard.

3. **Click New Note (or Ctrl+N) to create a new note.**

4. **Paste your image into the note area.**

5. **Crop the unwanted portions out of the screen shot.**

   If you want to make adjustments, you need to open the image in a photo-editing program. To do so, right-click the image, select Open With, and then pick a program from the applications offered.

See Chapter 17 for information about using the Skitch application to edit images that you've attached to notes.

Attaching a Video

All users can save video files to notes as attachments, subject to note-size limitations. Using an attachment may not be quite the same as having the item readily available on the notes screen, but an attachment requires only one extra click or tap to play.

Currently, a note is limited to 25MB for free accounts or 100MB for Premium or Business accounts, so it's suitable only for relatively short video clips. Using your mobile device, you can record a short video and e-mail it directly to your Evernote account or use iTunes as the conduit. (When you sync iTunes, the video is copied, and you can drag it into a note.) For longer videos, you can use one of the low-priced, nifty pocket cameras and then transfer the video via a computer to your Evernote account or use an Eye-Fi card (see Chapter 18).

If your plan imposes limits on e-mail size then you can transfer longer videos from your mobile device to your computer and then to Evernote to work around the situation. But keep in mind that the file and any additional info in the note need to be less than the note limit for your Evernote account type.

It all adds up!

Although you can store unlimited data in your Evernote account, monthly uploads are limited. Currently, free accounts are limited to 60MB a month, Premium accounts are limited to 1GB, and Business accounts are limited to 2GB. Although that amount of storage sounds like a lot, be aware that videos eat upload capacity. Be conscious of your monthly limits.

To see where you stand with regard to your monthly upload limit, do one of the following things:

✔ On a Windows PC, choose Tools⇨Account Info to see how much storage you've used and how much remains before the next cycle.

✔ On a Mac, choose Help⇨Account Settings. In the Usage section of the resulting window, check out the Current Monthly Usage bar, which shows how much of your allowance you've used and how much is available. (You need an active Internet connection, as you're being connected to www.evernote.com/User. action#summary.)

✔ Go to http://evernote.com, log in, and click Settings. Your storage amounts appear in the middle of the page.

If you're constrained by size limitations, you can increase your note upload allowance in 1GB increments to a maximum of 5GB for a single month, to a limit of 25GB additional per annual cycle for a small fee (currently $5.00), and you can do this up to five times a year. Increases are temporary and expire at the end of the month in which you bought the upgrade, whether you used up all of the storage space you purchased or not.

You also need an application on each computer or device that can play the file type you're storing. Evernote is your extended memory; it stores the clip, but it doesn't inherently play anything.

Reading Images and Image Recognition

One of the coolest things about Evernote is its ability to read images. If there's text in an image, including images embedded in PDFs, Evernote can read and catalog the information.

Evernote doesn't make images in PDFs searchable. Evernote's image recognition is performed on image files (JPEG, GIF, and so on); PDFs are separate cases. For Premium and Business users, Evernote uses optical character recognition to scan PDF documents. This process is optimized to make text documents searchable.

So where are the instructions for running this cool feature? That's where the program is really neat. Image recognition is automatic. Any image you add is automatically scanned for recognition. You don't have to do anything other than add the image to your Evernote account.

Want to remember the name of that dish you had at that quaint little restaurant in New York? Snap a picture of the menu with your mobile device, and you'll have it forever and can search for what you need. For another example of how Evernote's image-recognition feature can make your life easier, see the nearby sidebar "Grill shopping made easy." Read Chapter 8 for tips on searching Evernote.

Image recognition even works on handwritten stuff, but it's limited by the neatness of the handwriting. If you can't make out what you wrote, don't expect Evernote to be able to read your writing either.

Evernote doesn't run the image-recognition software locally over the application, but within its servers, so there'll be a delay from the time when you store the note until it's read. If you store a note and search for it immediately, you may not find it. Have patience. A subsequent search *will* recognize it.

You don't need to stay online for the file to process. After you store the note, Evernote recognizes that you've added a file for recognition. That file gets queued and processed. The next time you sync your account, the local database is updated, so a search on a web client (which synchronizes automatically) may see it first.

The amount of time it takes to process image recognition depends on file size and the load on the Evernote service. Business accounts are served from their own servers. Premium members' requests are processed ahead of requests from free accounts, so their files usually can be completed within a few minutes. In my experience, recognition often takes only a few seconds for a Business or Premium account. If you have a free account, it can occasionally take hours for the recognition servers to get around to indexing your documents. But hey, remember that you're getting the service free.

If you have only a paper copy of a document, simply scan it or take a picture of it with your smartphone to move it over to Evernote. Chapter 6 has more details on scanning.

Grill shopping made easy

Evernote's image-recognition feature can simplify your life, even when you're out and about. When I was shopping for a new grill, I used my smartphone to photograph grills, their product descriptions, and price tags, and then put all that information in a note in Evernote. Evernote read the pictures, even though I took them sideways.

When I searched for *Brinkmann,* for example, Evernote found the picture instantly, even though I inadvertently tagged the note incorrectly by leaving out the second *n* in *Brinkmann.* Because Evernote recognized the name in the photograph, the search instantly retrieved what I was looking for.

Chapter 6

Creating Notes from Other Media

In This Chapter

▶ Working with ink, e-mail, and Twitter notes

▶ Scanning notes into Evernote

▶ Creating notes on various devices

▶ Using the Kindle and Nook to create notes

*I*n this chapter, you explore applications and devices that you may not normally have thought of in connection with Evernote. But if you've ever sunk time into trying to locate an e-mail in your inbox or in your Sent Mail folder, or if you have a plethora of faxes, you know just how frustrating keeping track of everything can be. In this chapter, I tell you how to create notes from many programs, apps, and devices.

Exploring Evernote's Diversity

One reason why Evernote is useful is that it handles diverse media originating from diverse sources, not just that it works with a plethora of computer and mobile types.

Using Evernote with different devices

Here are some examples of ways you can use Evernote with different devices:

✔ If you're linked to a scanner, you can send the scanned document directly to Evernote as a PDF, and if you're a Premium subscriber, Evernote's servers will make the PDF searchable for you.

✔ If you have a tablet with a tool for taking notes, you can send the notes right into Evernote.

✓ Use your mobile device to take a picture and send that photo right into Evernote to save your memories instantly — and find them again easily later.

✓ Forward or carbon-copy important e-mails and deliver them as notes, with all the power of Evernote available for searching and retrieving them.

✓ Tweet to Evernote or save tweets from other people that you'd like to keep.

✓ Save information straight from your Nook or Nook Color to Evernote.

Use discretion. Evernote is for keeping important and useful stuff that you'll likely access again. It's easy to end up with too much of a good thing if you're not careful. If you signed up for lots of RSS feeds and direct them indiscriminately to your Evernote account, for example, you may find yourself with too many notes to handle — and may also exceed your monthly upload allocation. (You can click Settings to see where you stand in terms of your monthly upload allowance.)

Using Evernote with different apps

Application users can now share notes to Facebook and Twitter via the iOS app or by choosing Share⇨Post to Facebook or Share⇨Post to Twitter in Windows. For other platforms, you can still use the old web-clipping method to get content from the site into a note. See Chapter 2 for more information on the Evernote Web Clipper Internet browser extension.

By choosing to share a note, you're making the contents of the note publicly accessible. It's a small but important update that furthers Evernote's social direction.

Creating an Ink Note

This section applies to Windows 7 and Mac OS X; use the third-party InkNote app for Android. To download InkNote, point your browser to https:// play.google.com/store and search for InkNote in the top search bar.

Chapter 5 covers how to use image recognition and how to take pictures of notes that you hurriedly scribble. If you have an app for taking handwritten notes, a graphics tablet connected to a PC or a Mac, or a tablet supporting Windows 7, you can go one better by scribbling the note right into Evernote — no camera necessary.

Evernote for Windows lets you create an *ink note* — a note written on a graphic tablet — right inside Evernote. Click the InkNote option and then start scribbling with your Wacom or other supported tablet. After you're done, that ink note syncs to all other versions of Evernote that you use.

You can also use the ink technology built into Mac OS X. For detailed instructions, see `http://macobserver.com/tmo/article/Ink_Your_Macs_Keyboard_Alternative/`.

To create an ink note on a Mac, follow these steps:

1. **If you haven't done so already, connect your tablet to Evernote.**

2. **Start writing on your tablet to teach Evernote your handwriting.**

3. **Create a doodle.**

   This step is mostly for practice, but sketching something helps Evernote differentiate your writing from your drawing.

4. **In System Preferences, click the Ink icon.**

5. **Make sure that Handwriting Recognition is set to On.**

6. **Select Open Ink Help.**

   You're ready to start showing Evernote what all your chicken scratching or flowing lettering really says.

Other than as described in this section, Ink isn't supported on the Mac on iOS devices, as this book goes to press. Some support is provided by third-party applications such as Awesome Note (`http://bridworks.com/anote/en/ipad/features/index.php`), but that app doesn't sync directly with Evernote. An option I use myself is Evernote's Skitch application (read more in Chapter 18) to create a note or drawing and then drag it into Evernote (Mac and iOS only). If you use an Android device, you're in luck. Handwriting is now supported (see `http://blog.evernote.com/blog/2014/03/05/handwriting-arrives-evernote-android/`).

Creating and Forwarding Notes by E-Mail

Similar to the way you clip a web page (see Chapter 4), you can create an e-mail note. Evernote has made creating an e-mail even easier than clipping a web page, however, because you can have your e-mails delivered into the application as notes.

Creating an e-mail note

To create an e-mail note, follow these steps:

1. **Click Settings on your Evernote for Web home page.**

2. **Write down your incoming e-mail address.**

   When you created your account, Evernote generated an e-mail address for you. If you're using a desktop version of Evernote, you can find your e-mail address as follows:

   - **Mac:** Choose Evernote⇨Account Info.

   - **PC:** Choose Tools⇨Account Info.

   - **iOS devices:** Tap Settings⇨Evernote.

   - **Android:** Tap Evernote⇨Settings.

3. **In your regular e-mail account, add the Evernote-generated address to your contacts list to be sure that e-mail from Evernote isn't filtered out.**

   You might create a contact called Evernote with the e-mail address associated with your Evernote account. If you're setting up your note on an iOS device, you can tap Add to Contact below the e-mail address when you look it up in Step 2.

   For more on this address, see the nearby sidebar "Your Evernote-generated e-mail address."

4. **Create a new e-mail, add your Evernote e-mail address, enter** Test E-mail **as the subject, type** Test e-mail **in the e-mail body, and click Send to e-mail it.**

   The first part of your subject is the title of the note. After the title, type @ and the name of the notebook where you want the e-mail to be stored. If you'd like to add a tag as well, type # before the tag name. Even better, you can add multiple tags to the e-mail.

5. **Click the Sync button to resync your account and verify that the e-mail was filed properly.**

Evernote enables you to designate the target notebook and tags for an e-mailed note in the e-mail's subject line. For example, if you want your e-mailed note to appear in your Cooking notebook, simply append @Cooking to the e-mail subject. If you want to tag the note, just add tags to the e-mail subject by preceding them with the hash (#) sign, like this: #recipes #vegetarian #sometag. Note that when you want to designate the target notebook and also use tags when sending or forwarding an e-mail to Evernote, you have to enter the notebook name before typing the tag names. Precede each tag with a space and a #, as shown in the preceding example. Of course, any notebook or tags added to the e-mail's subject must already exist in your Evernote account; you can't create new ones this way.

Your Evernote-generated e-mail address

Evernote generates a unique but random address for your account. For your own protection, you can't choose your own. Allowing you to do so means that Evernote would have to let you know that an address you've been craving — say, `JenniferLopez@evernote.com` or `MarcAnthony@evernote.com` — is already taken. So Evernote decided that the best solution was to create and provide a random e-mail address to each user.

You're not stuck with the original Evernote-generated address, however. If you need to generate a different random e-mail address for some reason, navigate to Account Settings in the web version of Evernote, and click Reset Incoming E-Mail. Premium and Business users can contact Evernote support to have an address shortened to just *[username]*@m.evernote.com.

If you want to add items that require specific syntax, such as tags, you may have to practice a couple times to get the notes just the way you want them. The extra effort is well worth the time.

You can use the @ and # symbols only for existing notebooks and tags, so make sure that they're set up before you try to e-mail them. Also, always include the title of the e-mail first. In addition, if you have the @ or # symbol as part of the name of a notebook or tag, consider changing it. If you don't, you won't be able to file the e-mails the way you'd like.

Be mindful of the e-mail limits. You can send up to 50 e-mails per day from free Evernote accounts and 250 e-mails per day from Premium and Business accounts. When you share a note via e-mail or send an invitation to join a shared notebook, each e-mail going to a recipient counts as one e-mail from Evernote. (I've never hit the limits on Premium or Business accounts.)

Forwarding mail to another e-mail account

You may want to have your incoming e-mail forwarded automatically to Evernote for archiving and for rapid search. Gmail and some other e-mail systems let you forward incoming mail to another address automatically, if you like. Consult the help documentation of your e-mail provider for specific instructions.

Creating a Note by Scanning

You can create a note from scanned documents in several ways. The method you use doesn't necessarily depend on what computer you have. You must have a scanner for these steps to work, of course.

If you have a scanner but no software (it does occasionally happen), you can find and download several programs to use. Make sure to read the information on them for compatibility with your computer before you download.

Scanning into Evernote on a PC

Scanning into Evernote is as varied as the number of scanners out there, but you can generally apply the following instructions to most scanners. If you're in the market for a new scanner and want to make working with Evernote as easy as possible, see the sidebar "Evernote-compatible scanners."

Before you scan your first note, you should spend some time making sure that your scanner is set up properly and ready to go.

To scan a note into Evernote, follow these steps:

1. **Find your scanner settings (located in Control Panel or a stand-alone program).**
2. **Look for a way to configure the hardware buttons on the scanner.**
3. **Set a button to launch Evernote by pointing it to** `Evernote.exe` **(in most cases, in** `C:\Program Files\Evernote`**).**
4. **Save the settings.**
5. **Start scanning.**

    Evernote knows what to do with files sent to it from a scanner, such as image or PDF files. If Evernote isn't running, it launches and creates a new note from the received file.

Scanning into Evernote on a Mac

Image Capture is the technology built into every version of Mac OS X that transfers images from your digital camera or scanner to your Mac for use in iPhoto or Automator. Maybe you're already familiar with this feature. If so, life is good, as Image Capture automatically works with whatever scanner you've set up to work with your Mac. Image Capture is a default program, so you don't have to download anything to start scanning your note.

To scan your note with Image Capture, follow these steps:

1. **Start Image Capture.**

   This free application comes with Mac OS X and is located at /Applications/Image Capture.

   If your scanner is supported and turned on, you see a window similar to the one shown in Figure 6-1.

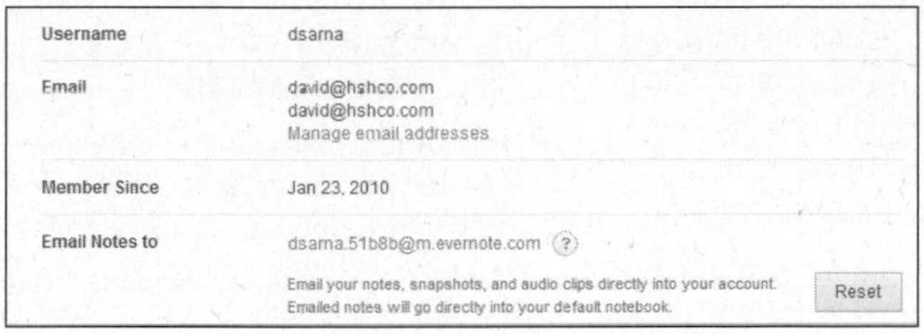

Figure 6-1:
Image
Capture.

Username	dsama
Email	david@hshco.com david@hshco.com Manage email addresses
Member Since	Jan 23, 2010
Email Notes to	dsama.51b8b@m.evernote.com (?)
	Email your notes, snapshots, and audio clips directly into your account. Reset Emailed notes will go directly into your default notebook.

2. **Select the area you want to scan by dragging a rectangle around the preview of the scan.**

3. **Set the quality of the scan to B/W or Color Photo, depending on what you're scanning.**

4. **Give your scan a title.**

5. **Choose PNG or JPEG as your scan's format.**

   If you'd rather scan to PDF, keep in mind that Evernote's image recognition doesn't recognize images embedded within PDFs but makes PDFs searchable for all subscribers.

6. **Select Evernote as the Automatic Task.**

   This step is the key step in this process.

7. **Click Scan.**

8. **Go into your Evernote account, and check out your newest note.**

Whatever options you choose the first time (scanner, image type, and automatic task) are retained as your default settings.

Evernote-compatible scanners

If you're looking to buy a new scanner, and you plan to use Evernote a lot, consider purchasing one that's Evernote-compatible. The following list includes some that you may want to investigate:

✔ **ScanSnap Evernote Edition:** ScanSnap Evernote Edition, produced by Evernote and Fujitsu, automatically rotates, de-skews, detects color and multiple pages, scans front and back, and saves pages into Evernote. Everything you scan is organized and autofiled into the appropriate notebook (documents, receipts, images, or business cards) for easy searching and syncing. See `www.evernote.com/market/feature/scanner` for details.

✔ **imageFormula P-150:** This scanner can run up to 15 pages of scans at a time. After just a few seconds of working in the optimization menu, you can make Evernote your default location for scans. From then on, everything goes into Evernote without your doing anything more than adding the page and

pressing Scan. Visit `www.usa.canon.com/cusa/consumer/products/scanners` to go to the Scanner section of the Canon website and perform a search for imageFormula P-150.

✔ **Doxie:** This ultra-portable, fully automatic scanner scans directly to Evernote. Just insert your paper, and Doxie sends your scans right into Evernote to share, sync, and access on the go. Find their wide range of scanners at `www.getdoxie.com/info/products.html`.

✔ **HoverCam:** This scanner combines a scanner and a camera, and enables you to take high-resolution image scans in less than a second. Using the HoverCam Flex software, you can send your scans to your Evernote account with a single click. You can find HoverCam scanning products at `www.thehovercam.com/products`.

For more on scanners, see Chapter 18.

Scanning handwritten notes

Scanners usually save images as PDF files or JPEG files. Many scanners also are bundled with software that can do optical scan recognition for you, too. None of this software processes handwritten text, but Evernote can help. If you're scanning pages of printed or handwritten notes, Evernote's image-recognition servers can read them and make them searchable.

Image recognition on the Evernote servers can take time (less if you're a Premium subscriber); don't expect to discover that your scanned notes are searchable immediately after you synchronize. Eventually, though, scanned notes are read and are made searchable via the Evernote indexing system.

Currently, Evernote's indexing system processes images, PDFs, and digital-ink documents. For Premium and Business users, any attached document, presentation, or spreadsheet created using Microsoft Office and iWork also shows up in your search results.

Creating a Note from Cameras with Eye-Fi

Today, most devices — BlackBerry, Android, and iOS devices, and Mac and PC computers — have built-in digital cameras. The quality of the cameras varies from very good to blah, but few take pictures with the quality of a good digital camera and a high-quality lens. (See Chapter 18 for a full discussion.)

To take high-quality digital pictures, you need a quality digital camera. Until recently, to get pictures into Evernote, you had to remove the card from the camera and insert it into the card reader on your computer, or you had to take along a cable and transfer files from the camera to your computer. No longer. A company called Eye-Fi makes it possible to hook up your camera with Evernote, even without hooking up the camera to your computer.

Despite the rhyming name, Eye-Fi doesn't require a Wi-Fi connection to work in direct mode. When you put the Eye-Fi X2 card in your camera, it creates its own Wi-Fi network and then uses a free app (which you can download from `http://support.eye.fi/features/direct/mobile-applications`) to transfer pictures and other files to your computer or mobile device.

The Eye-Fi card comes ready to be configured in a USB reader. The software you need to get started is included.

Preparing to use Eye-Fi mobile apps for Android

To use Eye-Fi on your Android device in direct mode, you need to have the following items:

- Eye-Fi Center version 3.3 or later
- Eye-Fi Card with firmware version 4.5021 or later
- Computer with an Internet connection
- Android device running Android 2.1 or later
- Eye-Fi app for Android

For instructions on setting up Eye-Fi Direct Mode with an Android phone or tablet, navigate to `http://support.eye.fi/mobile-applications/eye-fi-android-app`.

Preparing to use Eye-Fi mobile apps for iOS

To use Eye-Fi on your iOS device in direct mode, you need to be sure that you have the following before you begin:

- ✔ An iOS device running iOS 4.0 or later
- ✔ Eye-Fi app for iPhone or iPad

For instructions on setting up Eye-Fi Direct Mode with an iOS device, navigate to `http://support.eye.fi/mobile-applications/ios-eye-fi-app`.

Using Eye-Fi

To use Eye-Fi, follow these steps:

1. **Follow the instructions that come with the Eye-Fi card to set up an Eye-Fi account.**

2. **Insert the Eye-Fi card into your camera.**

3. **Power on your camera.**

4. **Add the wireless networks the Eye-Fi card will use to upload your media.**

   You can add up to 32 networks, even if they're not in range, but you need IDs and passwords to add them.

5. **Choose your destinations, and customize which computer and folders are used to store media.**

   If your Eye-Fi card supports online sharing, you also need to customize where on the web your photos are to be wirelessly transferred. Link the Eye-Fi card to your Evernote account as a destination (probably as the preferred destination).

6. **Take pictures.**

   Eye-Fi and Evernote do everything else.

After you're done taking hundreds of pictures of baby's first step or a collection of business cards or receipts, go into your Evernote account, and start determining which photos are keepers and which ones you don't need. The notes created retain the filename assigned by the camera as the note title. As with any other note, you can retitle the note, add descriptive information, and add tags at will.

Be mindful of monthly upload limits — 60MB for free accounts and 1GB for Premium. Digital photos, especially from higher-resolution cameras, can chew up bandwidth. In months when you're on vacation and may be taking lots of high-resolution pictures, you may want to increase your upload allowance, 1GB at a time, with a limit of 5 increases in one month and up to 25GB in a single year. You can easily check your usage in the web version of Evernote by choosing Settings⇨Usage. Click Increase Upload Allowance to add more bandwidth.

Using E-Readers with Evernote

E-readers such as the Kindle and Nook are lightweight and optimized for book reading. They're very popular and can interface with Evernote.

Using the Kindle with Evernote

Although the Kindle and Evernote are a match made in heaven, no one remembered to tell the designers. As a result, depending on your Kindle, getting information from the device into Evernote on your PC or Mac can be a bit of a challenge. Kindle doesn't directly support copying and pasting into Evernote. A free service, ClippingsConverter (`http://clippingsconverter.com`), lets you easily pull quotes and text from your Kindle and save them to Evernote as notes, as I discuss later in this section.

In this section, I assume that you have a basic knowledge of how to use the Kindle.

If you're new to the Kindle, *Kindle Paperwhite For Dummies,* by Leslie H. Nicoll and Harvey Chute or *Kindle Fire HD For Dummies,* by Nancy Muir and Bernard W. Taylor (both from John Wiley & Sons, Inc.) are great books for discovering how to get the most out of your Kindle.

Clipping quotes and text

Have you ever been reading a book or a newspaper on your Kindle and wanted to clip a few words to refer to later? You can do that by using ClippingsConverter.

For detailed information on creating clippings on your Kindle, see `www.clippingsconverter.com/kindle-clippings-faqs`.

After you sign up for an account at `www.clippingsconverter.com/`, this free site lets you publish your clippings as notes to Evernote after you have authorized ClippingsConverter to access your Evernote account.

Here's what to do:

1. **Select the text you want to highlight on your Kindle. Pick Add a Note or Highlight from the menu that pops up on your screen.**

   The clipping you highlighted is saved in a file called `My Clipping.txt` that is accessible from your computer. You can also see the note or highlighted text by tapping the top of the screen and selecting Go To. Then tap the Notes tab from the drop-down box that appears.

2. **Access the `My Clipping.txt` file by connecting your Kindle to your computer via the supplied USB cable.**

   Click Open in response to the invitation to open the device, and look for a directory named documents. Or if you are using a Mac, open your Finder and select the Kindle option under the Devices heading.

3. **Copy the `My Clippings.txt` file to your computer's desktop.**

4. **First ensure that you are logged into your ClippingsConverter account and then navigate to `www.clippingsconverter.com/Explorer`. Click the import button at the top to upload the `My Clippings.txt` file you saved in Step 1.**

   A window opens to prompt you to select the source of your upload. Click the Click to Upload button in the bottom right.

5. **Choose the `My Clippings.txt` file that you copied to your desktop.**

   Your clippings have now been imported into your MyClippings account.

6. **While still on your MyClippings home page, select Export then Evernote from the drop-down menu on the top right. Click Start Export.**

   Your clippings have now been exported to your Evernote account.

You can review your clippings later, search for words or terms you clipped, and transfer the `My Clippings.txt` file to your computer. This clipping technique is a great way to capture your favorite quotations to share with others.

Sending Kindle content to Evernote by e-mail

One huge disadvantage of the mobile Evernote website is that although you can create a new note, you can apply a title and tags to it only on the latest Kindle. Currently, you can't place any text in the main section of a note.

If you want to use your Kindle to add notes to Evernote, the best method is to send notes via e-mail. Here's how:

1. **Locate your Evernote e-mail address.**

   If you're not sure what your Evernote e-mail address is, on your PC or Mac, go to www.evernote.com, and click Settings. The Evernote e-mail address is located below E-Mailing to Evernote.

2. **On your Kindle, log in to your online e-mail account.**

3. **Use the Kindle web browser to compose your note.**

   The subtitle section of your e-mail is the note title, and the content of your e-mail becomes the body of the note after you open it in Evernote.

4. **Copy and paste each note into your Evernote account.**

5. **Send the e-mail to your Evernote e-mail address.**

How you organize your notes is entirely up to you. If you want to store all your notes in a single notebook, great. If you want to create a separate notebook just for the books you read on your Kindle, great. If you want to create a notebook for each book you read (which seems a little excessive!), you can certainly do that.

Publishers set a clipping limit of around 10 percent of a book. When you reach that limit, you can't highlight any more passages. You won't know what the limit is until you reach it and get the `Clipping limit reached` message.

You can also save your `My Clippings.txt` file. Hook your Kindle up to a computer and simply copy the file into Evernote.

Creating notes directly on the Kindle

The Kindle Fire has a version of Evernote that you can download from the Amazon Apps for Android store at no charge. Click here to download it: www.amazon.com/dp/B004LOMB2Q/ref=cm_sw_su_dp.

Using the Nook and Nook Color

The Nook Color is a 7-inch tablet based on the Android platform, and the Nook is a similar black-and-white version. Both models support Evernote. All Evernote features for Android tablets should work the same way on the Nook and Nook Color. Go to www.barnesandnoble.com/w/evernote-evernote/1102538597 to download the free Nook app for Evernote. See Chapter 15 for more on using Evernote with an Android device.

Skitch, the related Evernote drawing application discussed in Chapter 18, is also supported on the Nook.

You can't do anything on the Nook or Nook Color involving GPS or camera features, but you can do the other regular Evernote stuff.

Nook is based on the Android platform and always requires an SD card to function.

Part III
Managing Information

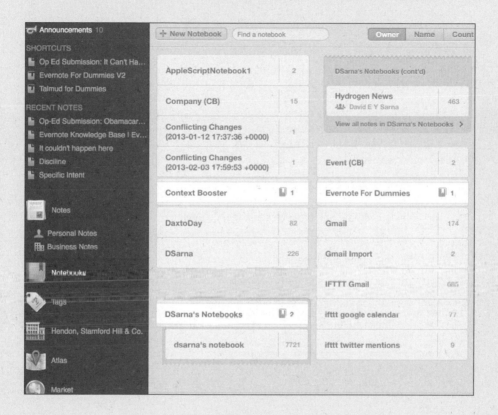

If you want to read more about other ways you can use and customize Evernote, visit
www.dummies.com/webextras/evernote.

In this part . . .

- ✔ Using Evernote on computers and mobile devices
- ✔ Organizing your notes so you can easily find them later
- ✔ Sharing notes and notebooks
- ✔ Encrypting and exporting your notes
- ✔ Connecting your account to other applications
- ✔ Troubleshooting

Chapter 7

Customizing Evernote at Home and Away

*I*n this chapter, you discover how to work on Evernote on your desktop computer and how to get yourself organized. Organization is the whole point of Evernote, of course, so I show you how to move and organize your notes.

You also find out about using Evernote on your mobile devices. I tell you about texting, taking snapshots, working with camera rolls, and recording on different types of mobile devices.

Working with Evernote on Your Desktop Computer

You love working on Evernote wherever you go, but what happens when you hit an area that doesn't have an Internet connection or your Internet connection is down? Or perhaps you just want to do a few things and don't want the temptation of checking e-mail or surfing the Net.

In both situations, Evernote has you covered. When you signed up, you downloaded Evernote to your computer, so you can work right from your desktop or laptop computer (and on some smartphones) even if you don't have an Internet connection.

In cloud computing, nothing is stored locally; in classic desktop computing, everything is stored locally. Evernote is a unique blend. Everything is stored on Evernote's servers, but many devices on which Evernote runs also store local copies. The two copies — local files and the notes stored on Evernote's servers — are synchronized, as discussed in Chapter 9.

If you find yourself without Internet access (by choice or not!), enjoy being on your little desert island for a while, and take some time to get yourself organized. When you return to the busy, civilized world of Internet access, Evernote syncs everything you did, so what's on your local device and what's on Evernote's servers are once again identical.

Exploring your view options

One of the first organizing tasks you'll want to tackle is personalizing Evernote on your computer. You can change Evernote's look and feel by choosing the settings that work best for you.

When you open Evernote's View menu, you see several options that you can customize. At first glance, they look very different. They're similar, in fact, but the Mac version has several new features that haven't migrated to the Windows version at this writing.

Table 7-1 describes the options available on the View menu.

Table 7-1	Options on the View Menu	
Command	*Shortcut Keys*	*Description*
Hide Toolbar (Mac only)	Cmd+⌘+T (Mac)	Hides the toolbar. (The default setting is for the toolbar to show.)
Hide Sidebar	Cmd+⌘+S (Mac)	Hides the left sidebar. (The default setting is for the sidebar to show.)
Sidebar Options	None	Customize the sections shown in the left sidebar.
Customize Toolbar	Right-click the top toolbar and choose Customize Toolbar (Windows) from the contextual menu; no shortcut for Mac	Allows you to add any features of note manipulation to the bar, such as the Sync button or All Notes.

Command	Shortcut Keys	Description
List View	Ctrl+F5 (Windows); no shortcut for Mac	Provides a view of your notes in a list (see Figure 7-1). You can drag the window down to show more notes. The right side has more details on the note highlighted in the list.
Snippets View	Ctrl+F6 (Windows); no shortcut for Mac	Shows you part of the title, the note date, a few more details, and a thumbnail of your notes (see Figure 7-2).
Card View	Ctrl+F7 (Windows); no shortcut for Mac	Shows you a thumbnail of the note and the first few words of the title (see Figure 7-3). You can drag the window to the right to see more thumbnails.
Show Search Explanation	Ctrl+F10 (Windows); no shortcut for Mac	Hides the main icon toolbar — the one that helps you manipulate notes.
Show Note List (Show All Notes)	F11 (Windows); up arrow+⌘+A (Mac)	Shows all the notes in the selected notebook.
Enter Full Screen	^+⌘+F (Mac); no shortcut for Windows	Makes your Evernote window fill the entire screen.
Jump to Notebook	Shift+Alt+N (Windows); ⌘+J (Mac)	Takes you to whatever notebook you select, the same as clicking it.
Back	⌘+[(Mac); no shortcut for Windows	Returns you to the previous screen.
Forward	Command+] (Mac); no shortcut for Windows	Becomes enabled after you click the Back button; returns you to the screen from which you backed out.
Jump to Tag	Shift+Alt+T (Windows); up arrow+⌘+J (Mac)	Opens a menu of tags being used in the selected notebook so you can jump to the location of the tag.

(continued)

Table 7-1 *(continued)*

Command	Shortcut Keys	Description
Show Status Bar (Windows only)	None	Shows the details about your note at the bottom of the screen (see Figure 7-4). Details include word count and characters for the notebook you have highlighted.
Show Note History (Windows only)	None	Shows you the history of your notes. (This feature works only for Premium members.)
Show Note Panel (Windows only)	Ctrl+F11	Shows or hides the note preview in the right pane.
Show Related Notes (Windows only)	None	Shows notes related to the note you're currently viewing. Evernote selects notes to show you based on the tags you assigned the notes.

Figure 7-1: If you like lists, List View is for you.

All Notes ▾						
Created	Updated	Title	Notebook	Tags	Sync	Size
Yesterday 6:44 PM	3 minutes ago	Mac View Menu	Evernote For Dum...		•	77.1KB
Yesterday 5:42 PM	Yesterday 5:42 PM	Image From Snagit 3/3/2014 5:42:...	Evernote For Dum...			200KB
Yesterday 4:46 PM	Yesterday 4:47 PM	New FaceTime Camera Note	Evernote For Dum...			75.4KB
Yesterday 11:14 AM	Yesterday 11:15 AM	Adding voice to an existing note	Evernote For Dum...			159KB
Yesterday 11:05 AM	Yesterday 11:06 AM	Create New Audio Note from File ...	Evernote For Dum...			69.0KB
Yesterday 11:00 AM	Yesterday 11:01 AM	New Audio Note on Evernote File ...	Evernote For Dum...			47.7KB
Yesterday 8:25 AM	Yesterday 8:25 AM	Recorded Audio Note	Evernote For Dum...			56.3KB

Date

Title

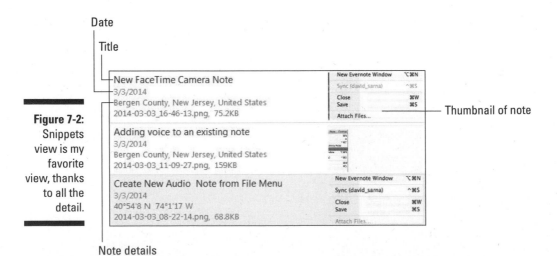

Figure 7-2: Snippets view is my favorite view, thanks to all the detail.

Thumbnail of note

Note details

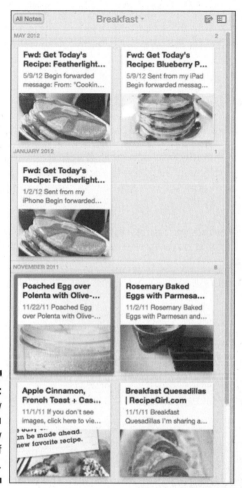

Figure 7-3:
Card View
shows you
the first few
words of
each note.

Figure 7-4:
The status
bar lets you
see where
you stand
on number
of notes,
number of
images (if
any), word
count, and
file size.

Number of notes   Word count   File size

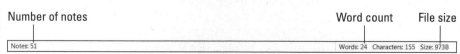

I like Snippets view best. It gives you the most details, even if it does show you fewer notes at a time. You can drag the window farther to the right to see more details. You can find more details on your selected note below the list.

Customizing your Evernote toolbar in Windows

As you play around with the installed version of Evernote in Windows, you may wonder whether there's any way to make the icons on the top bar specific to your needs. There is, of course! The process is simple and takes only a matter of moments.

To customize the Evernote toolbar in Windows, follow these steps:

1. **Choose Tools⇨Customize Toolbar.**

   The menu gives you icon options to customize your toolbar as shown in Figure 7-5.

Figure 7-5: The available Toolbar customization icons.

◀ ▶	🔄 Sync	🎪 Market	📝 New Note ▾	📝 New Note
🖊 Ink Note	🎤 Audio	Ⓢ Webcam	🖵 Screenshot	🗒 All Notes
✉ Share ▾	✉ Email	🌐 Copy URL	🖶 Print	🗑 Delete
Usage	Activity	👤 User ▾	| Separator	

To customize your toolbar, add buttons by dragging them to the toolbar. Drag them off to remove.   Done

2. **Drag the icons that you want on your toolbar into the Evernote toolbar area at the top of the screen.**

   If you change your mind and want to remove icons, simply drag them back into the menu with the toolbar customization icons.

   Place all of your often-used icons on the left end of the toolbar. Otherwise, as you add more and more icons and run out of space, a down arrow appears on the right end of the toolbar, and you have to click that arrow every time you want to access those icons.

3. **Click Done.**

Organizing Your Notes

If you've been clipping, taking pictures, scanning, and recording without paying attention to organization, your notes may look as bad as my pre-Evernote office desk. Whether you keep your notes online in Evernote or on sticky notes around your desk, you won't be able to find what you need without organization.

Lose something? The Notebook shortcut in the left sidebar shows all the notes you have saved. If you have multiple notebooks and aren't sure where you saved something, start by checking each notebook (that is, if you haven't already generated a ton of notes!).

To keep your notes organized, you can move them, copy them, or (if you're a Premium member) even refer to older versions of them.

Moving and copying notes

Fortunately, even if you didn't start off organizing your clips, pictures, and more, you can do so now. You can move notes from folder to folder in the same way that you move files around in Windows Explorer and the Mac Finder.

In Evernote, you can move a note in two ways:

- Drag and drop your note into the appropriate folder.
- Highlight the note, and choose Note⇨Move⇨*Notebook Name* (see Figure 7-6).

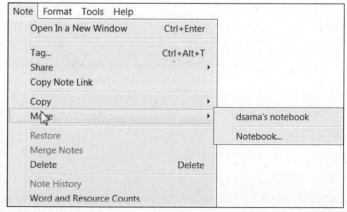

Figure 7-6:
You can move notes to a new folder.

Either way, the note moves from the original notebook into the new notebook.

To copy the note to another folder instead of moving it, choose Note➪Copy➪ *Notebook Name*. This way, you have copies of the note in two folders.

Referring to a previous version of a note

If you're a Premium or Business subscriber, you can check out an older version of a note. Open the current version of that note and then follow these steps:

1. **Choose Note➪Note History.**

   Evernote retrieves the previously saved version of your note (see Figure 7-7.)

2. **Do one of the following:**

   • Click the version of the note you want to open. The note's content appears in a preview box.

   • If you already know the version you want, click the Import link to the right of the filename and skip to Step 4.

   Depending on how old your note is and how many times you've changed it, you may have several versions to choose among, represented by the dates and times when the file was saved.

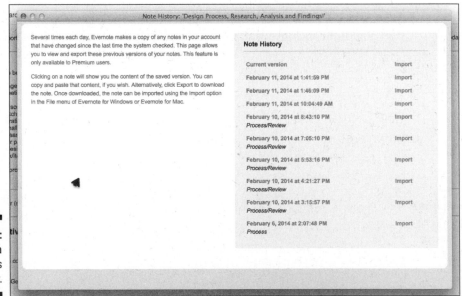

Figure 7-7:
View a
note's
history.

TIP

You can switch to a new version of the note by choosing a new date from the drop-down menu at the top of the preview box or by clicking the Older and Newer links on either side of the drop-down menu (see Figure 7-8).

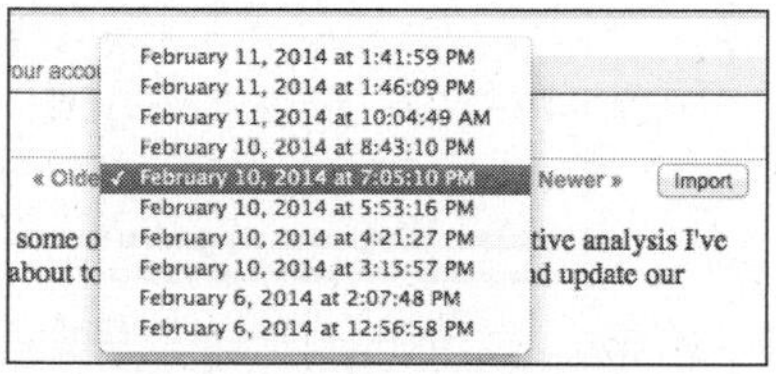

Figure 7-8:
Choose a
new date
from the
drop-down
menu.

> our acco
> February 11, 2014 at 1:41:59 PM
> February 11, 2014 at 1:46:09 PM
> February 11, 2014 at 10:04:49 AM
> February 10, 2014 at 8:43:10 PM
> « Olde ✓ February 10, 2014 at 7:05:10 PM   Newer »   Import
> some o   February 10, 2014 at 5:53:16 PM   tive analysis I've
> about to February 10, 2014 at 4:21:27 PM   d update our
>   February 10, 2014 at 3:15:57 PM
>   February 6, 2014 at 2:07:48 PM
>   February 6, 2014 at 12:56:58 PM

3. **When you find the note you're looking for, copy the content to the clip-board to paste it elsewhere, or click the Import link in the preview box.**

   Clicking the Import button downloads the note and places that selected version of the note in a new local notebook called Import _Note Name._

4. **If you clicked the Import link, a dialog box appears, asking whether you want to place the note in a synchronized notebook.**

   Clicking Yes makes your newly imported note accessible from any device on which you use Evernote. Clicking No keeps the note on the device on which you downloaded the note.

5. **If you copied the content to paste elsewhere, click the blue X in the preview box on the top right of the note to close the note.**

   You're taken back to the Note History window, where you can select a different version of the note to view or import, or click the red Exit X on the top left of the dialog box to close it.

TIP

If you want to go back to an earlier update but have updated content that you don't want to lose, as a safety precaution, copy the content of the target note and paste it into a new note. This option saves your newest version and keeps the old one.

Using Evernote on Your Mobile Phone

Evernote has a fairly standard view that it displays on mobile devices includ-ing iPhones, Android phones, BlackBerry devices, and Windows Phone. Tablets are slightly different, but the standard setup pretty much holds.

In the following sections, I provide a general discussion of features and point out the different functionalities of various mobile devices.

Although the iPod touch isn't a phone, it can do almost anything that the iPhone can do, so the iPhone instructions work for the iPod touch, too.

Except for texting, the following methods save attachments to your note. When you open Evernote, you see the new note you just created from your mobile device. Attachments and their extensions are added to new notes.

Texting

If you want to text, you need your Evernote-generated e-mail address. (See Chapter 6 if you're not sure what yours is.) If your mobile device doesn't have texting, of course, you can ignore this section.

To text a note to Evernote, follow these steps:

1. **On the device you use for texting, enter your Evernote-generated e-mail address in a new text message.**

   Although the iPod touch doesn't have texting capabilities, you can download the free app TextNow (www.textnow.com), which doesn't require a data package. This app lets you send pictures and text without paying a dime. You do need a Wi-Fi connection to send texts.

2. **Type** Test.
3. **Tap Send.**

After your Evernote account syncs up, you receive the nifty note that you texted to yourself.

See a recipe you want to try? Snap a photo, add a little detail, and text it right into your notes.

Adding pictures to notes

Most people have adopted their phones as their primary cameras because — let's face it — people are rarely without their cellphones. For example, if you're in a grocery store and find an item that you think would work for a recipe but aren't sure, simply snap a picture of the item in Evernote, and *voilà* — you have an image to refer to when you need it.

To add a picture to a note on a mobile device, follow these steps:

1. **Open Evernote on your mobile device, and tap the appropriate icon.**

   On an iPhone, for example, the icon is the circle icon labeled *Text;* on an Android device, the icon that looks like a piece of paper with a plus sign (see Figure 7-9).

   A new text note is created.

iPhone text option   Android text option

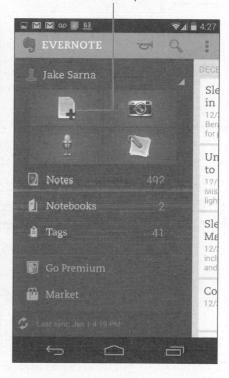

Figure 7-9:
Evernote
text note
icons for
iPhone and
Android.

2. **Tap Note in the top-left corner of the screen, and enter a title.**

   If you don't change the title, your note will be saved with the title (yup, you guessed it) Note.

3. **Below the note's title, tap the notebook icon to select the notebook in which the note will be saved.**

   This opens up a new notebook selection screen. You can select a different notebook, or you can create a new notebook by entering a title in the gray box at the top of the screen that says "Find or Create Notebook" and clicking the plus sign to the right of the notebook's name (see Figure 7-10).

Figure 7-10:
Enter a
descriptive
title (top)
and select
a notebook
(bottom).

Tapping the More link to the right of the notebook name brings up a
screen where you can add tags or a location to your note.

4. **Tap the New Note link to get back to the note page.**

5. **Tap inside the content box where you see the words *Tap to Edit*.**

   A menu bar appears at the bottom of the screen.

6. **Tap the Camera icon.**

   Your phone's camera opens, ready to take a picture.

7. **Take a picture.**

   You have the opportunity to retake the picture if you don't like the first,
   second, or tenth try. You can take as many pictures as you need until
   you're satisfied or have used up your battery.

8. **(Optional) Tap the Camera icon again to take additional pictures.**

   Evernote lets you add up to four photos to your note, so keep snapping!

9. **When you finish, tap the check mark in the bottom-right corner of the
   photo preview screen to save the photo.**

   Evernote inserts the photo into your new note and also saves it in the
   camera roll on your phone so you can access it outside Evernote.

10. **(Optional) Tap anywhere inside the note to write text.**

    Type something that describes the photo, such as a caption or location
    (see Figure 7-11).

Figure 7-11:
Add some detailed text about your photo note.

11. **Tap Save in the top-right corner of the screen.**

The new note containing your picture is saved to your Evernote account.

Using your photo collection

If you've already taken pictures with your iOS device or Windows Phone, you can send those pictures to Evernote from your camera roll. Here's how:

1. **Open Evernote on your mobile device, and tap the Text or New Note icon.**

2. **Tap Note to enter a title.**

If you don't change the title, your note will be saved with the title of your phone's photo collection.

3. **Below the note's title, tap the notebook icon to select the notebook in which the note will be saved (refer to Figure 7-10 earlier in this chapter).**

You can also create a new notebook at this point by entering a title into the gray box at the top of the screen that says "Find or create notebook" and clicking the plus sign to the right of the notebook's name.

4. **Tap the icon that looks like a framed picture on the bottom menu bar.**

   Your device's photo collection opens so you can see every picture that's currently saved on that device.

5. **Select the photo you want, and tap Use in the top-right corner.**

   The selected photo is saved into your new note.

6. **Repeat Steps 4 and 5 to select as many pictures as you want.**

   You can select up to 25MB in a free Evernote account or 100MB in a Premium or Business account.

7. **Tap Save.**

When adding images from your phone's photo collection, you can choose to attach multiple images to a single note or create a note for each image. To select multiple images, tap the Select link in the top-right corner of the photo collection screen, tap the notes you want to include, and tap Done.

If you decide to make multiple notes, the title, notebook, and tag settings associated with the note you're creating are applied to all the new image notes automatically.

Creating a note from a business card

Premium Evernote users can use the built-in camera of an iPhone or iPad to scan a business card. Evernote uses optical character recognition to detect the name and contact information on the card and then stores this information, along with a photograph of the card, inside an Evernote note. You can enhance this note by pulling in your contacts' LinkedIn or Facebook profiles for cross-referencing, in addition to including data from your address book.

To scan a business card, follow these steps:

1. **Tap the Camera icon.**

2. **Swipe left on the camera screen.**

3. **Center the business card inside the rectangle on the camera screen.**

4. **Tap the screen to ensure that the card is in focus.**

5. **Tap the green button to scan the business card.**

   All the information is captured.

6. **If your initial scan doesn't capture properly and you want to repeat the scan, tap the Trash icon, and repeat Steps 3 through 5.**

   The earlier scan is sent to the Trash.

7. **To accept the scan, tap the check mark in the bottom-right corner.**

Evernote scans the card, focuses it, and deskews the image. It recognizes the text pretty accurately but not perfectly, and converts it to editable text for easy editing. It also attempts to figure out, based on the content of the card, likely fields, such as Email, Fax, Phone, Company, and Title. Evernote also captures the card image. It can't decipher logos, however. Still, it's an easy edit and a huge timesaver for the bulk of the information that it gets right.

Scan dark cards on a light background and light cards on a dark background. Tilt shiny cards to minimize glare.

Linking business cards to LinkedIn

Optionally, you can connect your Evernote account to LinkedIn. Evernote cross-references the information read from the card you scanned with LinkedIn to make a richer note that even includes a photo of the person you've met. The information picked up from LinkedIn is shown with the LinkedIn logo.

Chapter 8

Organizing and Searching Your Notes

*T*he whole point of saving useful information is to be able to find it later.

You have several ways to get your notebook or notebooks situated for easier searching and storing.

In this chapter, I discuss how to store your content for ease of retrieval and how to effectively and quickly find what you need, every time.

Tagging

Evernote offers several fantastic methods for organizing your notes. See Chapter 7 for a preview of some of these tools. Tagging is one of those many methods, and a very important one. (Tagging and titling are also discussed in Chapter 3.)

 The ways to tag a note are as numerous as Evernote-compatible devices and apps. Because you have so many choices of how you can tag a note, I group the types of devices and the best method of tagging for each type. Regardless of which device you're using to access Evernote, you need to look for the tag icon.

Tagging is meant to be helpful; that's why you can apply multiple tags to every note. If, however, you tag every note with a unique label, go overboard on tagging, or add the same tags to every note, you'll find that the feature doesn't work very well. Before you begin tagging notes, consider how you want to set up your tags based on the types of notes you know you'll use most often (such as by research project, book you're reading, list or chore type, note type, and so on).

Here are a few tips I've found useful for tagging:

- **Don't overtag.** Evernote has a great and speedy full-text search engine. You usually don't need to tag words that are in a note's title.

- **Tag related notes with the same tag.** Tagging is most useful for making sure that notes containing different words for the same thing are retrieved together, even if only one of the terms appears in any single note. I suffer from chronic kidney disease, for example, and I use Evernote to save information I come across that's related to the disease, which is sometimes referred to as CKD ESKD (end-stage kidney disease) or renal failure. I tag all related notes with the *CKD* tag.

- **Keep the tags short.** Brevity is the soul of wit, and short tags reduce typing and make it easier for you to tag as you go along.

- **Words in the document or title will be found by a search; you don't need to tag them specifically.** I use the tag *Medical David* for all prescription and lab-test results because the phrase isn't in the body of the note and wouldn't be found when I search for *Medical David*.

- **Notes can have more than one tag.** Up to 100 tags per note are supported; 2 or 3 are usually adequate.

When you start typing the tag, Evernote automatically provides tags that begin with the same letters you type. The feature is kind of like autocorrect, except that it doesn't try to replace what you've done; it just helps you along by reducing how much new material you have to type. Also, if (like me) you're a poor typist or have an inexact memory, Evernote's helpful suggestions let you click to select tags you've already saved, which prevents you from having multiple similar tags for the same thing.

Tagging on computers and tablets

Tagging is fundamentally similar for all platforms and is extremely useful as you dash about trying to enter notes on whatever device you're using at the time.

To create a tag for a note on a computer or tablet, follow these steps:

1. **Highlight the note you want to tag.**

   If you're creating a new note, refer to Chapter 3.

2. **Click or tap the Tag icon or the Click to Add Tag link.**

   A small box opens, as shown in Figure 8-1.

Figure 8-1:
Adding tags
to a note.

3. **Enter your tag name.**

   Your tag name can be a new tag or an existing tag. If you create a new tag, Evernote includes it in its collection of possible tags to use in the future.

4. **Click or tap anywhere outside the area (or press Enter or Return on a computer), and save the note.**

As you create more and more tags, you may lose track of tags you've already created. When you click or tap Tags in the side panel, you see all the tags you have and how many notes are associated with each one (see Figure 8-2).

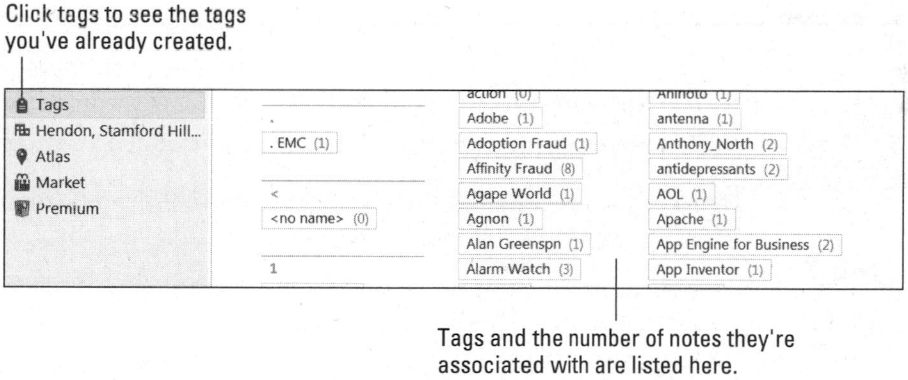

Click tags to see the tags
you've already created.

Figure 8-2:
The side
panel helps
you keep
track of your
tags.

		action (0)	Anmoto (1)
Tags		Adobe (1)	antenna (1)
Hendon, Stamford Hill...	.EMC (1)	Adoption Fraud (1)	Anthony_North (2)
Atlas		Affinity Fraud (8)	antidepressants (2)
Market	<	Agape World (1)	AOL (1)
Premium	<no name> (0)	Agnon (1)	Apache (1)
		Alan Greenspn (1)	App Engine for Business (2)
	1	Alarm Watch (3)	App Inventor (1)

Tags and the number of notes they're
associated with are listed here.

Tagging on smartphones

Tagging on a smartphone is even easier than tagging on a computer. With a little practice, you'll become adept at getting the tags set up.

The tagging feature for smartphones is pretty universal, regardless of what device you use. Follow these steps:

1. **Tap New Note.**

2. **Enter whatever information you need (pictures, recordings, and so on).**

more...

3. **Tap the More link and then the Add Tag link, and add your tag (see Figure 8-3).**

   You can create a new tag or tap the plus (+) sign to select the name of an existing tag.

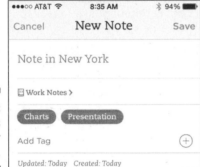

Figure 8-3:
Adding tags
on your
smartphone.

4. **When you finish, tap the Close link.**

5. **Complete your note and save it after you've added your tag.**

Tagging is just like adding a title, but it gives you a little more information to narrow the results of your searches.

On the Home screen, you can check out all your tagging options. Tap the Tag icon and review the notes specific to each tag.

Sorting Lists of Notes

Evernote provides several criteria by which you're able to sort a list of notes. The group of notes in question doesn't make a difference, whether you're viewing the contents of a notebook or the results of a search. Any group of notes is sorted the same way.

Sorting on a computer

To sort a group of notes in Evernote for Windows, make sure you're viewing either all of your notes or a specific notebook and then choose the Sort Menu⇨Sort Notes by⇨*your selected Sort option* (see Figure 8-4). The default setting sorts notes by the date they were created. Several other sorting options are available, including title, size, and author.

Figure 8-4:
The options
for sorting
a group of
notes in
Windows.

Sorting notes in Evernote for Mac works similarly to sorting in Windows. Choosing the Sort Menu⇨Sort Notes by⇨*your selected Sort option* shows the list of potential sort criteria that you can select.

Sorting on an iOS device

When you view a collection of notes on an iPhone, you can tap the Options button to access the various sorting options available (see Figure 8-5). Your options are pretty much what you'd expect from a sorting method, such as title, date, and size.

Figure 8-5:
Tapping
the Options
button
shows you
your sorting
options.

When you're working on an iPad or iPod touch, tapping Options also shows you a list of sorting options. You can sort by note-creation date or the last time notes were updated, for example.

Sorting on an Android device

On an Android device, you can tap anywhere on the Notes bar or tap the small down-pointing arrow to the right of the list of notebooks to see the available view options:

- ✔ Tap Date Updated to sort by the last date the note was updated.
- ✔ Tap Title to sort notes by title.
- ✔ Tap Other to see the full menu of sorting choices (see Figure 8-6).

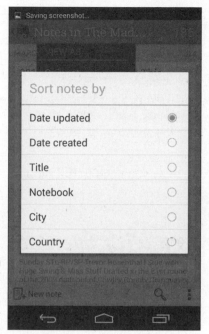

Figure 8-6:
Sort Notes
By menu.

Conducting a Simple Search of Your Notes

You can search your notes in many ways, some of which are more effective than others. You can start by doing a simple search by keyword, title, or tag.

A *simple search* is exactly what it sounds like — pretty simple. Regardless of your device, you can quickly type a keyword or phrase and run a search over all your notes or notes in a specific notebook.

Keep these tips in mind when conducting a simple search:

✔ If you want to review the notes that include your simple search by tag, check out the Tags pane on the left side of your screen. If you have a tag called Projects, all the notes that have that tag (and only the notes that have that tag) appear when you click that tag.

✔ If you want to run a simple search on more than one topic, go to the search box, and type the word you're searching for. To find notes with both the words *Android* and *iPhone,* for example, type **Android iPhone**. Evernote returns everything that has both words in it.

✔ Don't type extra words in your search. Words such as *the, and, or,* and *a* are highlighted and become part of the search requirement. So if you want to find a comparison between Android and iOS, go ahead and type **A Comparison**. Evernote returns only the messages that contain all these words.

When you're done with a search, you need to clear it by deleting the text or clicking the X to the right of the search box. If you delete all text from the search box, you see all existing notes because you've cleared the contents of the search box.

The following sections give you the tools you need to run rudimentary searches on different platforms.

Doing a simple search with Evernote

Every version of Evernote, on every platform, has a search icon (magnifying-glass icon) and a search box. The search takes place on Evernote's servers and works the same way on all platforms.

To do a simple search in Windows or on a Mac, follow these steps:

1. **In the search box, to the right of the search icon, type the word or phrase you want to search for.**

   Suppose that you're getting a new phone and have researched both Android phones and iPhones. You can see what notes you've already saved by typing **Android**. Evernote displays all the notes in this particular notebook that contain the word *Android*, including handwritten entries. So cool!

   The search isn't case-sensitive, so don't worry about including both *android* and *Android* in the search. Misspelling is another issue. If you type **Androd**, you're not likely to have any results displayed unless you also misspelled the word in your notes.

2. **Press Enter or Return.**

3. **Start reviewing the notes.**

   Evernote highlights all instances of *Android* in each note. This search includes any notes that have *Android* in the title or in the tag.

Doing a simple search on a mobile device

On a mobile device, no matter which type it is, the procedure is very similar, with a few added features. Follow these steps:

1. **Open the Evernote app.**

2. **Tap the magnifying glass in the top-right corner of the screen.**

   The search area opens. If you haven't run a search before, you won't have much to look at. If you *have* run a search, you see a list of all words that you've searched on, as well as the notebooks that you included in the search.

3. **Type the words you're looking for in the search box, and tap the Search button in the bottom-right corner of the screen.**

   If you type **Android iPhone**, the search returns all notes from all notebooks with the words *Android* and *iPhone,* regardless of the capitalization you used.

Searching by title or tag is even easier. Follow these steps:

1. **Click the magnifying glass.**

   You return to the search area.

2. **Click the clock (title search) or the tag (tag search).**

   If you searched for *iPhone* and *Android,* the clock looks for notes with *iPhone* and *Android* in the title. If you click the tag, the tag looks for notes with *iPhone* and *Android* in the tag.

Searching on Autogenerated Attributes

Autogenerated attributes are labels that Evernote places on notes automatically, providing details about their creation, such as the date of creation or update, where a note was created, or the notebook in which a note was saved. Evernote lets you search on those autogenerated attributes (examples of which are visible at the bottom of Figure 8-3 earlier in this chapter).

Searching on autogenerated attributes is no different from searching on attributes you assign yourself.

Evernote creates or updates these attributes automatically every time you create or update a note.

Sorting by attributes

The autogenerated attributes that you can sort and search on include the following:

- ✔ **Title:** Sorts by — what else? — the note's title.
- ✔ **Date Created:** Sorts by the date the note was created.
- ✔ **Date Updated:** Sorts notes in order of the most recently updated.

✔ **Source URL:** Sorts by source URL. (If you return to a website often or have a few locations you're using for research, this option makes life a lot easier.)

✔ **Size:** Lists a range by 100KB (100KB to 200KB, 200KB to 300KB, and so on), making it easier to isolate merged notes, notes with attachments, or notes with images or recordings. Smaller notes are grouped by 10KB or solo because most people don't tend to have as many of them.

Sorting by organization

You can also sort on organization of the notes, as follows:

✔ **Reverse Sort Order:** The default is descending order, so choosing this option gets the opposite order from what you usually get for a search. (Every time you choose this option, the search order is reversed.)

✔ **Show in Groups:** If you don't want your files grouped, you can show them all as stand-alone notes.

Why can't I find it?

Sometimes you know that you saved information in a note, yet a search doesn't turn it up.

We humans recognize our names, for example, and understand intuitively that *David* is the same whether it's written in small or large letters, bold, plain, or italic typeface, and in a variety of fonts (or even in no font at all when the name is handwritten).

For computers, recognition isn't so easy. Computers are good at making exact matches because they're digital, which means that they store numbers only. Text is stored by assigning codes to numbers.

For searching, descriptive additional coding showing attributes such as bold and italic are fine, and if there's an exact match between the text you've stored in Evernote and what you're searching for, Evernote finds it irrespective of size, font, and other attributes.

Documents that begin as pictures enter Evernote as scanned documents, which means that they're really just pictures, or as various picture formats (such as JPEG, PNG, and BMP). Evernote also supports and reads documents in Portable Document Format (PDF), an open standard pioneered by Adobe. In each case, Evernote has to "read" these images by using its image-recognition technology, reverse-engineer the dots into letters, and then assign the letters to the appropriate text symbols.

Although in my experience, Evernote does an amazing job of reading most documents accurately — even those that started out as handwritten notes — the results aren't guaranteed or foolproof. If you want to be sure that a term in a scanned document can be retrieved in a search, tag it yourself.

The City, State, Country, and Address sorting options display notes with an unknown location first, which isn't very helpful if the vast majority of your notes don't have known origins. Most notes created on mobile phones include geolocation information, but notes created on computers don't. If you have a notebook that includes only geotagged photos from a phone or a digital camera that captures geolocation information or uses an Eye-Fi card (see Chapter 18), using one of these sorting options can be very helpful indeed.

After the notes are reordered as you like, you can do anything you want with them: e-mail them, print them, move them, and so on. Using one of the previously mentioned sorting options is just another way to view your note collection.

Doing a Simultaneous Search

One of the coolest things about Evernote is that you can search any of the three big search engines — Google, Bing, and Yahoo! — and your notes at the same time. This feature works in Chrome, Firefox, and Safari.

This feature is available only to Premium members. Also, you must have the Evernote Web Clipper installed for the browser you're using; see Chapter 4.

Here's how to do a simultaneous search.

1. **Open the desired search engine in your browser.**

2. **Type your desired search term, and click the Search (magnifying-glass) icon next to the address.**

   If you don't see the Evernote results on the right side of the search results, you have to enable this feature as follows:

   • In Google Chrome, click the Customize and Control icon (three horizontal lines) in the top-right corner of the browser window, choose Settings⇨Extensions, and click the Options link (which is next to the Allow in Incognito check box).

   • In Firefox, choose Tools⇨Add-ons⇨Extensions⇨Evernote Web Clipper⇨Preferences, and check Related Results. Then click Save.

   • In Safari, click the Web Clipper icon in the top menu bar and then click your Evernote username on the bottom of the Clip menu⇨Options⇨check Related Results. Then click Done.

   With Simultaneous Search is enabled, when you search Google, Bing, or Yahoo!, the same query is also run on Evernote.

3. **Restart your browser and perform a search.**

   Now whenever you run a search in one of these search engines, you see a window showing the number of notes in your notebooks that contain the same information. Check out Figure 8-7 for an example.

Google results   Evernote results

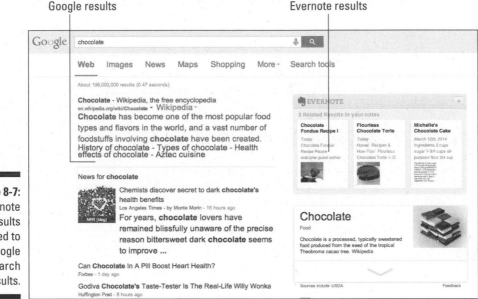

Figure 8-7:
Evernote
results
added to
Google
search
results.

Doing a Descriptive Search

Evernote has a really powerful search language, but like SQL, its power comes with a somewhat steep learning curve. The truth is, most users never bother to master it, which is a pity.

The nice folks at Evernote are well aware of this limitation and have been hard at work developing better ways to hide or simplify the complexity. They've christened their new baby *descriptive search*. This feature works by allowing you to describe what you're looking for by using common terms, which makes creating a complex search incredibly straightforward.

At the time of this writing, descriptive search is available only for the Mac and in English. Evernote promises that this feature will be making its way to other languages and versions of Evernote soon. I've found descriptive search to be incredibly useful, and I look forward to seeing it on the other platforms I use regularly.

When descriptive search is available, clicking the search box brings up a helpful window to guide your search (see Figure 8-8). The first section shows your last five searches, and the next section lists your saved searches. (See "Saving Searches" later in this chapter for more information on this feature.)

Figure 8-8:
Descriptive
search.

You can also narrow down the search results by choosing different criteria. Click Show Less to hide most of them. Figure 8-8 shows the additional options visible when the Add Search option is clicked. Another window opens, allowing you to further constrain the search. In Figure 8-9, I selected notes that contain audio files.

Figure 8-9:
Descriptive
search
for notes
containing
audio files.

If you don't select a different option in this window, Evernote searches your entire account, which is the default setting.

Here are some examples of descriptive searches that Evernote handles with aplomb:

✔ *"Images from Rome since 2012":* This search brings up all your notes since 2012 that contain images with Rome as the location.

✔ *"Recipes with photos tagged* vegetarian*":* This search shows any notes that Evernote classifies as a recipe that contain an image and have the tag *vegetarian*.

✔ *"Powerpoint from last week":* This search returns all notes with attached Microsoft PowerPoint presentations since last week. (***Note:*** Capitalization is ignored in searches.)

Figure 8-10 shows other ways to constrain a descriptive search to find just what you want. These options are on the drop-down menu you see when you click the search box.

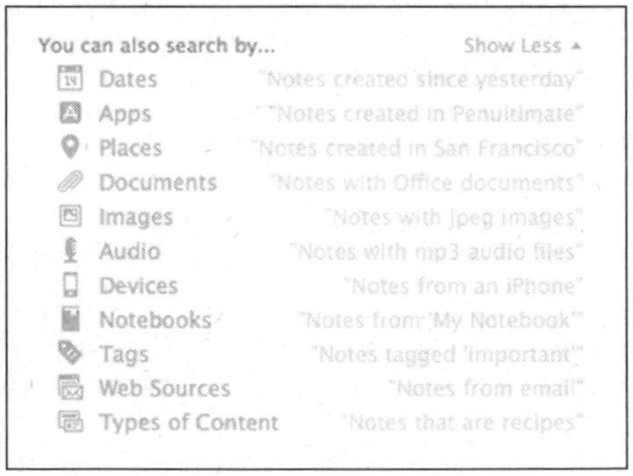

You can also search by...	Show Less ▲
🗓 Dates	"Notes created since yesterday"
Ⓐ Apps	"Notes created in Penultimate"
📍 Places	"Notes created in San Francisco"
📎 Documents	"Notes with Office documents"
🖼 Images	"Notes with jpeg images"
🎙 Audio	"Notes with mp3 audio files"
📱 Devices	"Notes from an iPhone"
📓 Notebooks	"Notes from My Notebook"
🏷 Tags	"Notes tagged 'important'"
🗐 Web Sources	"Notes from email"
🗐 Types of Content	"Notes that are recipes"

Figure 8-10:
Constraints
for
descriptive
searches.

Doing an Advanced Search

If you're feeling a little brave, you can master the native Evernote search syntax. Your reward will be your ability to carry out advanced searches when you have an idea of what you're looking for but don't remember exactly how you stated it. This type of search relies on the use of Evernote search syntax to find what you need.

Syntax, as you may recall from English-grammar classes, is the principles and processes by which sentences are constructed in particular languages and especially in formal languages such as programming languages. The search syntax of Evernote, is, I freely admit, a little inscrutable, and Evernote's documentation (`http://dev.evernote.com/doc/articles/search_grammar.php`) definitely isn't for anyone whose native language isn't C++ or Linux. Still, examples help, and with a little practice with a notebook whose contents you're familiar with, you'll get the hang of advanced search quickly. The results will be worth the effort.

In a search, *syntax* means the parameters and words you use to execute the search. Tag syntax, for example, looks like this:

```
Tag: "name of tag"
```

A basic search starts at the beginning, but when you add the syntax (everything that appears up to the colon, such as `Tag`), you free Evernote from the constraint of matching the exact text.

You can run these types of searches on titles or tags, your to-do list, and many other items. Table 8-1 lists some of the most basic and useful types of syntax.

Table 8-1	Basic Syntax
Syntax	*Description*
`Intitle`	Searches for and returns notes based on their titles
`Tag`	Searches for and returns notes according to their associated tags
`-Tag`	Searches for and returns notes that aren't associated with tags
`Source`	Searches for and returns notes based on the source media in which the notes were generated, such as e-mail, picture, or typed text
`Any`	Searches for and returns notes based on any of the criteria entered in the search
`Todo`	Searches for and returns notes that have a check box

The advanced search is nearly identical across platforms, with the method of accessing it matching the type of device, as discussed in "Searching on Autogenerated Attributes" earlier in this chapter. You can type **intitle:bills** in the search box to pull up every note within a highlighted notebook that has *bills* in the title, for example.

Table 8-2 provides examples of advanced searches that work, as well as some that don't work.

Table 8-2	Advanced Search Syntax		
Syntax Element	*Example*	*Search Matches*	*Search Doesn't Match*
Space embedded in quoted text	"San Francisco"	"The hills of San Francisco"	"San Andreas Fault near Francisco Winery"
- (hyphen)	-potato	"Mash four potatoes together"	"Sweet potato pie"
`tag:` `[tag name]`	tag:cook*	Any note with a tag that starts with "cook"	Note tagged with "cook"
`created:` `[datetime]`	-created:day	Notes created before today	Notes created today
	created:day-1-created: day	Notes created yesterday	Notes created before yesterday

Don't add punctuation if you didn't originally include it in the title. The colon is the only piece of punctuation that you should use. You also should avoid adding extraneous spaces.

Saving Searches

At first, the simple and advanced searches are enough to cover what you need for your notes. After you've used Evernote for a while, however, you'll have so many notes that you'll find yourself periodically running the same searches repeatedly. Well, you probably don't want to have to remember exactly what you typed two months ago. If you soon realize that you're using the same searches, saving them can really speed your ability to find notes quickly, particularly if you're running advanced searches often.

Recent searches are saved automatically and are displayed when you click the search box (see Figure 8-11).

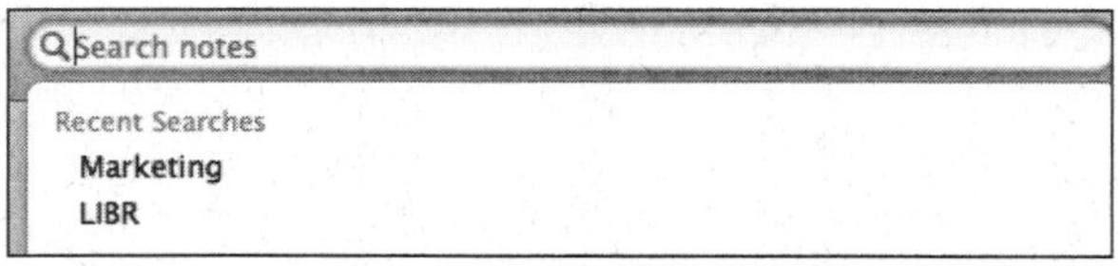

Figure 8-11:
Recent
searches.

Q Search notes

Recent Searches
Marketing
LIBR

Saving searches in Windows

To save your searches in Windows, follow these steps:

1. **Click the search box, and choose Save Search from the drop-down menu.**

   The Create Saved Search dialog box opens.

2. **Enter the name you want to give the search (see Figure 8-12).**

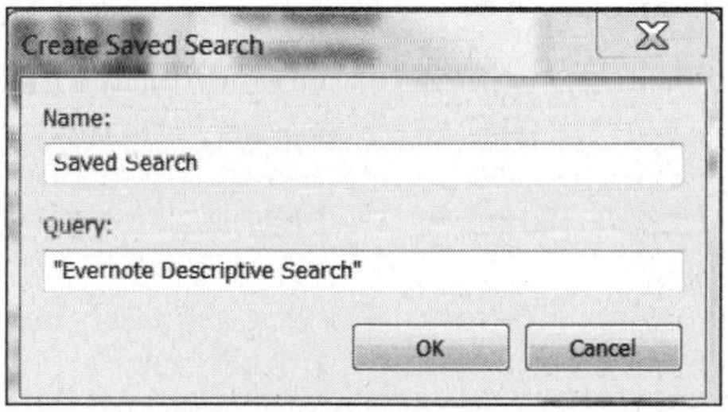

Figure 8-12:
The Create
Saved
Search
dialog box.

Create Saved Search ✖

Name:
Saved Search

Query:
"Evernote Descriptive Search"

OK   Cancel

3. **Click OK.**

   Your search is saved. From now on, anytime you click the search box, you see it in the list of saved searches (see Figure 8-13). You can have a maximum of 100 saved searches.

Figure 8-13:
Saved
searches.

Saved searches
Aluminum Gallium
David's Favorite Search
Gallium Alumium
Saved Search
WoodallTech

4. (Optional) Delete unwanted saved searches.

If you want to keep your saved searches list neat and organized, and then simply right-click and select Delete or hover your mouse over the saved search and click the Edit button to the right.

Saving searches on a Mac

To save your searches on a Mac, follow these steps:

1. **Type your search term in the search box in the top-right corner of the screen, and press Return.**

2. **Choose Edit⇨Find⇨Save Search.**

A dialog box pops up, asking you to give your search a name.

3. **Name your search, and click the OK button.**

The dialog box closes, and you're taken back to your search results. You can have a maximum of 100 saved searches.

4. **(Optional) Delete unwanted saved searches.**

To keep your saved searches list neat and organized, simply hover your mouse over the saved search you want to delete and click the Edit button that appears to the right of the search term. Then click the Delete Saved Search button at the bottom of the dialog box that appears.

Saved searches can also be made into shortcuts, which saves you even more time. Instead of using the search box to pull up your saved searches every time you need one, simply drag the saved search term from the Search menu and drop it into the Shortcuts section of the left Sidebar. That way, your favorite searches are always available.

Evernote takes searches on a Mac a step (or two) further, though. When you click the search box, Evernote responds interactively and guides you through the process. Think of this process as saved searches on steroids. The feature is called *type ahead,* and it saves keystrokes by completing your thoughts based on the words and phrases you use frequently in Evernote. Figure 8-14 shows what happens when I type **Descriptive**.

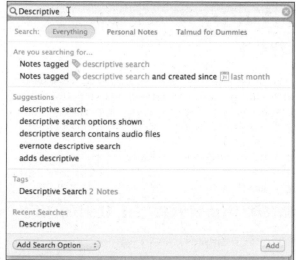

Figure 8-14:
Type-ahead
search on a
Mac.

Saving searches on smartphones and tablets

Evernote automatically saves your searches on all smartphones and tablets, so the first time you run a search, you've saved a search. You also see searches that you've saved manually on other platforms.

Searching on smartphones and tablets is easy. Follow these steps:

1. **Open your Evernote app.**

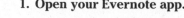

2. **Tap the magnifying glass in the top-right corner of the screen.**

   You see the old familiar search area. It shows you searches you've recently run on your phone as well as the notebooks that you included in the search. Better yet, even if you run a simple search, Evernote saves an advanced search.

3. **Tap the blue Search button at the bottom of the screen.**

   Your search results are loaded.

4. **Tap the magnifying glass with a plus sign icon in the bottom-right corner of the screen.**

   A Saved Search dialog box appears.

5. **Enter the name of your search and tap Save.**

   The dialog box disappears and you are taken back to your search results.

Working with Multiple Notes from Your Search

After you have completed a search, you may want to work with multiple notes. Working with multiple notes is extremely useful if you have notes spread over several notebooks that you need to merge into a new notebook or want to print for a meeting, export, or combine into a single note.

This section discusses working with multiple notes.

Tagging multiple notes in Windows

Follow these steps to tag multiple notes in Windows:

1. **Open Evernote.**

2. **Highlight the notes that you want to work with (holding the Shift key down to select multiple notes) and right-click the highlighted notes.**

   To highlight notes out of sequence, hold down the Ctrl key, and click the notes you want to highlight.

   The selected notes are grouped and shown in a "pile" as shown in Figure 8-15.

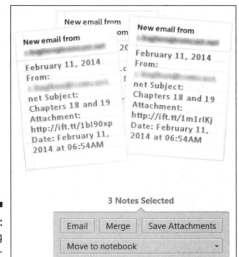

Figure 8-15:
Working with multiple notes.

Underneath the pile of notes you have several options in a dialog box, as shown in Figure 8-15.

- **Email:** Sends the notes to an e-mail account. When you click the Email button, you get something that looks like Figure 8-16, with the subject being the title of the first highlighted note. You can change the Subject line. Don't forget to add the e-mail address, and feel free to add a message to your notes. Check the box titled CC Me on This Email if you want.

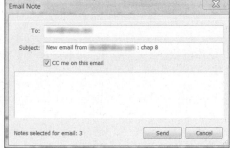

Figure 8-16:
Email Note
options.

- **Merge:** Merges your notes. See "Merging notes," later in this chapter.

- **Save Attachments:** If the notes you selected have attachments, then clicking this button lets you save those attachments to a location on your computer.

- **Move to Notebook:** Gives you options on where to move the files. Check out Chapter 7 for details.

- **Click to Add Tag:** Tags several notes at a time. This feature is the coolest of all. Tags already created are shown. Click the Click to Add Tag link at the bottom of the notes option box to globally add additional tags to selected notes.

Printing a combined list on a computer

To print a combined list of notes in Windows or on a Mac, follow these steps:

1. **Select the notes.**

2. **Do one of the following:**

   - *Windows:* Right-click the selected notes and choose Print Notes from the contextual menu.

   - *Mac:* Option-click the selected notes and press ⌘+P.

If you change your mind and don't want to print a combined list, click any note to cancel the multiple selection.

3. **Click Print in the dialog box that appears.**

   Printing a combined list of selected notes doesn't merge the notes.

Merging notes

If you've captured notes that are similar in content and that you plan to use on the same project, you can use Evernote's merge feature to put them all in one place.

You can merge on desktop and laptop computers and on iOS and Android tablets.

After you merge notes, you can't unmerge them. Make sure that merging is truly the best option.

To merge your notes, follow these steps:

1. **Open the notebook that contains the notes you want to merge.**

   If you're not sure which notebook contains the notes you want to merge, open All Notebooks on the side panel so that all notes are visible.

2. **Highlight the notes you want to merge.**

3. **Do one of the following:**

   • *Windows:* Right-click the highlighted note and choose Merge Notes from the contextual menu.

   • *Mac:* Choose Note⇨Merge Notes.

Chapter 9

Synchronizing Notes

*O*ne of the nicest things about Evernote is that it lets you save items individually on all supported devices and then access everything you've saved on any device. The only requirement is that all your devices be in sync, which usually occurs without your needing to do anything.

In this chapter, you get the inside scoop on Evernote's synchronization mechanisms, settings, and methods. This chapter contains fewer directions than the other ones in this book. Think of this chapter as an information download that you can use to better understand how Evernote works and to be confident of its capability to work for you.

Working with Evernote Servers

The core of the Evernote service is a farm of servers that Evernote calls *shards*. Each shard handles all data and all traffic (web traffic and traffic generated by other apps connected to Evernote) for approximately 100,000 registered Evernote users. Because more than 80 million people use Evernote (at this writing), the math translates into around 800 shards.

Because each user's data is completely localized to one (virtual) shard host, Evernote can run each shard as an independent island with virtually no crosstalk or dependencies. As a result, the issues on one shard don't snowball to other shards.

Despite all the precautions and redundancies, problems are bound to happen occasionally because nothing is foolproof. Evernote understands these odds and has created a web page for you to check the status of its network: `http://status.evernote.com`. If you're having issues with syncing, you may want to check out this page to make sure that the problem isn't something on Evernote's end.

You can find details on the Evernote architecture at `http://blog.evernote.com/tech/2011/05/17/architectural-digest`.

Synchronizing Notes Automatically

A primary benefit of Evernote is that it enables you to access the most recent versions of all your notes, regardless of what device you're using — even when you're logged in to a library computer to double-check a grocery list because your phone battery is dead. Evernote's ability to synchronize notes on all devices is a reliable service, and you no longer need to try to cram everything onto your smartphone. This ability to have synchronized devices and a centralized network to store everything is probably the main reason why you chose Evernote in the first place.

Best of all, this automatic synchronization usually happens for you under the covers; Evernote saves you from having to do anything most of the time. Because the default setting is automatic synchronization, Evernote automatically syncs your notes on the web, regardless of your device or platform. (I discuss how to change these options in "Setting Sync Preferences," later in this chapter.)

Evernote can juggle so much information supported by so many devices because it operates on what's called a *hub-and-spoke system*. The Internet or web serves as the hub: a single centralized location for all the data, files, and information to be stored. The spokes are your devices that you access to update your notes. You can have as many spokes as you need.

Suppose that you have a Windows desktop computer, a MacBook Pro, a BlackBerry for work, an iPhone for personal use, and a couple of tablets. In that situation, you're really experiencing the marvel of Evernote's system. Every time you sign in to work on your notes, Evernote syncs the hub to the spoke you're using to ensure that the next time you access your account, you have everything at your fingertips. When you're at the grocery store an hour later, the grocery list you typed on your Windows computer is on the iPhone you're toting, even though the systems are ordinarily notorious for being pretty standoffish.

Understanding synchronization

Synchronization is a fundamental and powerful feature of Evernote. Most of the time, it happens for you automatically, and you needn't give it a second thought. But there are a few things you should keep in the back of your mind when it comes to how Evernote synchronizes your data:

- ✔ Premium subscribers (see Chapter 2) can save notebooks locally and work offline on Android and iOS devices. All users can work offline on Mac and Windows computers.

- ✔ You can limit synchronization. Suppose that you have a notebook dedicated to storing your online passwords. It ought to be encrypted (discussed in Chapter 11), but even so, you probably don't want this information stored anywhere that it may be accidentally posted or shared. If you lost your cellphone, for example, someone may find it and access information in your Evernote account, especially if you chose an easy-to-guess password. Therefore, you can choose not to synchronize that particular notebook.

 Choosing whether a notebook is synchronized is a one-time election that you make when you create a notebook; you can't change this setting later. If you choose not to sync, this information is never synced by Evernote, and you're on your own with regard to backing up the notebook. (A USB dongle that you carry on your keychain is an obvious possibility as an alternative backup.)

- ✔ Limiting synchronization to what Evernote calls *local-only notebooks* removes a primary reason for using Evernote, so consider whether it's something you actually want to do before you save a local-only notebook. Usually, encryption is adequate.

- ✔ When you create or update a note on one device, you see it on that device only until it contacts the Evernote server, which gets the note to the Evernote cloud. The next time another device synchronizes with the Evernote cloud, the change is propagated to that device.

- ✔ Working on a note when the network is down or when you're not connected to the Internet means that whatever you work on is saved locally and synchronized after connectivity is reestablished. You may want to initiate a sync manually as soon as connectivity is reestablished to make sure that you get those changes back up to the secure Evernote servers ASAP.

Forcing synchronization

Synchronization occurs at preselected intervals in the background on any device on which Evernote is open. The default on Mac and Windows computers is every 15 minutes, but you can change that setting (as discussed later in the chapter). Sometimes, however, you may want to force synchronization, and Evernote makes that easy.

 To force synchronization at any time, click the synchronization icon for the device you want to synchronize.

 On your desktop computer (Windows or Mac), you can change the default synchronization frequency by choosing Tools⇨Options⇨Sync (Windows) or Evernote⇨Preferences⇨Sync (Mac) and then adjusting the settings in the Options dialog box (see Figure 9-1). For information on how to adjust the sync settings on your mobile device, see "Setting Sync Preferences" later in this chapter.

Figure 9-1: Adjusting sync options in Windows.

Managing conflicting changes

It's a rare occurrence, but if you edit a note from a second device before sync occurs, you may accidentally create two versions of one note. To explore what can happen in such situations, I ran a test. In my test, I updated a note from my iPhone and saved it. While the phone was thinking and syncing, I bounced over to my iMac and started adding information to the same note, knowing full well that the copy on my iMac wasn't synced. Moments after I saved the note, I got the error message shown in Figure 9-2.

Figure 9-2:
Conflicting-
changes
error
message.

When Evernote noticed the conflict, it put the note in a new local notebook called Conflicting Changes (see Figure 9-3). This notebook is where Evernote puts all notes with conflicting changes. Conflicting changes are rare, given how often Evernote syncs, so you can decide whether or not to keep this notebook.

Figure 9-3:
Conflicting
Changes
notebook.

Here's what to do to resolve a conflict:

1. **Click the Notes icon in the left sidebar to view all your notes.**

   The original note and the one from the Conflicting Changes note-book appear next to each other in the list (see Figure 9-4).

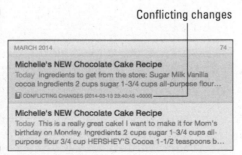

Figure 9-4:
Note
list with
conflicting
changes
(top) and
original
(bottom).

2. Click the original note to open it.

The original note doesn't have *Conflicting Changes* in the bottom-left corner, as shown in Figure 9-4.

3. Scroll down the original note until you find a clear dividing line, as shown in Figure 9-5.

The top of the page is the original note, and the bottom of the page (below the dividing line) is the note with the conflicting changes included.

4. Copy and paste anything that has changed from the bottom portion of the note to the top portion of the note.

You have to compare the two notes visually. If you're a lousy proof-reader, try copying both documents to a word processor that supports comparing document versions, such as Microsoft Word.

5. Highlight the conflicting note below the dividing line, and press the Delete key.

You have one clean note with all the changes incorporated.

6. Delete the `Conflicting Changes` folder and note when you're satisfied that you've resolved the issue.

The page break separates the original
note from the conflicting changes.

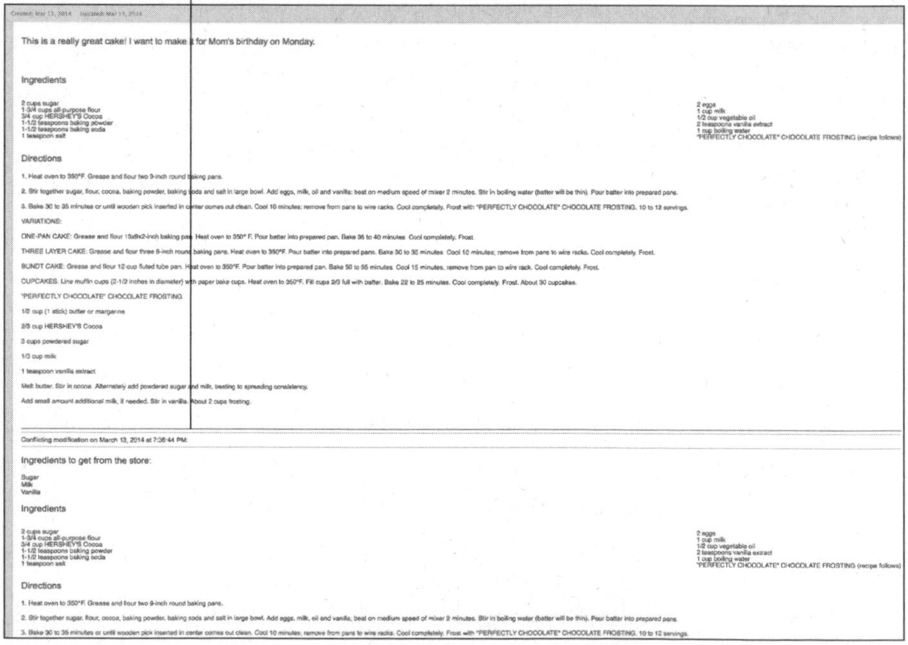

Figure 9-5:
Original
note
(top) and
note with
conflicting
changes
(bottom).

Evernote asks you a couple of times whether you're sure you want to delete the folder, so make sure that you're ready to delete before you do so. I recommend that you delete the conflicting note, though. Having two copies of the same note is what got you into this mess in the first place!

Although the preceding instructions are much the same for managing conflicts on a mobile device, I highly recommend you perform this task on a computer to save the time and frustration of having to continuously scroll to compare and move the text.

Check out Chapter 13 or the Evernote User Forum (http://forum.evernote.com) if you're still experiencing syncing issues.

Setting Sync Preferences

One of the most useful features of Evernote that runs in the background is automatic syncing of your files. As with nearly every other aspect of Evernote, you can personalize the sync preferences to occur as often as you feel is necessary.

If you don't spend much time in Evernote, you probably aren't going to need the notes to be synced often, so changing the settings so that Evernote syncs less frequently won't be a problem. If you spend hours in Evernote, you probably want to sync a little more often to make sure that your changes aren't lost.

Evernote's default setting is to sync automatically when you open it, so if you usually work on one device and then open Evernote on another, you may end up spending a little bit of time waiting for the sync to complete, although sync has gotten much faster recently. If you have shared notebooks linked to your account that are updated frequently, you may want to set them to update manually. If you keep Evernote open (but minimized), Evernote synchronizes in the background while you work on other things. I leave Evernote open all the time.

Syncing on Windows and Mac computers

The default setting for both Windows and Mac computers is for the sync to occur every 15 minutes. You can go into the sync preferences and change that setting (and a couple of others). Here's how:

1. **Open Evernote on your computer.**

2. **In Windows, choose Tools⇨Options; on a Mac, choose Evernote⇨Preferences.**

   The Options dialog box appears.

3. **Click the Sync tab.**

   You see the sync preferences (see Figure 9-6).

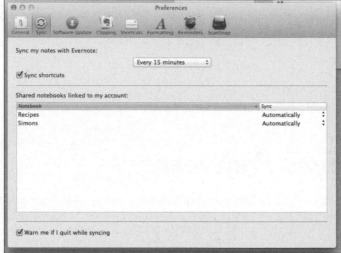

Figure 9-6:
The Sync
tab of the
Preferences
dialog box
on a Mac.

4. **Choose a new time interval between syncs from the Synchronize Automatically drop-down menu.**

   You can choose manual synchronization or automatic synchronization every 5 minutes (Mac only), every 15, 30, or 60 minutes, or once a day (Windows only).

5. **(Optional) Update your shared-notebook sync times individually.**

   • In Windows, double-click the notebook you want to update. Figure 9-7 shows the sync preferences for a notebook.

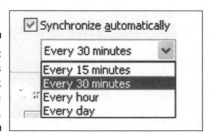

Figure 9-7:
Windows
notebook
sync
options.

• On a Mac, click the area next to the notebook you want to update, and choose a new update frequency in the resulting dialog (see Figure 9-8).

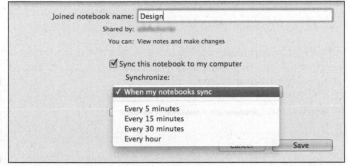

Figure 9-8: Mac note-book sync options.

6. **Click OK to close the Options dialog box when you're done setting sync options.**

Syncing on Android devices

Setting up the sync settings on an Android device is quick and easy. The default setting is every 60 minutes. If you'd like to change the setting, follow these steps:

1. **Open Evernote, and tap the Profile icon.**

   This icon is the one bearing your name in the top-left corner of the screen.

2. **Tap Settings.**

3. **In the Settings window, tab the Sync Notes tab.**

4. **Scroll down to Sync Automatically, and choose a new sync interval.**

   You have five choices: No Background Sync, Every 15 Minutes, Every 30 Minutes, Every 60 Minutes, and Every 1 Day.

   I don't recommend choosing No Background Sync, because if you do, you have to sync your information manually every time you need to have your notes synced to the system (see the next section).

5. **Exit the Settings window by tapping the Back icon.**

You have two sync options other than auto sync. Choose Wi-Fi Sync Only to make your Android device sync only when it's hooked up to Wi-Fi, or choose Sync Data on Power-Up to begin syncing your device as soon as you turn it on.

Syncing notes manually

You don't need to sync Evernote when you access it from a web browser. You're directly accessing Evernote's servers in the cloud. Here's how to synchronize your notes manually:

- ✔ **Windows:** Click the sync icon or press F9.
- ✔ **Mac:** Click the sync icon or press Control+⌘+S.
- ✔ **iOS device:** Tap the Sync icon in the top-right corner of your Evernote home screen.
- ✔ **Android device:** Tap the Sync icon in the bottom-left corner of your Evernote home screen.
- ✔ **Windows Phone:** Tap the Sync button to sync all your changes.
- ✔ **BlackBerry:** Swipe down on the screen from top to bottom, to reveal the manual sync option.

You should use the sync feature over Wi-Fi to extend your bandwidth, which increases your Internet speed and makes syncing finish faster.

Maximizing Mobile Sync Performance

Syncing often ties up your mobile device and slows everything else you're doing. Lengthy syncs can kill your battery and create a lag in getting your information into the hub.

Evernote has been working diligently to ensure that syncing is not only stable and reliable, but also convenient. Synchronization is efficient on all platforms but is limited by the communication speed of the device. Android phones and iPhones have the best syncing performance among small mobile devices. The latest BlackBerry release is much improved, too.

Running sync in the background means that it runs much faster. The more often you sync, the less data your device has to transfer at a time. After all, you aren't going to be able to update 250 notebooks in the amount of time you've set for autosync (refer to "Setting Sync Preferences," earlier in this chapter).

The sync feature is also robust, which means that you're less likely to encounter problems with conflicting notes. In the example in "Synchronizing Notes Automatically," earlier in this chapter, I had to move quickly and deliberately to create a conflict and get a conflict message. As long as you keep your autosync setting at a time limit that's reasonable for the number of updates you make in a day, you're unlikely to have much of an issue with duplicate saved notes. (For more on this topic, see "Managing conflicting changes," earlier in this chapter.)

Sync handles really large databases. The sync feature does have a few limitations, but it's unlikely that you'll encounter them. If you ever do hit a limit, please write to tell me what you're doing that exceeded an Evernote limit. These restrictions are mostly theoretical and shouldn't be an issue as long as you keep autosync running in the background on your devices:

✔ **You can sync only 100,000 notes.** If you have autosync set to function daily, this limitation shouldn't be a problem. If you turned off autosync, however, you could have issues. (The average Evernote user has fewer than 5,000 notes, so in all likelihood, you won't have an issue.)

✔ **Evernote can't sync more than 250 notebooks.** That amount should be more than ample, but be aware that you don't want to get crazy with the number of notebooks you create if you sync among several devices.

✔ **You can sync only 100,000 tags but 100 per note.** That number is certainly more tags than I'd be able to follow, and odds are that you won't have nearly that many tags either. But that limitation is something to keep in mind when you're getting organized.

✔ **Evernote syncs up to 100 saved searches.** If this limitation is a problem, consider organizing your notebooks to reduce the number of saves you need. If you keep your bills organized in Evernote, for example, keep them in one notebook, which means that you don't need to save as many searches.

Seeing Your Sync Status

The sync status displays at the top (iOS devices, Mac computers, and Windows computers), bottom (Android devices), or top right of the screen (BlackBerry devices). This message let you know that the sync is working as you expected, running in the background and storing your updates without your having to do a thing.

The following list describes how you know that a sync happened on various devices:

- ✔ **Windows computer:** Your computer generates messages along the way and displays a pop-up window when every sync (manual or automatic) is complete.

- ✔ **Mac computer:** The arrows on the Sync icon rotate when a manual or automatic sync is occurring.

- ✔ **iOS device:** With Evernote active, tap the Profile button in the top-left corner of the screen. The first option in the resulting Settings screen shows you the date and time of the last update and indicates whether sync is occurring.

- ✔ **Android device:** When you update a note, the Evernote icon appears in the top-left corner of your screen with a check mark. You can tap this icon and get a pull-down menu to show you which notes you've updated. When your Android device is syncing, it displays a downloading bar at the bottom of the screen. When syncing is complete, you see Last Sync, followed by the month, day, and time.

Chapter 10

Sharing Notes and Notebooks

• •

In This Chapter

▶ Sharing over many platforms and media

▶ Sending notes to others

▶ Sharing over the Internet

• •

*I*n this chapter, you find out about the many ways of sharing your notes with family, friends, and professionals. Evernote gives you numerous options, from e-mail to social media, for getting your lists, research, and pictures out to a wider audience. Evernote isn't just about organizing yourself; it's also about making it easier to share what you know with others.

What kind of application would Evernote be if it didn't let you share information with the major social networks? No more just talking about that big fish you caught. You can actually take a picture from the lake while the fish is still on the line, record an audio note to go with it, and post it to any number of places.

Sharing information is by far one of the most exciting aspects of Evernote. Mom always said you need to share; Evernote has given you a means to do as she said.

In this chapter, I tell you what you need to know to share and publish notebooks.

Sharing Notes on Social Networks

You can share notes on social networks in several ways, which means that you're not limited by the network or to sharing with just one friend. The only limitations are the number of networks you've joined and the number of contacts you have.

Sharing on Facebook

Facebook, which was founded in 2004 by Mark Zuckerberg in his Harvard dorm, is one of the leading social networking services. Its website has 1.4 billion active users every month, which goes a long way toward fulfilling Zuckerberg's vision of "connecting the world." Many Facebook users want to connect Facebook to Evernote. Now it's easy.

One thing to keep in mind about Facebook (and Twitter, discussed later in this chapter) is that others may be able to see the notes you post. Use common sense when posting information to social networks, and keep all private notes off these types of sites.

Sharing on PCs and Macs

Sharing a note with Facebook is easy from both Windows PCs and Macs. Follow these steps:

1. **In the Note panel, highlight the note you want to share.**

2. **Click the Share button, or choose Share⇨Facebook (see Figure 10-1).**

Figure 10-1: You can share your notes through Facebook.

3. **If asked, enter your Facebook password.**

   When your Facebook page appears, you're free to update information as you normally would before sharing the link on your News Feed.

4. **Click the Share button.**

   The note is shared to your Facebook News Feed (see Figure 10-2).

Figure 10-2: Sharing to your Facebook News Feed.

Sharing on iOS devices

With just a few simple steps on your Apple mobile device, you can share any note you like. Ensure that the Facebook app is installed on your device, and follow these steps:

1. **On your phone tap Settings⇨Facebook.**

   You have to scroll down to find Facebook toward the bottom of the screen.

2. **Under Allow These Apps to Use Your Account, ensure that sharing to Facebook is allowed (see Figure 10-3).**

   Tap the circle to the right of Facebook to activate the feature. When the area containing the circle turns green, Facebook is activated.

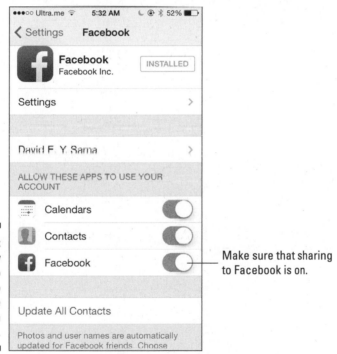

Figure 10-3:
Allow
sharing to
Facebook to
let Evernote
write on
your wall.

Make sure that sharing
to Facebook is on.

3. **Open the Evernote app and select the note you want to share.**

4. **Scroll to the bottom of the note, tap the three-dot icon, and select Share from the pop-up menu.**

5. **Tap the Facebook icon (see Figure 10-4).**

   An editable note is created, ready to post to Facebook (see Figure 10-5).

6. **Enter text (if you have something you want to say about the note) and then tap Post to share the information.**

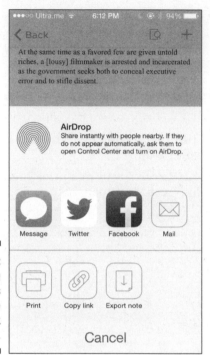

Figure 10-4:
The sharing options in the Facebook app.

Figure 10-5:
This note is ready to be edited and posted to Facebook.

Sharing on Android devices

Starting with the Gingerbread version (Version 2.3), the Android operating system enables users to share notes and notebooks (groups of notes). Follow these steps to share notes with Facebook from Evernote for Android:

1. **Press and hold the note you want to share until the editing menu appears.**

2. **Tap Post to Facebook.**

3. **Enter your Facebook login information.**

4. **Enter any text you'd like to post with your note.**

5. **Tap Share.**

   You're done.

You may be happy to know that after you've posted your first note to Facebook, the sharing process becomes much simpler. If you're already in a note and have previously shared with Facebook, the steps for sharing your notes are much faster:

1. **Tap the Menu button at the bottom of your Android device.**

2. **Tap Post.**

3. **Tap the Post to Facebook button in the Share with the World section.**

4. **Complete the Facebook sharing process.**

Sharing on Twitter

This section walks you through the process of linking your Evernote account to Twitter and then helps you tweet a note.

Tweeting on PCs and Macs

To share to Twitter from your desktop or laptop computer, follow these steps:

1. **Highlight the note you want to share in the Note panel.**

2. **Click the Share button or choose ⇨Twitter.**

3. **Enter your Twitter username and password.**

4. **Update the text you want to tweet.**

   Evernote automatically inputs your note's title, so if you have something else to say, make sure that you update it before you tweet (see Figure 10-6).

When you post to Twitter, you're creating a public link to a note that anyone who has access to the link can view. On Twitter, anyone — not just your followers — can view your posts, so by posting to Twitter you are in effect making your note public. *Be sure that this is your intention.*

5. Click Tweet.

You get a confirmation message saying your tweet has been sent.

Figure 10-6:
Tweet text.

Tweeting on iOS devices

To share to Twitter from an iPhone, iPad, or iPod touch, follow these steps:

1. Open the note you want to share.

2. Scroll to the bottom of the note, tap the three-dot icon, and select Share from the pop-up menu.

3. Tap Twitter.

If you realize that you've selected the wrong note or don't want to share on Twitter, you can tap Cancel.

4. Do one of the following:

- If you've already linked your Twitter account to your iOS device, skip to Step 5.

- If you've never linked your Twitter account to your iOS device, enter your Twitter account information and then tap Allow.

5. Tap Post.

6. Go to your Twitter account to check out your post.

Connecting social media and Evernote

Sharing between Evernote and social media (in both directions) greatly enhances your overall experience. You can routinely gather information in Evernote that you want to share, and you can share notes in Evernote with others via social media.

Two services make it simple to command and control applications, push data between web applications, and automate a lot of annoying recurring tasks:

- ✔ **IFTTT:** IFTTT (which stands for *If This Then That*) is a free service that connects two services of your choice to create an automated

flow called a *recipe.* Recipes are great for automatically adding content from various social networks and services to your Evernote account. For more information about IFTTT, visit `https://ifttt.com`.

- ✔ **Zapier:** This powerful service enables you to automate your workflow by connecting Evernote with social networks and web services. A limited amount of its power is free; subscription services cost $15, $49, or $99 per month and include support. Visit `https://zapier.com` for more information.

Tweeting on Android devices

You aren't exactly out of luck if you want to share a note through Twitter on an Android device, but at this writing, it's a bit more difficult than it is on other platforms.

To share with Twitter, make sure that the Twitter application is installed on your Android device. Then, to share, tap Menu⇨More and choose Share. Twitter is one of the options.

Sharing Notes with SMS

Android and iOS device users can share notes with SMS, too — assuming, of course, that the Android devices support SMS. Follow these steps:

Sharing via SMS on iOS devices

To share via SMS from an iPhone, iPad, or iPod touch, follow these steps:

1. **Scroll to the bottom of the note, tap the three-dot icon, and select Share from the pop-up menu.**

2. **Tap the Message icon.**

3. **Enter the recipient's phone number.**

4. **(Optional) Edit the message that will be sent to the recipient.**

   Evernote automatically composes a message containing a link to the note to the cellphone number you selected, but you can edit the message to include additional information if you want.

5. **Tap Send.**

Sharing via SMS on Android devices

To share via SMS from an Android device, follow these steps:

1. **Tap the share icon on the top-right corner of the screen. It looks like two dots connected by lines.**

2. **Select SMS in the share menu that appears.**

3. **Enter the recipient's phone number.**

4. **(Optional) Edit the message that will be sent to the recipient.**

   Evernote automatically composes a message containing a link to the note to the cellphone number you selected, but you can edit the message to include additional information if you want.

5. **Tap Send.**

Sharing Notes with Gmail (Web Only)

If you use Gmail, Google's e-mail service, Evernote can work amiably with your Gmail account so you can share notes easily in your e-mail messages.

Configuring Evernote to work with Gmail

To configure Evernote to work with your Gmail account, follow these steps:

1. **Log in to your Evernote account on the web.**

2. **Click the Settings link at the top of the page.**

3. **Choose Connected Services from the options on the left.**

4. **Click the Connect button next to the Google logo.**

   Google may display the following message: `This app would like to: Have offline access`. If so, click Accept. If you have multiple accounts, Google offers the option to select the account that you want to connect. To connect to a different account, click Add Account.

5. **Log into your Gmail account.**

   You are taken back to the Connected Services page and the web version of Evernote has access to your Gmail account.

Sharing with Gmail

To share a note with Gmail, follow these steps:

1. **Choose Share⇨Email.**

   A new e-mail window opens.

2. **In the Send To section, start typing the e-mail address.**

   Evernote autocompletes it, based on matching entries from your Gmail contacts.

3. **Type a message, if you want to.**

4. **Select the recipient's address.**

   You can also send the note to multiple people by separating their addresses with commas.

5. **Click Email to send the note.**

Sharing Notebooks

The principles for sharing complete notebooks are the same as for sharing individual notes, but sharing a notebook is a little more complicated.

You can share only notes from mobile devices — not entire notebooks. To share a notebook, you must do so from a desktop or laptop computer.

To share a notebook, follow these steps:

1. **Select the notebook you want to share (see Figure 10-7).**

2. **Right-click the notebook you want to share, and select Share Notebook from the menu.**

3. **Click Create a Public Link or Share with Individuals (see Figure 10-8).**

   For this exercise, click Share with Individuals. When you do, you see the dialog box shown in Figure 10-9.

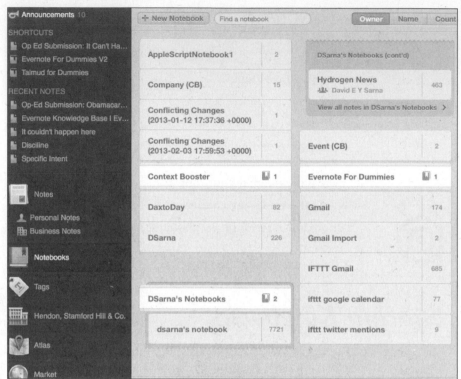

Figure 10-7:
Selecting a
notebook for
sharing.

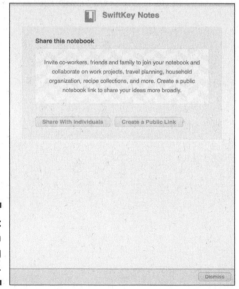

Figure 10-8:
Select a
sharing
option.

Grant permissions.

Add e-mail addresses for
people who can share the notebook.

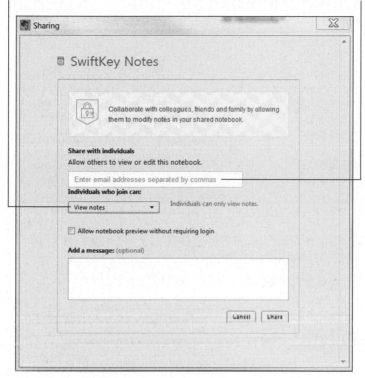

Figure 10-9:
Inviting
individuals
to share and
granting
rights.

4. **Enter e-mail addresses for sharing invitations, separating the addresses with commas.**

5. **Grant permissions for the shared notebook.**

   The default is View Only. Premium and Business users can also allow users to view notes and activity, invite others as well as modify notes.

6. **(Optional) Add a message for the share invitation.**

7. **(Optional) Select the check box titled Allow Notebook Preview Without requiring login.**

   By checking this box, you are allowing the recipient to view the Evernote notebook you are sharing without logging into her account.

8. **Click Share.**

9. **Click Dismiss.**

   Addressees receive an e-mail similar to Figure 10-10.

Additional sharing options for Premium subscribers

Premium and Business subscribers have an incredible advantage when it comes to sharing: They can save notebooks that others can modify. So if you have a project that you need to coordinate, and you divvy up the tasks, everyone on the project can make changes without a network. You can be at the store snapping pictures and uploading them while a friend records and loads some audio and a third friend is adding text and websites from home. Better yet, only one of you has to be a Premium subscriber to make this happen. The Premium subscriber grants the other users access so they can start loading content into the notebook.

Here's a nice bonus: Additions made by other users don't count toward the subscriber's monthly allowance for uploads.

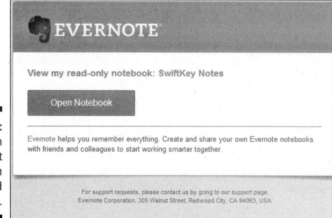

Figure 10-10:
Invitation
to recipient
to open
a shared
notebook.

Making Notes Available on the Internet

An alternative to sharing through Facebook, Twitter, or Gmail, or sharing directly with other Evernote users, is sharing a single note at a specific URL. The most common use of this feature is to publish a list of links on a web page. Follow these steps to create a link on the Internet:

1. **Log in to Evernote Web.**

2. **Highlight the note you want to share.**

3. **Choose Share⇨Link.**

   A unique (but lengthy) URL is available for your note. You can share it via e-mail, instant messaging, or any of the social-media methods your heart desires.

You can paste the lengthy URL that Evernote creates into a URL link shortener, such as `https://bitly.com` or `http://goo.gl/`, to shorten the link before you share it.

You have several options:

- ✔ Click Copy to Clipboard to copy the URL.
- ✔ Click Stop Sharing if you no longer want the note to be public.
- ✔ Click the Open Note URL link to see how it looks to the party you're sharing with.
- ✔ Click Close to close the properties dialog box.

Sharing on Mobile Devices

Evernote makes it easy to share notes from your mobile devices when you're on the go. This can only be done with notes, however. In order to share notebooks, you must do so from your desktop computer. Here is how you go about sharing notes from your mobile devices.

iOS devices

To share a note from your iPhone, iPad, or iPod touch, follow these steps:

1. **Tap a note to open it.**

2. **Tap the three-dot icon.**

3. **Tap Share.**

4. **Tap the method you want to use to share (see Figure 10-11).**

   The available options depend on the applications you have installed.

5. **End sharing by tapping Stop Sharing.**

   You may need to swipe right to see that icon if, as in Figure 10-11, the Stop Sharing icon is partially or completely hidden.

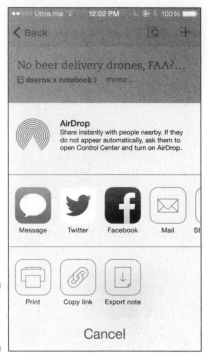

Figure 10-11:
Sharing from
an iPhone.

Android devices

Follow these steps to share notes on an Android device:

1. **Find the note you want to share.**

2. **If you see snippets of notes, tap a note to open it.**

3. **Scroll to the bottom of the screen and tap the Share icon (three vertical dots).**

   The share screen opens (see Figure 10-12).

4. **Tap the service you want to share your note to.**

   Options vary according to what is installed on your device.

   For this example, tap Gmail. An e-mail with a link to the note opens, as shown in Figure 10-13.

5. **Enter the recipient's address.**

6. **(Optional) Add a comment.**

7. **Tap Send.**

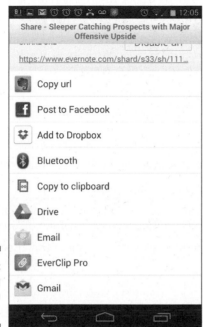

Figure 10-12:
Sharing
a note in
Android.

Send button

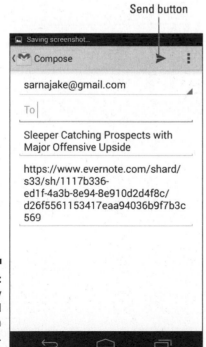

Figure 10-13:
Note ready
to edit and
send via
e-mail.

E-Mailing Notes from PCs and Macs

Sometimes, you have notes that would be perfect to e-mail. Thank goodness Evernote has taken that fact into account and has made it very easy to e-mail your notes to anyone.

To e-mail from a desktop or laptop computer, follow these steps:

1. **Highlight the note you want to e-mail in the Note panel.**

2. **Choose Share⇨Send by Email (Windows) or Share⇨Email Note (Mac).**

3. **Enter your intended recipient's e-mail address.**

   If you're e-mailing someone who is in your contact list, just pull that contact up from the address book. Otherwise, type the full e-mail address.

   To e-mail a copy of the shared note to yourself, select the check box titled CC Me on This Email.

4. **Click Send.**

   Your note is sent, and you're good to go. If you decide against e-mailing, just close the message, and all is forgotten.

Chapter 11

Exporting, Importing, and Encrypting Notes

In This Chapter

▶ Exporting notes from Evernote

▶ Importing notes into Evernote

▶ Encrypting your notes

▶ Securing your information

---

*E*vernote has several useful — although perhaps little-known and less-used — features that help make the experience more complete, safer, and more enjoyable. Importing and exporting notes can be extremely helpful for storing information as an archive, and encrypting notes ensures that your private information is secured.

Exporting Notes

Evernote's three Laws of Data Protection are

 ✔ Your data is yours.

 ✔ Your data is protected.

 ✔ Your data is portable.

Evernote has no data lock. Evernote is committed to making it easy for you to get all your data in and out at any time. The Evernote desktop software lets you export all your notes and content in human-readable HTML as well as in fully documented machine-readable XML format.

Evernote offers a free application programming interface (API) that lets you access all your data via programs, as discussed in the appendix. The company believes that if you're confident that you can leave at any time, you'll be confident enough to want to stay.

Exporting is a desktop or laptop activity; it can't be done from mobile devices or even from Evernote Web (the version of Evernote accessed directly from a web browser at `http://evernote.com`). Exporting lets you back up your notes outside Evernote so that you can retrieve them easily. Exporting is useful if you decide to stop using Evernote, when Evernote's system is down, or when you want to export notes to another application.

Exporting from a PC

You can export a single note, a notebook, or all your notes. The process is the same for each item after you select what you want to export.

To export a note, follow these steps:

1. **Highlight the note or notes you want to export.**

   If you want to export a notebook, highlight the desired notebook. You can also right-click the note or notebook to see a contextual menu of choices.

2. **To export a note, choose File⇨Export.**

   To export a notebook, choose Export Notes from *Notebook Name* or from All Notebooks. If you right-clicked, choose Export Notes from the contextual menu.

   This step archives all your notes from that particular notebook or (in the case of All Notebooks) all your notes.

3. **Change the format, if desired, and click Export.**

   Figure 11-1 shows the Windows version of the dialog box for exporting notes. Figure 11-2 shows the different settings you can choose to export or ignore.

   You have four options for saving your archive:

   • *Export As a File in ENEX Format* (see the nearby sidebar) archives your information in a single file without links (`.enex`).

   • *Export As a Single HTML Web Page* archives your information as a single web page (`.html`).

   • *Export As a Web Archive* saves your information as a web archive and separates your notes but keeps them in a single file (`.mht`).

   • *Export As Multiple Web Pages* exports the selected note or notes as multiple web pages (`.html`).

   Clicking the Options button lets you control what to export. The default is to export them. When you're exporting as a web archive or multiple web pages, you have more control of what's exported. Attributes that can be exported include note title, created date, updated date, author, location, tags, and source URL.

Unless you have a reason not to, such as a need to import to another program, you may as well export a note with all its attributes.

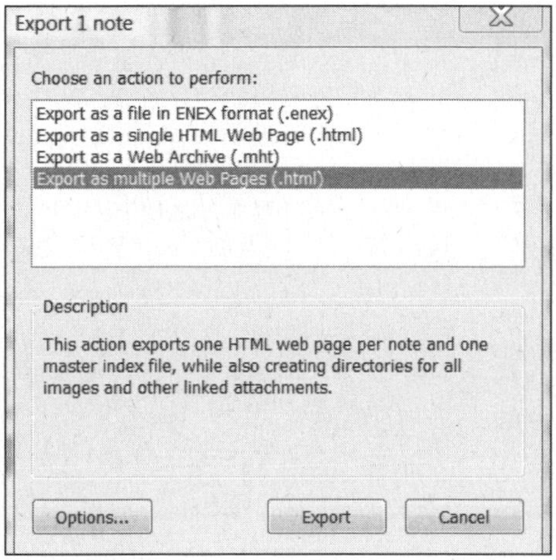

Export 1 note

Choose an action to perform:

Export as a file in ENEX format (.enex)
Export as a single HTML Web Page (.html)
Export as a Web Archive (.mht)
Export as multiple Web Pages (.html)

Description

This action exports one HTML web page per note and one master index file, while also creating directories for all images and other linked attachments.

Options...   Export   Cancel

Figure 11-1:
Windows
export.

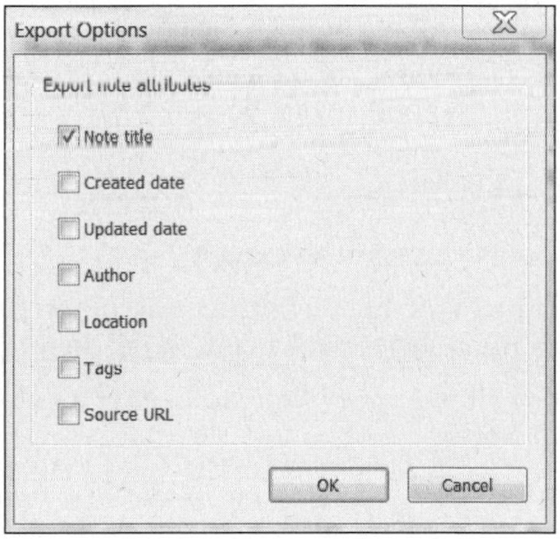

Export Options

Export note attributes

☑ Note title

☐ Created date

☐ Updated date

☐ Author

☐ Location

☐ Tags

☐ Source URL

OK   Cancel

Figure 11-2:
Windows
export
options.

4. **Select a destination for saving the file, and give the file a name that will be easy for you to remember.**

5. **Click Save.**

Evernote does the rest and lets you know when the task is complete.

Exploring the .enex and .html file types

Both Windows and Macintosh computers offer `.html` and `.enex` file types. Saving your archives with an `.html` extension ensures that you can always access the notes, even if you drop your Evernote account. The archive creates a link to attachments, so you don't have to worry about losing them. The price is that you lose the ability to use Evernote's optical-character and image-recognition features, which make it easy to scan your PDFs and pictures, so be aware that they won't function quite the same way after they're saved outside Evernote's system.

The `.enex` file type is Evernote XML. It keeps all your information in a single file, and you don't have to follow links to access them. An `.enex` file includes everything in code, however, so unless you know XML, pretty much the only way to use it is to load it into another system.

Windows also has `.mht` and multiple-page `.html` files, which work similarly to `.html` files. Feel free to experiment with the different file types to see which one best serves your needs.

Exporting from a Mac

You can export a single note, a notebook, or all your notes. The process is almost the same as in Windows except for what you select when you export.

To export a note, follow these steps:

1. **Highlight the note or notes you want to export.**

   If you want to export a notebook, highlight the desired notebook. You can also click Notes and right-click to get a contextual menu.

2. **To export a note, choose File⇨Export Note; to export a notebook, choose File⇨Export All Notes.**

   This step archives all your notes from that particular notebook or all your notes. You can also right-click and choose the applicable option from the contextual menu that appears.

3. **Enter a name you can remember, select a save location, and change the format if desired.**

   Figure 11-3 shows the Mac version of the dialog box for exporting notes. The default filename is My Notes, so if you've exported before, enter a distinctive name so that you don't overwrite your older archives.

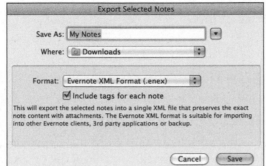

Figure 11-3:
Setting
export
options on a
Mac.

You also need to specify the file type for the export:

- *Evernote XML Format* archives your information in a single file without links (.enex).

- *.html* archives your information as a web page.

4. **Click Save when you're satisfied with the name, location, and file type.**

Evernote does the rest and lets you know when the task is complete.

Importing .enex Notes into Evernote

Using any Evernote desktop client, you can reimport any archived .enex file that you created into the same account or another account.

Importing to a Windows PC

To import an .enex archive on a PC, follow these steps:

1. **Choose File➪Import➪Evernote Export Files.**

   A pop-up window appears.

2. **Browse to the .enex file you'd like to import.**

3. **(Optional) Import the tags included in your archive file by selecting or deselecting Import Note Tags.**

4. **Click Open.**

You can import Microsoft OneNote archives the same way. Simply choose File➪Import➪Microsoft OneNote in Step 1.

Importing to a Mac

To import an `.enex` archive on a Mac, follow these steps:

1. **Click File➪Import Notes for Archive.**

   A pop-up window appears.

2. **Browse to the archived file, and click Open.**

   You can double-click the file to start it. If you'd like to include tags, select the Import Tags check box at the bottom of the pop-up window.

   The import process begins, and the notes are initially placed in a temporary notebook. A dialog box informs you of this temporary location and gives you the chance to add the notes to a synchronized notebook.

Protecting Information Through Encryption

Security and privacy are important concerns when you're working with Evernote, which contains all your valuable information. You have the ability to encrypt your own notes, making it easier to protect billing information, bank and credit cards, or your tax information.

The process and the mechanics are very similar on Windows PCs and Macs, so I discuss the subject as a whole and let you know when the steps are different.

Figure 11-4 shows an example note that you may want to encrypt.

To encrypt the note, follow these steps:

1. **Highlight the text to be encrypted.**

2. **Right-click the highlighted text and choose Encrypt Selected Text from the contextual menu.**

   Alternatively, press Ctrl+Shift+X (Windows), or Control-click (Mac) and choose Encrypt Selected Text from the contextual menu.

   The Note Encryption dialog box appears.

3. **Enter an encryption passphrase, verify it, and click OK (see Figure 11-5).**

   Use a passphrase that you can remember easily. I like to save passphrases to a spreadsheet, but this method may not be the best one for you. You don't want to save your passphrase as a note, because that would defeat the purpose of encrypting it.

| Created: | 7/ 4/2011 11:42 PM | Updated: | 7/ 4/2011 11:47 PM | Author |

Click to set location...

Click to set URL...   Project Timeline

Arial   13   B I U

Pay the bills
    Car - 1840402734
    Power - 358702305 with credit card 1111 1111 1111 1111
    Water - PS98894952 with credit card 1111 1111 1111 1111
    Rent - bank account 123456789
Complete Chapter 4
Finish 11 hrs
Spend time with Mom and G

Figure 11-4:
A note
before text
encryption.

Note Encryption

Choose an encryption passphrase (note that passphrases are
case sensitive):

Re-enter encryption passphrase:

WARNING: Evernote does not store a copy of your encryption passphrase.
If you forget this passphrase, Evernote cannot recover your encrypted
content.

Optional: enter a hint to help you remember your passphrase (the hint will
not be encrypted):

☐ Remember passphrase until I quit Evernote

Cancel   OK

Figure 11-5:
Passphrase
and options.

Select the hint option if you're at risk of forgetting the passphrase.
Evernote can't recover your passphrase, so I strongly recommend that
you use this feature in case you don't remember your passphrase when
you need to get into the note.

Your text is now encrypted and looks something like Figure 11-6. You will know there is encrypted text in a note when you see a series of dots, but you won't be able to read it, and nothing indicates how much text is hidden.

Complete Chapter 4
Finish 11 hrs
Spend time with Mom and G

Figure 11-6: Successful encryption.

To see the encrypted text, right-click (Windows) or Control-click (Mac) the encrypted text symbol (the series of dots), and then choose Show Encrypted Text from the contextual menu. To remove encryption, right-click (Windows) or Control-click (Mac) the encrypted selection, and then choose Decrypt Text Permanently from the contextual menu. If you want to decrypt permanently, you'll be prompted to enter the passphrase.

Evernote does *not* store your password and can't recover it. If you forget it, you can't access the text if you close out of Evernote. Write down your password!

Ensuring Privacy and Security

Some large heists of personal data have been splashed all over the news in recent years, including massive hacker thefts of customer data from Target, Neiman Marcus, and Michael's. These reports have (understandably) put all of us on edge about the security of our data.

Evernote, as the keeper of many secrets, is most aware of these issues, especially because the founders made a good living in cryptography for many years before founding the company.

Evernote's privacy policy

Detailed disclosure about what data Evernote collects and maintains about you is available in Evernote's privacy policy (`http://` `evernote.com/legal/privacy.php`). It's not mumbo-jumbo, and you should take the time to read it.

Two-step verification

Evernote offers users two-step verification (known in the industry as *two-factor authentication*), which is designed to keep your account secure even if someone discovers your password. It does this by requiring a verification code whenever you're asked to provide your username and password. This request usually occurs only when you log into Evernote Web or install the app on a new device. This combination of something you know (your password) and something you have (your phone) makes two-step verification a significant security improvement over passwords alone.

What makes two-step verification powerful is the six-digit verification code. This code is delivered to your mobile phone via text message or, if you prefer, generated by an app that runs on your smartphone, such as Google Authenticator. Evernote also gives you a set of one-time backup codes for use when you're traveling. Don't keep these codes exclusively in Evernote because you'll need them in situations when you may not have access to your Evernote account.

If you have a free account, you have to install an authenticator app on your phone in order to set up two-step verification. A good option is Google Authenticator (see `https://support.google.com/accounts/` `answer/1066447`). If you are a Premium user then you also can have the code delivered to you as a secure text message via Telesign (`http://www.` `telesign.com/`).

Access history

Your *access history* is a running list of all the times your account was accessed over the past 30 days. This list includes all the versions of Evernote that you've used, along with locations and IP addresses. If you ever suspect that your account was accessed without your knowledge, you can check the history.

To reach your access history, follow these steps:

1. **Choose Help➪Account Settings.**

2. **Click Security Summary.**

3. **When you're prompted to do so, enter your password.**

4. **In the Two-Step Verification section, select Enable.**

5. **Click Access History to see how and when your Evernote account has been accessed in the past 30 days (see Figure 11-7).**

   You can see the application that accessed Evernote, when, and the IP address of the device that had access. You can also review other services to which you've granted access rights (not shown in the figure).

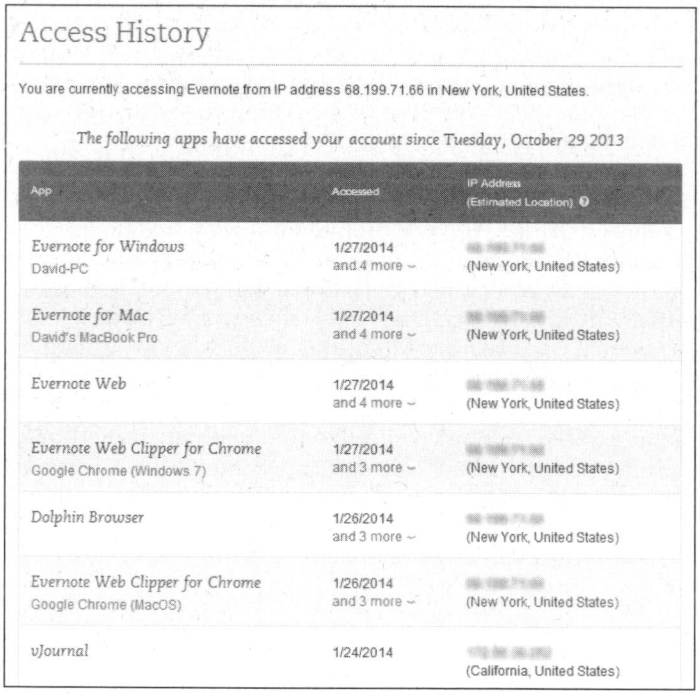

Access History

You are currently accessing Evernote from IP address 68.199.71.66 in New York, United States.

The following apps have accessed your account since Tuesday, October 29 2013

App	Accessed	IP Address (Estimated Location) ❓
Evernote for Windows David-PC	1/27/2014 and 4 more ⌄	(New York, United States)
Evernote for Mac David's MacBook Pro	1/27/2014 and 4 more ⌄	(New York, United States)
Evernote Web	1/27/2014 and 4 more ⌄	(New York, United States)
Evernote Web Clipper for Chrome Google Chrome (Windows 7)	1/27/2014 and 3 more ⌄	(New York, United States)
Dolphin Browser	1/26/2014 and 3 more ⌄	(New York, United States)
Evernote Web Clipper for Chrome Google Chrome (MacOS)	1/26/2014 and 3 more ⌄	(New York, United States)
vJournal	1/24/2014	(California, United States)

Figure 11-7: Fragment of an access log.

If two-step verification ever becomes too burdensome for you, repeat Steps 1 through 3, and select Disable in Step 4.

Passcode lock

Premium and Business subscribers who use certain devices can now lock the Evernote app with a Passcode lock. Whenever you return to the app, you're asked to enter your code. A Passcode lock is a great option if you share your phone or tablet with other people and want to keep them from accessing your notes. One cool thing about this feature is that you can still create quick notes via a widget (a mini app that lives on your Home screen) even when the app is locked; you just won't be able to view or search your notes until you enter your passcode.

You can set up Passcode Lock on your mobile device through your account settings by tapping your name in the top-left corner of the screen and then selecting Premium from the menu. On the following page tap Passcode lock to turn the feature on. You are then prompted to choose a passcode. To change or disable the Passcode lock, return to the Passcode Lock screen, and reenter the PIN. If you mistype your Passcode three times, you'll be asked to enter your password.

At this writing, the PIN Lock feature is exclusive to Windows Phone, Android devices, and iOS devices. Perhaps it will be extended to other platforms in the future.

Chapter 12

Interfacing with Other Products

*E*vernote works with many applications, as well as with many devices and platforms. Trying to figure out the many ways of interfacing with Evernote can be overwhelming. In this chapter, I focus on what you need to do to set up other applications you use to interface with Evernote.

Interfacing with Twitter

Twitter and Evernote are very much in sync. You can share from Twitter to Evernote or from Evernote to Twitter. You can even capture notes from tweets written by people you're following on Twitter.

Before you can have Evernote and Twitter interact, you need to set up accounts in each service. I'm assuming that you've already set up an Evernote account (see Chapter 2) and that you have a Twitter account.

myEN, which used to let you save tweets to your Evernote account, is no longer supported.

I discuss more general alternatives to integrating Evernote and Twitter, IFTTT, and Zapier in Chapter 10. You can also investigate We-Wired Web (http:// wewiredweb.com), elastic.io (www.elastic.io), and CloudWork (https:// cloudwork.com). At this writing, I've found that IFTTT and Zapier are most robustly integrated with Evernote.

Interfacing with E-Mail

One of the greatest things about Evernote is that you can treat it just like a contact, sending e-mails to your notes or attaching information that arrived over e-mail without having to perform half a dozen steps to get it saved to your notebook. The following sections help you set things up so that your e-mail and Evernote work together.

Adding your Evernote e-mail address to your contacts

Your Evernote address is automatically generated to provide better security. The address contains elements of your name to make it easy enough to remember, plus a few random numbers to ensure that it won't be duplicated. In other words, Evernote's autogenerated address appends a number that's truly random and doesn't indicate how many others have your address.

The location where you can find your Evernote e-mail address varies for each platform and device. Use the following information to locate your Evernote-generated e-mail address, and then add it to your contacts:

✔ **Online:** Log in, click your username, and then click Account Settings in the top-right corner of the screen. The e-mail information is located on the Account Summary tab, in the Email Notes to section.

You can do something else cool here. Evernote strives to protect you from spam. If your account starts to receive spam, you can click the Reset button. Evernote generates a new e-mail for you. Don't forget to put the new address in your contacts list.

✔ **Windows:** Open Evernote, and choose Tools⇨Account Info. You can also upgrade your account, see how much you've used Evernote, and check out how much more you can do before you reach your limit. This command is good to use when you need to see basic information in one place.

✔ **Mac:** Open Evernote, and choose Evernote⇨Account Info. You can also upgrade your account, see how much you've used Evernote, and check out how much more you can do before you reach your limit. This command is good to use when you need to see basic information in one place.

I added my Evernote address to my contact list, and I routinely copy my important outgoing e-mail to it. I also forward incoming e-mail to that address when I want to be sure to save it.

Adding your address to contacts from mobile devices

Mobile devices have very easy one-click solutions for saving your Evernote e-mail address to contacts. The following sections cover individual devices.

Adding your address to iOS devices

On an iPhone, iPod touch, or iPad, follow these steps to add your e-mail account to your contacts:

1. **Open the Evernote app.**

2. **Tap your username in the top-left corner.**

3. **Tap General.**

4. **Scroll down to Evernote Email Address.**

   You see your e-mail address for Evernote.

5. **Tap the arrow to the right of the address.**

6. **Tap Add to Contacts.**

   The Add to Contacts button adds your Evernote e-mail address to your contact list. Now you don't have to worry about your e-mails winding up in your junk mail.

You can also choose to copy your Evernote e-mail address to the Clipboard in case you want to give it to someone or store the address someplace else on your device.

Adding your address to Android devices

On an Android device, follow these steps to add your e-mail account to your contacts:

1. **Tap your username at the top of the Evernote home screen.**

2. **Tap Settings.**

   Below this heading, you see the entry Evernote Email Address. The address listed below this area is your autogenerated e-mail address.

3. **Tap Add to Address Book.**

4. **Choose whether you want to save the address to your device or to your Google account.**

   Note: You must have a Gmail account for the latter option to work.

5. **Enter contact information for your account.**

   Yes, this step seems to be mostly a formality, but it's worth the minute or two it takes to enter a minimal amount of information so that you don't lose information to your junk box.

6. **Tap Save.**

   Now whenever you e-mail from your Android device, you can avoid having to hunt for your Evernote e-mail address.

Adding your address to BlackBerry devices

On a BlackBerry device, follow these steps to add your e-mail account to your contacts:

1. **Navigate to `http://evernote.com` in your BlackBerry browser.**

2. **Log in with your username and password.**

3. **Scroll to the bottom of the page, and tap Settings.**

4. **Scroll down to Incoming Mail Address.**

5. **Highlight the address, and copy it to the clipboard.**

6. **Tap Contacts➪New Contact.**

7. **Paste the e-mail address that you copied in Step 5.**

8. **Press the BlackBerry key, and tap Save to save the address in your contacts.**

TECHNICAL STUFF

Delivering RSS feeds to Evernote

At this writing, the easiest, most efficient, guaranteed way to get RSS feeds into Evernote is to e-mail them. If you need to save only the web address and page, that task is relatively simple to accomplish. Here's a free way to do it:

1. **Highlight the URL, and copy it to the clipboard.**

2. **Navigate to `www.feedmyinbox.com`.**

3. **Paste the copied RSS URL into the Feed URL field.**

4. **Paste your Evernote e-mail address into the Your Email Address field.**

   Remember to use your Evernote e-mail address.

5. **Click Feed My Inbox.**

All notes are delivered to your default notebook.

Notes created from feeds (whether or not you use FeedMyInbox) go against your monthly upload allowance (1GB per month for Premium subscribers and 60MB per month for free accounts). Also, you're limited to 250 e-mails per day in an Evernote Premium account and 50 e-mails per day in a free account. Therefore, you should use the RSS once-a-day feed option, if it's available.

You can also use a site such as `http://habilis.net/dailyfeed` to generate a daily feed from any website. Feeds appear as new notes in your default notebook. Habilis is a simple way to save a page so that you can come back to it and catch up on the latest news.

Blogging with Evernote

If you're one of the many people who has a blog, wouldn't it be fantastic if you could coordinate your blogs with Evernote to save duplicating your work? Evernote has already thought of bloggers and gives you just that option. Those of you who have multiple blogs can now use Evernote as a centralized work location to draft your blog posts and coordinate your various blogging endeavors.

You can set up and track your blogs any way you like, of course, but here are some very cool things you can do to make your blogging life easier:

- ✔ **Create new notes as you come up with new ideas.** If you have multiple blogs, it may be easiest to have a template tag as well as tags for each of your blogging sites. You can always set up different notebooks for each blog source, but working with multiple notebooks may become a bit confusing as you try to remember what you said on which blog. Tags are slightly easier to track because you can deal with all the blogs within a single folder instead of having to search in the All Notes section because you accidentally filed it in the incorrect folder.

- ✔ **Save research to a `Blogging` folder.** This folder doesn't have to be just for writing. For most bloggers, a good bit of research goes into blogging. Even if you don't do research because you blog about yourself, you probably have pictures and websites that you regularly include in your blogs.

- ✔ **Create a new note from the template when you're ready to start preparing a blog.** You've saved your ideas. You've modified your template as you realize what you need. That should be everything you need to start populating your blog.

You'll soon find that blogging takes far less time than it did in the past because you've used Evernote to get organized.

A service called Postach.io (`http://postach.io`), which I discuss in Chapter 17, allows you to tag notes created in Evernote on any platform and then publish them on your Postach.io blog. Postach.io blogs support all the content that Evernote supports, including audio, video, text, and photo posts.

Chapter 13

Troubleshooting Problems

In This Chapter

▶ Dealing with common issues

▶ Getting help from other users

▶ Taking advantage of Evernote's many troubleshooting resources

As with most software, it may take you a while to get used to all of Evernote's many features. You're bound to encounter unanticipated issues and may need help finding answers quickly. Besides, Evernote is software, and software bugs are common.

The good news is that Evernote has established several areas on its website to assist you with troubleshooting. In this chapter, I offer solutions to common problems and also let you know where you can find additional help.

Finding Solutions to Common Problems

Although a section on possible issues could take up a book all on its own, I focus on what I consider to be the top ten issues not covered elsewhere in this book and suggest solutions for them. For more complicated problems, check out the other sections in this chapter, or contact Evernote support (http://evernote.com/contact/support).

This section is meant to handle generic questions, so I don't cover issues specific to any one platform or device. Instead, I discuss problems that you may encounter as a newbie or that may recur.

My confirmation code never arrived

After you have signed up, and after you complete the registration process, a confirmation code is sent to the e-mail address you provided while signing up for your Evernote account.

If this e-mail gets lost or isn't delivered, follow these steps to recover your confirmation code:

1. **Check your e-mail program's spam or junk folder.**

   This folder is far and away the most common place for confirmation e-mail messages to end up (aside from the inbox).

2. **If you can't find the e-mail in your spam folder, visit the Password Reset page (`www.evernote.com/User.action#password`) and enter the e-mail address you used when registering for your account.**

   The confirmation e-mail will be re-sent to you.

3. **If these steps didn't work, contact Evernote support (`http://evernote.com/contact/support/`) for assistance.**

   I cover Evernote support options in "Getting Help from Evernote" later in this chapter.

Evernote won't open

When Evernote won't open (a rare occurrence), you face a very frustrating situation. You really have only one way to fix the problem: Uninstall Evernote, reboot your system, and reinstall the Evernote software. (You can try simply rebooting before uninstalling, but I haven't seen that technique alleviate the problem.)

Syncing occurs frequently and is mostly automatic unless you've disabled the sync feature. If you sync as often as you should — and you should sync your notes at least twice a day — you won't lose anything by uninstalling Evernote. If you have unsynced notes, however, this drastic remedy may cause you to lose any notes you wrote that haven't been synced. Unfortunately, for some problems, you have no other solution.

I forgot my password

You use Evernote to help you remember everything, but what happens when you forget your password? It's like you can't get into the safe where you're storing all your jewels right before the guests arrive for the party!

If you forget your password, follow these steps:

1. **Open Evernote on your desktop or laptop computer.**

2. **Click Sign In.**

3. **Click Forgot Password below the login information boxes.**

4. **Enter either the username or e-mail address associated with your Evernote account.**

   Evernote sends you instructions for resetting your password (see Figure 13-1). If you haven't added Evernote to your safe contact list, make sure to keep an eye on your junk-mail folder.

   This link works for only two hours, so you need to use it quickly to reset your password.

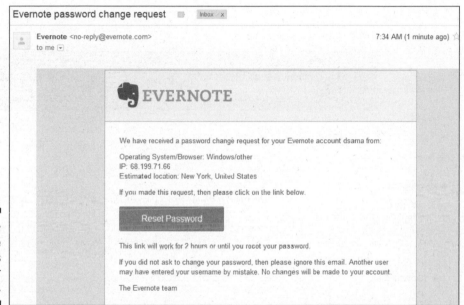

Figure 13-1:
Follow the instructions to reset your password.

Changing your password affects your login on every device you use with Evernote. If you change your password, you need to reset it on all your devices: iPhone, iPad, Android phone, Windows Phone . . . you get the idea.

My password doesn't work

If you just changed your password, and you're trying to access your account from a phone or other mobile device, make sure to enter your new password.

Everything is synced, even the password.

If you haven't changed your password recently, and your password is rejected, check to make sure that you don't have Caps Lock on. Otherwise, see the preceding section for instructions on resetting your password.

The server is acting up

Occasionally, something happens that makes your account on the Evernote servers inaccessible. You can find help on the Evernote customer support website at `http://evernote.com/contact/support/` (see Figure 13-2). The top-right corner shows the server status, which gives you an easy way to find out when the server is having trouble. Click the More link if you need additional details; the link takes you to the status page (`http://status.evernote.com`).

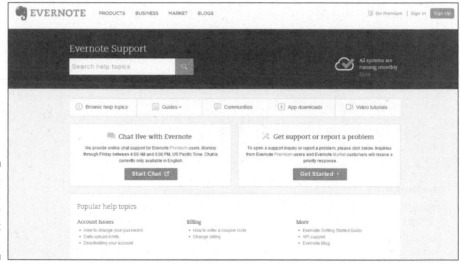

Figure 13-2: Evernote's customer support page.

You also can browse help topics; view the guides, discussion forums, and video tutorials; and download the latest product releases.

You don't have to be logged in to an Evernote account to get the answers you need.

Most of the time, the message looks something like `Ok: All systems are running smoothly`. If you find that upgrades or interruptions have occurred while you were creating or syncing notes, make sure that you resave your changes. Evernote tries to minimize downtime, but server outages can happen from time to time.

The alert box shows only the five or six most recent status updates, so if you have reason to suspect that something is wrong, check here as early as possible during your diagnostic procedures.

My notes are out of sync

Suppose that you created a new note on your phone earlier today. Now you're on your computer and want to update the note. The problem is that you don't see the note.

Odds are that your settings should be adjusted so that Evernote syncs more frequently. Syncing is different by platform and device, so for full details, check out Chapter 9. For a more immediate fix, try these steps:

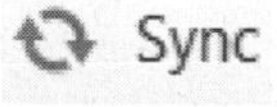

↻ Sync

1. **Click the Sync button at the top of the screen.**

   The exact location of this button depends on the version of Evernote you're using.

   When the sync arrows quit spinning, the sync is complete. If you still don't see the note, go to the next step.

2. **Open Evernote, and make sure that you saved the note.**

   A saved note appears on your notes screen in the list of notes in your notebook. If you didn't save the note, it may still be open. If you didn't save it, and the note isn't open, you've probably lost your work in that note.

I can't display all my notes

You know you have a lot more notes than you see below All Notebooks. Where did they go?

Check out the search box to see whether you've recently run a search, which hides the notes that don't meet the filter criteria. If the search bar has text in it and looks like Figure 13-3, you have a search running and should delete the text in the search box. (Click the X after the search item or items.)

Figure 13-3:
You have
a search
running.

| Q ▾ evernote ios | × |

If the search bar below the menu is empty and looks like Figure 13-4, you may want to make sure that your computer is synced (see the preceding section).

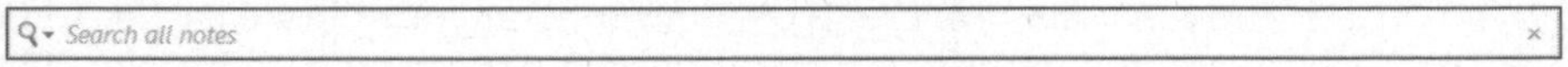

Figure 13-4:
No
searches
appear to be
running.

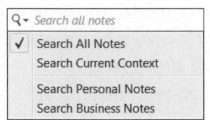

Q ▾ *Search all notes*   ×

My searches aren't working

Are you having problems with your searches? Try one of the following solutions:

✔ Click the down arrow to the right of the Search magnifying-glass icon (see Figure 13-5) and select the appropriate notebook, or choose Search All Notes before starting a search.

Checking Search All Notes rules out the possibility that you are searching in only one notebook, for example, which will greatly limit your results.

Figure 13-5:
Choose
search
restrictions
correctly.

Q ▾ *Search all notes*
✔ Search All Notes
Search Current Context
Search Personal Notes
Search Business Notes

✔ Check to see whether you already have a filter running that is further reducing your notes (see the preceding section). Compare your Evernote bar with Figure 13-3, earlier in this chapter. If your search bar has text in it, you have one or more searches running. Click the X beside the searches you don't want.

Clear your search box when you're done. If you don't, what you type is appended to the search you've entered. (Honestly, this one trips me up time and again.)

No one but the creator can update shared notebooks

You've shared a notebook with friends or colleagues, or they've shared one with you, but only the creator can update the notebook. The problem is that the person doing the sharing isn't a Premium subscriber.

Notebook modification by multiple users works only for Premium subscribers, who are the only ones with the power to grant editing rights to the people they share notebooks with. Everyone else can share so that others can read the shared notes. Other users who had the notebook shared with them can even clip information from a shared note and create their own notes to share (the owner of the note should attempt this cautiously, lest the note soon mushrooms into so many versions that you'll never be able to track it), but access remains read-only.

I have a problem after installing a new release

This issue is an ongoing one, as Evernote releases updates frequently. No matter how much beta testing occurs, releases always fix some problems while creating some unexpected issues. For applications such as Evernote that cross over to so many platforms and devices, odds are even greater that issues will occur with a new release.

If you encounter problems following a new release of Evernote or even an update to your platform/device, the best place to start looking for answers is the user forum (see the next section). You'll likely find either a solution or a known issue on the subject.

Finding Answers Online

Many questions can be answered online, saving you the time it takes to participate in an online chat or submit a trouble ticket. Also, chat is not always available.

Searching the user forum

The user forum is a good source of answers. Users visit the forum to get answers to specific questions. Most answers are provided by other users, although Evernote does monitor the forum. Odds are that you won't be the first to encounter a problem. Think of the user forum as being a form of crowdsourcing for answers.

Here's how to access and search the user forum:

1. **Go to** `http://evernote.com/contact/support`.

2. **Click the Communities link.**

   You are now on the Evernote user forum home page that shows all of the active user discussions. Topics include Recent Topics that are the most active and specific Evernote product discussions forums.

   Figure 13-6 shows a screen shot of a day at the Evernote General Discussion forum. To access a more specific subject without having to comb through the discussions, go to the next step.

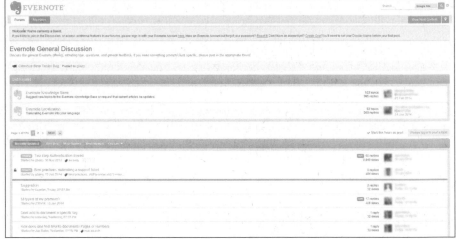

Figure 13-6:
The main page of the Evernote General Discussion forum.

3. **Enter a subject in the search box in the top-right corner of the forum page, and click Search.**

   The notes matching your search criteria are displayed.

Suppose that the Evernote elephant icon disappeared from your browser's menu bar after you downloaded the newest version of Evernote. Here's what you'd do:

1. **Type** My icon disappeared **in the search box and then click Search.**

   Figure 13-7 shows example results for this search topic. You may need to narrow your search so that you aren't plowing through a bunch of posts to get your answer. But you should start by looking at previous posts before asking your own questions.

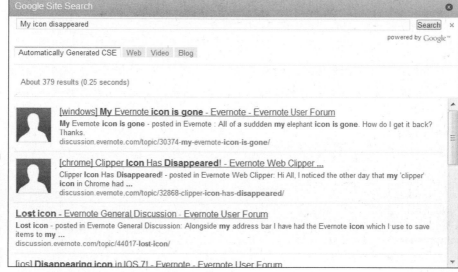

Figure 13-7: Searching the forum for disap-pearing-icon issues.

2. **Scroll through the questions and answers.**

   Your issue probably isn't new, so a diligent search should help you narrow your possible solutions.

3. **To do an advanced search, click the wheel to the right of the search box.**

   An advanced search form opens (see Figure 13-8).

4. **Make the search as restrictive as you like, limiting results by specific phrase, tags, author, date range, product, and other search criteria.**

Figure 13-8: Advanced search options in the user forum.

Navigating the forums

You can quickly navigate the forums by following these steps:

1. **Click the Navigate icon.**

   The Quick Navigation menu opens (see Figure 13-9).

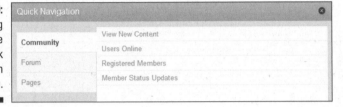

2. **To restrict whose contributions to see, click Community and then select one of these options:**

   • View New Content shows you only new posts to the forum.

   • Users Online shows you only the content posted by users who are currently online and active in the forum.

   • Registered Members shows registered members. After selecting this option, you can select Add As Friend, PM (private message) this member, or Find Content, which shows you all of the posts this member has added to the forums.

   • Member Status Updates shows information the members post about what they're currently up to, similar to a status update on a social media site like Facebook or Twitter. For example, "I'm heading off to work for the day."

3. **(Optional) Click Forums to see the forums, Pages to see daily news (Paper.li), or Wiki (at this writing, a work in progress).**

   Clicking a forum takes you directly to that forum.

4. **Select what you want to see from the menu bar (see Figure 13-10).**

   At the top of each forum is a menu bar that gives you several options for accessing posts, as well as an option to create a custom filter.

Recently Updated   Start Date   Most Replies   Most Viewed   Custom ▾   Show un/answered ▾

Searching the Knowledge Base

If you have a particular question in mind, you can search the Knowledge Base (see figure) for an answer.

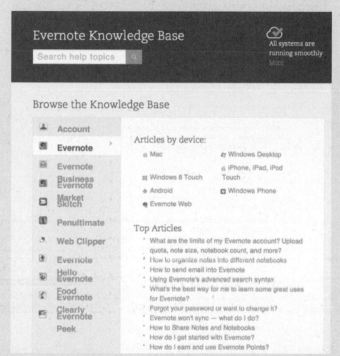

1. **Navigate to** `http://evernote.com/contact/support/kb/.`

2. **Type a question in the Search box.**

   For this example, I typed **export notes**.

3. **Click Search.**

   Although my question returned more hits than I would have liked, one result is obviously on point (see figure).

You can also browse the Knowledge Base. Click any category to browse the Knowledge Base for entries related to that topic. In addition, the same page that contains the search box for the Knowledge Base (`https://support.evernote.com/ics/support/KBSplash.asp`) also shows the most popular and most recent articles. Visit it often.

(continued)

(continued)

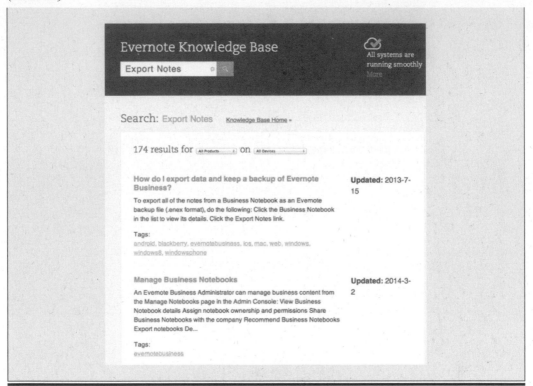

Getting Help from Evernote

At the time of this writing, Evernote doesn't offer telephone support at any price. Premium and Business users can chat online, however, and every user can submit a trouble ticket. I've found these options to be adequate for my needs.

Chatting with Evernote

At this writing, chat support is available only to Premium and Business users. The service is available in English 24 hours a day Monday through Friday. To chat with Evernote, follow these steps:

1. **Navigate to** `http://evernote.com/contact/support/`.

2. **Click Start Chat.**

   A dialog box opens.

3. **Select the product (Evernote), enter a short problem description (used for routing your request), and click Submit.**

   During business hours, you see the message `Just a moment . . .` until an Evernote representative replies.

Submitting a support request

Evernote has set up a user-friendly way of requesting help to solve your problems quickly when you can't locate an answer in the user forum or Evernote Knowledge Base. To submit a support request, follow these steps:

1. **Go to `http://evernote.com/contact/support/`.**

2. **Scroll down to the box on the right that says Get Support or Report a Problem.**

3. **Click the Get Started button.**

   The Get Help Form opens (see Figure 13-11).

4. **Fill in the required information.**

   Make sure to attach any files that would be helpful.

5. **Click Submit.**

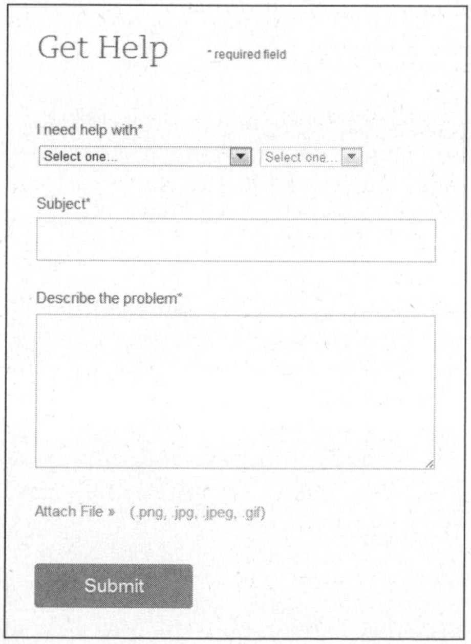

Figure 13-11: Form for submitting a help request.

Get Help   *required field

I need help with*
[Select one... ▼] [Select one... ▼]

Subject*
[   ]

Describe the problem*
[   ]

Attach File » (.png, .jpg, .jpeg, .gif)

[Submit]

The Evernote staff replies to you as quickly as possible. If you're a Business or Premium subscriber, you can rest assured that you'll get a response within one business day. (Sorry — you shouldn't expect an answer if you're having issues right after church on Sunday.)

Make sure that your response didn't arrive in your junk-mail folder, especially if you keep rather strict filters on your inbox. After you receive an answer, if you find that it was delivered to junk mail, make sure to add the address to your safe list.

Viewing the instructional videos

Evernote offers you an entire library of videos, including tutorials, stories, tips, overviews, and demonstrations of a whole ecosystem of third-party products. You can access the Evernote videos at www.evernote.com/video (see Figure 13-12).

Figure 13-12:
Watch the
Evernote
overview
video.

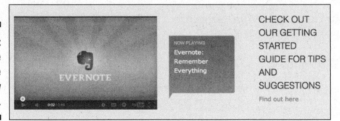

New features are frequently added to Evernote. Illustrative how-to videos often accompany these feature announcements, and you can access them by clicking the appropriate links (see Figure 13-13). Navigate to https://evernote.com/video/ in your browser. You will find tutorials, as well as stories and tips.

You can also access the videos from YouTube. You can find the official Evernote YouTube channel at www.youtube.com/user/EvernoteVideos.

Figure 13-13:
Go to
https://
evernote
.com/
video/ to
check out
Evernote's
many
instructional
videos.

Part IV
Just For You: Device-Specific Features

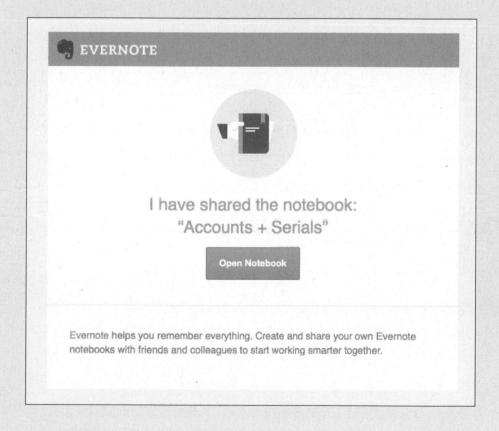

Explore the cool feature of Evernote for Android that enables you to store handwritten notes in Evenote by visiting www.dummies.com/webextras/evernote.

In this part . . .

- ✔ Using Evernote on Windows and Mac computers
- ✔ Using Evernote on tablets and smartphones
- ✔ Using Evernote Web
- ✔ Discovering best practices for making the most out of Evernote on your device

Chapter 14

Computers: Windows and Mac

. . . .

In This Chapter

▶ Pointing out the differences for Windows devices

▶ Taking advantage of extra features for Macs

. . . .

*T*he features of Evernote are discussed throughout this book, especially in Parts I, II, and III. In this chapter, I look at Evernote features as they relate to Windows and Mac computers. Evernote Web (for all platforms) is discussed in Chapter 16.

Evernote discovered that some device-specific features are generally useful and implemented those features across all platforms. Nearly all Evernote features are available cross-platform. Still, some differences in the experience remain, and this chapter is where I discuss them.

Discovering Windows-Only Features

Evernote supports many devices. Some support, however, is unique to Windows, as I discuss in this section.

Working with ENScript.exe

One Windows-only feature is ENScript.exe, a command-line interface available in all versions of Evernote for Windows beginning with version 4.0 and supported by all versions of Windows. The file is installed automatically when you download and install Evernote. You can use ENScript.exe to create new Evernote commands and applications that look and feel like stand-alone applications. (See Chapter 19 for more information about using ENScript.exe.)

Creating a shortcut to ENScript.exe

To create a shortcut to `ENScript.exe` in Windows, follow these steps:

1. **Navigate to the location or folder where you want to create the shortcut.**

2. **Right-click an empty location of the folder or screen, and choose New⇨Shortcut from the contextual menu.**

   The Create Shortcut Wizard appears (see Figure 14-1).

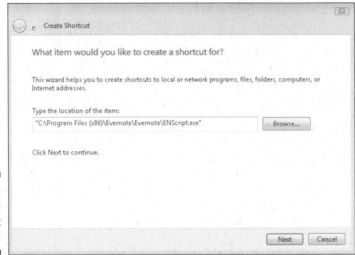

Figure 14-1:
The Create
Shortcut
Wizard.

3. **Enter (or browse to and select) `ENscript.exe`, and then click Next.**

   On my computer, for example, `ENscript.exe` is located in `C:\ Program Files (x86)\Evernote\Evernote`.

   As a security measure, Windows 7 and Windows 8 don't allow users to create files in the `Program Files` folder. Windows wants you to use the `Downloads` folder in your user profile (`C:\Users\<username>`). Older versions of Windows may not have this security feature.

4. **In the next window, name your shortcut (see Figure 14-2), and click Finish.**

   The shortcut is created where you specified.

Figure 14-2:
Name
your new
shortcut.

5. **Right-click the new shortcut's icon, and choose Properties from the contextual menu.**

   The Properties dialog box opens.

6. **Click the Shortcut tab, if it isn't already open.**

7. **Click the Change Icon button to assign your shortcut a custom icon.**

   Ignore the message `The file . . . ENScript.exe contains no icons.`

8. **Click OK to close the error dialog box.**

   The Change Icon dialog box opens, showing some available icons (see Figure 14-3).

Figure 14-3:
Assign an
icon to the
shortcut.

9. **Browse to** `Evernote.exe`, **and select any Evernote-developed custom icon you see, or select your own icon from any location on your computer.**

   `Evernote.exe` is located in the same folder as `ENScript.exe` and is represented by the Evernote elephant icon. You can also select an icon from the initial Change Icon dialog box.

10. **Click OK to accept the icon.**

    The icon appears in the Properties dialog box.

11. **Click Apply to update the properties.**

    The shortcut has been created, sits where you put it, and sports the icon you selected.

12. **Click OK to close the Properties dialog box.**

Getting a script into a shortcut

After you cause `ENScript.exe` to execute, you need to edit the target in the shortcut you created to add your query after the filename. This edit creates a stand-alone executable instance of `ENScript.exe` that loads and executes your script. Here's an example of a simple query you can store in this fashion that lists all the notes created in the notebook *Evernote For Dummies:*

```
"C:\Program Files (x86)\Evernote\Evernote\ENScript.exe" showNotes /q
         "notebook:\"Evernote for Dummies\""
```

A collection of `ENScript.exe` scripts that you can install is available at `www.howtogeek.com/howto/26100/make-evernote-more-approachable-with-custom-windows-7-taskbar-integration`.

The syntax of command-line commands isn't very forgiving. Make sure that you have your quotes placed correctly around the path to `ENScript.exe` if there's a space in the path. Also, you need to use quotes for the search string and for the notebook name, if your notebook name has a space in it, as in the preceding example.

If you think you'll use a script often, you can pin it to the taskbar. Simply right-click it and choose Pin to Taskbar from the contextual menu. Then you can execute it any time by clicking the icon on the taskbar. If your version of Windows doesn't give you the option to pin to the taskbar by right-clicking alone, hold down the Shift key and right-click again.

Taking webcam notes

If Evernote detects an installed webcam, the New Webcam Note option is available on the File menu. Choosing this option lets you preview a picture. When you're happy with the preview, click Take Snapshot to take the picture. (Otherwise, click Cancel.) Then you can click Retake Snapshot, Save to Evernote, or Cancel, as shown in Figure 14-4.

Figure 14-4:
Taking a webcam note.

Save to Evernote creates a new note with the title Webcam Note and the snapshot. You can edit the note as you would any other.

Using Evernote on a Mac

Evernote has strived to accomplish two seemingly contradictory goals: Make Evernote for Mac OS X a natural Mac application (one that's intuitive for Mac users and takes full advantage of the Mac's capabilities) while also minimizing the learning curve for those who (like me) use Evernote on Windows computers and on mobile devices. I think that the company has accomplished this difficult jujitsu with aplomb.

Some important features are specific to the Mac version of Evernote, however, and I describe them in this section.

Using AppleScript

AppleScript, Apple's scripting language, is a powerful but easy way to extend your use of Evernote. It's built into OS X, is supported by Evernote's Open Scripting architecture, and is easier to work with than `ENscript.exe` for Windows. See Chapter 19 to find out more about AppleScript.

Sharing Notebooks

Sharing notebooks on a Mac is really easy, and it's similar to the way the process works in Windows. The best part is that you don't have to do it online. You can share your notebooks and view other people's notebooks right from Evernote on your Mac. For more information on sharing notebooks, see Chapter 10.

Customizing shared notebooks

In addition to sharing your own notebooks, you may want to access notebooks that other people have shared and customize the settings for your own Evernote account. Follow these steps to start syncing with a shared notebook:

1. **Click Notebooks in the left sidebar.**

   All your notebooks appear in the Evernote window.

2. **Hover over the name of a shared notebook to see options you can customize for the notebook.**

   Any notebooks you are sharing will have an icon that looks like the silhouette of people beneath the notebook name (see Figure 14-5).

 3. **Click the Settings icon, which looks like a gear.**

   Figure 14-6 shows the dialog that appears.

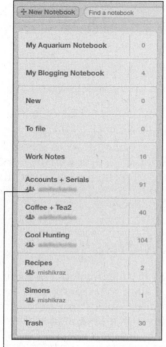

Figure 14-5:
Evernote
shared
notebooks.

Indicates a shared notebook

Figure 14-6:
Customiz-
ation
options
for shared
notebooks.

Joined notebook name: Accounts + Serials

Shared by: adellecharles

You can: View notes and make changes

☑ Sync this notebook to my computer

Synchronize:

When my notebooks sync ↕

☐ Subscribe to reminders in this notebook

Cancel   Save

4. **Make sure that the check box titled Sync this notebook to my Computer is selected.**

   Selecting this option ensures that the shared notebook is added to your account and syncs with the rest of your Evernote data.

5. **(Optional) Adjust the other settings as desired.**

   You can rename the notebook or decide whether to subscribe to reminders from this notebook.

6. **Click Save.**

   After you add a notebook, your Mac automatically starts syncing. Watch as the notes start piling up.

If you're a Premium or Business subscriber, you can enjoy even more special treatment. When you share notebooks, you can offer write access as well as read-only access, making note sharing a lot more user-friendly because you can get others' opinions right in your notebook instead of having them e-mail responses to your notebook and notes.

Working with notebook stacks

Using notebook stacks is just as easy as organizing your bookshelf. If you have several blogging projects that you want to keep together, for example, you can use Evernote to organize your notebooks. You can place them in alphabetical order so that your blogs are spread out all over the notebook screen. Or, if you like to experiment in the kitchen, you may be annoyed to have notes about recipes mixed in with notes about to-do lists and bills. Notebook stacks take care of this problem by enabling you to drop related notebooks in a stack.

Stacking is as easy as dragging and dropping or ⌘-clicking the notebook and choosing Add to Stack from the contextual menu.

Follow these steps to group multiple notebooks:

1. **Click one notebook and drag it to another.**

2. **Repeat Step 1 for as many notebooks as you want to group.**

   The order in which you drag notebooks really doesn't matter. Evernote puts them in alphabetical order in a new notebook called `New Stack` (see Figure 14-7).

Figure 14-7:
A newly
created
notebook
stack.

New Stack	📙 2
Recipes 👥 mishikraz	2
Simons 👥 mishikraz	1
Trash	30

3. **Ctrl+Click** New Stack, **choose Rename Stack from the contextual menu, and give the notebook an appropriate name.**

   Now you can start creating new notes to go into the notebooks.

4. **To create a new notebook within the stack, Ctrl+Click the notebook stack, choose New Notebook from the contextual menu, and enter a name.**

Using notes on a Mac

Evernote works very smoothly on a Mac. It fully supports Mac-specific features such as FaceTime and the older iSight, built-in audio, and the high-resolution graphics for which the Mac is famous. While the goal of Evernote is to have the same features on both Mac and PC platforms, the reality is that many times updates and improvements for the Mac platform are rolled out earlier, sometimes months ahead of their PC counterparts. This gives Mac users some bragging rights when it comes to enjoying the latest and greatest that Evernote has to offer.

Audio notes

Audio notes are available in Windows, too (see "Taking webcam notes" earlier in this chapter), but creating them is really intuitive on the Mac. I find audio notes to be fantastic tools for creating lists or quickly capturing ideas when I don't have time to type them. No matter how fast you type, you'll almost always be able to speak your notes faster than you can type them. See Chapter 5 for more information on creating audio notes.

FaceTime notes

FaceTime notes use the built-in camera included with Macs that were manufactured at the end of 2010 or later. This feature makes note-taking infinitely easier because you don't have to scan or do a whole host of things to get information into a note. Simply take a picture, and Evernote does the rest.

The process of creating a note by using iSight or FaceTime notes is relatively simple. Follow these steps:

1. **Open Evernote, and select the notebook to which you want to add the video note.**

   If you don't select a notebook, the image will be put in your default notebook.

2. **Click the Take Snapshot icon or choose File⇨New FaceTime Camera note.**

3. **When the camera opens, point it at the object that you'd like to photograph, and click Take Snapshot.**

   You can retake the picture as many times as you please until you're happy with the results. You can even take a couple of shots for the same note if you want to compare the pictures to make sure that the text is as easy to read as possible for Evernote.

4. **When you're satisfied with the picture, click Use to save it to your notebook.**

   Now you can check out what you and Evernote have created.

Computers versus mobile devices in the cloud

In Evernote, mobile devices communicate directly with the Evernote servers. Limitations of bandwidth and memory mean that certain great features for Windows and Mac aren't available on mobile devices. Mobile devices do have at least one very useful compensating advantage, however: the geotagging feature that records geographical identification metadata (the longitude and latitude coordinates) of the note. Evernote tags the notes with geotagging when that feature is available, and the note can then be searched, as described in Chapter 8.

Here are a few differences between computers and mobile devices that you should be aware of:

✔ You can't initiate a notebook share from some mobile devices; you have to initiate a share from a computer or mobile device that supports iOS or Android and then access the shared notebook from any device.

✔ You can't create web clips in mobile browsers.

✔ Not all formatting that's visible or editable on a computer is visible or editable on mobile devices. If a feature isn't visible on your mobile device, it isn't available.

✔ Drag and drop isn't available for mobile devices.

✔ Unlike mobile devices, few computers capture location information (geotag) when you create notes, as geotagging requires reception of Global Positioning System (GPS) satellite data. GPS reception on desktop computers is available only via an add-on device such as Emprum's UltiMate GPS accessory (www.emprum.com/ultimategps.php).

Chapter 15

Working with Evernote on Tablets and Smartphones

Nearly 2 billion smartphones and tablets have been sold worldwide. Android, Apple, and BlackBerry devices make up more than 90 percent of them and hold ever more prominent places in computing. Many people use only these devices. I still use a desktop and a laptop, too, but I rarely walk around with anything but a tablet and a smartphone, and increasingly, I carry only my smartphone. I use an iPhone; my grown kids use Android devices; my wife uses a BlackBerry. We all use Evernote. Fortunately for us, Evernote embraces all devices and supports tablets and smartphones well.

Using Evernote on iPhones and iPod touches

Evernote's extraordinary connection to Apple products makes using Evernote on the iPhone and iPod touch nearly an addiction — especially with the iPhone 4 and later models. Siri (the personal assistant) is darn well like having your own private secretary for the price of the latest and coolest toy. The future has never been so close at hand.

Figure 15-1 shows the home screen of Evernote on an iPhone.

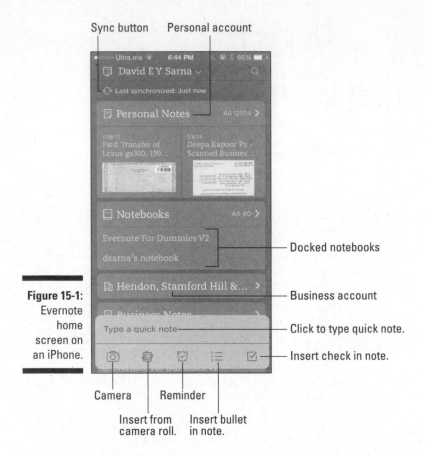

Sync button   Personal account

Docked notebooks

Business account

Click to type quick note.

Insert check in note.

Figure 15-1:
Evernote
home
screen on
an iPhone.

Camera   Reminder

Insert from   Insert bullet
camera roll.   in note.

Web clipping on an iPhone and iPod touch

Apple offers a secure, closed architecture on the iPhone and iPod touch. It doesn't directly support browser extensions for web clipping, as discussed in Chapter 4.

Fortunately, you have alternatives:

- Clip with a non-Apple browser that supports extensions.
- Use a third-party application such as EverClip.

All these techniques work, and I discuss them in the following sections.

With Dolphin

I've had the best luck working with the Dolphin browser (which is also available for Android. You can download Dolphin for free at http://dolphin.com. To install the Evernote add-in for Dolphin, go to http://dolphin-browser.com/add-ons/tools/evernote-share.

To clip with Dolphin, follow these steps:

1. **Navigate to the page you want to clip.**

2. **At the bottom of the page, tap the Dolphin clip icon, which has six squares.**

    A pane of options opens at the bottom of the page (see Figure 15-2).

Figure 15-2: Dolphin's options.

3. **Tap Share.**

    You may be prompted to log in with your Evernote account and allow Dolphin access to that account.

    When you do, the Clipped Note screen opens (see Figure 15-3), with a default notebook created (DSarna in the figure).

Figure 15-3:
Clipped
Note
screen.

4. **(Optional) To select a different notebook, tap the right-pointing arrow (>) to the right of the default notebook.**

5. **(Optional) To add tags, tap > to the right of Add Tags; enter the tags; and tap Done and then the Back button in the top left.**

6. **(Optional) To add text to the note, tap Add Comments; enter the text; and tap Done and then the Back button in the top left.**

7. **Tap Save to save the note to Evernote.**

   A `Successfully sent` message signifies that the note has been added.

A short film demonstrating web clipping with the Dolphin browser is available at www.youtube.com/watch?v=mOwrF0CuUWA.

With EverClip

EverClip by Ignition Soft (`http://clip.ignition.hk`) lets you clip a page from websites, PDFs, and images to Evernote on an iPhone, iPod touch, and iPad (iOS 6 or later). It also lets you clip a page and paste it into Evernote. EverClip supports adding titles and tags to notes. Like all Apple software, it's sold through iTunes and the App Store.

Previewing your notes

Snippets view is arguably one the easiest and most popular views to use in Evernote. (Check out Chapter 7 for descriptions of the different views.) It makes working in Evernote easier because you can see everything you need in one easy-to-access location. For example, if the note is a picture, you can see enough in the view to know what the note contains without having to open it. You can see all your notes from the unified home screen, so you don't have to open notes one at a time to tell what's what.

Better yet, Snippets view is now the default view of Evernote, so you don't have to do anything to set it up for your notes. Evernote version 4 and later offers users a unified home screen and Snippets view to view photos and drawings on their iOS devices. For images, the Evernote app places the picture to the right of the title so that you get all the information you need in one location that you can easily scroll.

Unsure how to add a title to a picture you've taken? Check out Chapter 7 to see how to take a picture and add text. Or scroll through your existing Camera Roll and save the picture to Evernote.

Using the note screen

The note information panel is crisp and clear, with the title and notebook right up top. You can open the note information panel to access the details of the note. Navigating the panel and tagging notes by using your keyboard are fast and efficient.

Adding notes manually

To create a note by using the sleek New Note screen, follow these steps:

1. **Open the Evernote app.**

2. **Tap the Text icon to create a new note.**

   The New Note screen opens, displaying available actions at the bottom (see Figure 15-4).

Figure 15-4:
iPhone
New Note
screen.

3. **To change from the default (or previously selected) notebook, tap the right-pointing arrow (>) to the right of notebook name.**

The notebook list is displayed (see Figure 15-5).

Tap here to return to the note.

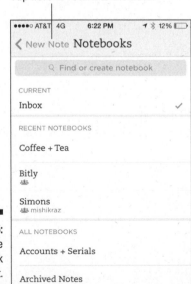

Figure 15-5:
The
Notebook
list.

4. **Tap the notebook where you want the note to be saved, and tap New Note in the top-left corner to return to the note.**

5. **(Optional) To edit the note, tap the More link.**

6. **To avoid storing location information with your note, tap Hide Info (see Figure 15-6).**

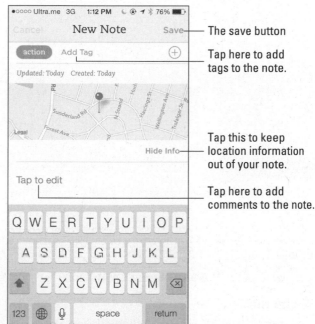

The save button

Tap here to add tags to the note.

Tap this to keep location information out of your note.

Tap here to add comments to the note.

Figure 15-6: Editing a note.

7. **Tap Add Tag, and add tags to the box.**

As you start to type a tag, Evernote displays all matching tags. Tap a tag to select it or tap + to show all tags. Tap Backspace to delete a selected tag.

8. **Tap Tap to Edit, and type text in the note.**

While you're editing, all of Evernote's text-editing features are available. You can also attach a file and apply list formatting. Figure 15-7 shows the formatting and attachment options, and Figure 15-8 shows an example of a formatted note.

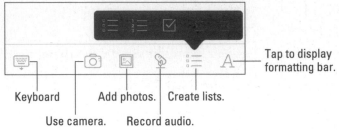

Figure 15-7:
Formatting
and
attachment
options.

Keyboard

Use camera.

Add photos.

Record audio.

Create lists.

Tap to display
formatting bar.

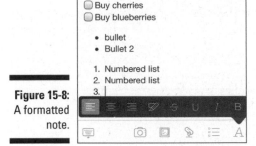

Figure 15-8:
A formatted
note.

9. **Tap Save (refer to Figure 15-6) to return to Snippets view, which shows all your notes.**

10. **To delete a note, swipe left and tap the Trash icon.**

Adding notes with Siri

Sure, everyone wants a personal assistant, but who can afford one? Well, if you own an iPhone 4S or later, you have Siri, an assistant built right into the device. All you have to do is make sure that you save your Evernote e-mail address to your contacts.

When you set up a note with Siri, you don't have to deal with tapping a Save button. If you're on the go and want to keep the process mostly hands-free, Siri is absolutely the best way to get things done. After you start using Evernote on Siri, you'll have no idea how you were able to survive without it.

Here's how to create a new note by using Siri:

1. **Launch Siri by holding down the home button on your iPhone.**

   To use Siri, you have to tap the microphone at the bottom of the screen before you start talking.

2. **Tell Siri, "Send e-mail to Evernote."**

   You can say whatever you like, of course, but Siri definitely understands this command.

3. **Dictate your note.**

   When you stop talking, Siri sends off the note. Expect to find the new note in your default notebook.

Selecting multiple Camera Roll images

Who wants to add one photo at a time to a note? It takes forever, especially if you've had your phone for years; no one has that kind of time. Well, you don't actually have to add one photo at a time. Evernote enables you to select up to ten pictures at a time. (You can add only ten pictures to a note anyway, so you don't need to be able to select more.)

Here's how you can select multiple photos and add them to a new note:

1. **Open the Evernote app.**

2. **Tap the Text icon, and enter information related to the photos.**

   Make sure that you enter the title and tags you want to associate with the note.

 3. **Tap the Picture Frame icon.**

   All the photos you have on your camera appear.

4. **Tap Select in the top-right corner of the screen.**

   This step lets your device know that you may want to add multiple pictures.

5. **Start tapping pictures.**

   All the photos you've tapped have a green check mark in the bottom-right corner so you can easily see whether you've inadvertently added an unwanted picture.

6. **Tap Done.**

   Your phone saves all the images to their own note, using the title and other information you entered in Step 2.

Browsing by notebook and tag

Being able to see all your notebooks at one time is a boon for getting work done. So is being able to check out all your tags in one location.

Here's how you can view your notebooks and tags:

1. **Open the Evernote app.**

2. **Tap Notebooks to get a quick view of all your existing notebooks.**

   From this view, you can see your favorite notebooks, view the contents of each notebook, or check out what's in the Trash.

   Tapping Edit in the top-right corner enables you to change the notebook's name.

3. **Tap Done in the top-right corner.**

4. **Tap Back in the top-left corner to return to the home screen.**

5. **Tap Tags to view all your existing tags.**

   You're not creating tags in this step — just checking them out — but you can edit them and see what notes each tag applies to.

6. **(Optional) Tap Edit, tap a tag, and edit it however you want.**

   If you want to change a tag universally, editing the tag is the easiest method.

7. **Tap Done in the top-right corner, and then tap Back in the top-left corner to return to the home screen.**

It takes about 30 seconds to do all this (unless you decide to rename all your tags, in which case you'd probably want to use a computer).

Searching

The problem with taking notes with paper and pen is finding them later. Searching your notes with the Search feature is so ridiculously easy that you'll never want to use paper notes again. Figure 15-1, earlier in this chapter, shows the Search box in the top-right corner of the screen. Simply tap it and start searching. Figure 15-9 shows the Search screen.

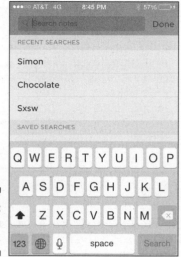

Figure 15-9:
The Search
screen.

Unsure how to work with searches? Check out Chapter 8.

Sharing notebooks

Chapter 10 provides the bulk of the information you need about notebook sharing. This feature is useful because it enables you to check out all the notebooks other people have shared, just as you can any other notebook you create. And, of course, if you're the one doing the sharing and you're a Premium subscriber, you can see what updates you have allowed others to make in your notebook.

Here's what to do to share a notebook from an iPhone or iPod touch:

1. **Tap Notebooks to go to the Notebooks screen.**

2. **Tap the Edit button in the top-right corner.**

 3. **Tap the Share icon to the right of the notebook you want to share.**

4. **Tap Share.**

Working with Evernote on iPads

When the iPad first arrived, many people questioned its usefulness. Well, when it comes to using Evernote, iPad is absolutely one of the best things ever. Bigger than a smartphone and smaller than a laptop, the iPad is portable without sacrificing many computer functions.

The following sections describe a couple of extremely helpful features that make having an iPad for use with Evernote much more enjoyable.

Web clipping on an iPad

Web clipping on an iPad is identical to web clipping on other iOS devices. See "Web clipping on an iPhone and iPod touch" earlier in this chapter.

Adding a snapshot to a note

Being able to take a picture with an iPad is an outstanding feature of the tablet, and adding photos to notes gives Evernote additional functionality. Many businesses now give their employees iPads for work, and taking pictures of a whiteboard or presentation really does increase productivity, especially when the presenter won't send the slides around for weeks (or not at all).

Taking a snapshot is simple. Press the Home button, and press and release the power button at the top of the iPad. The iPad makes a camera-shutter noise and takes the picture. Check out Chapter 5 to see how to capture a picture as a note.

Using Evernote on Android Devices

Apple products aren't the only mobile devices that get special treatment from Evernote. The Android platform has proved its worth and is a phenomenal asset for every Evernote user who has an Android device.

A convenient feature of Evernote on Android devices allows you to record the GPS location of each note (unless you've deliberately turned GPS off). You can tap on the Map pin (to the right of the search box) to see all the notes you created near a given geographical area.

Evernote on an Android device works nearly identically to Evernote on an iOS device, but the home screen looks different (see Figure 15-10).

Figure 15-10:
Evernote
home
screen on
an Android
phone.

Collaborating via mobile devices

If you enjoy the benefits of being a Premium subscriber, you can share your notebooks with others and allow them to have the same editing privileges as though you were sharing from a desktop computer.

You can access a notebook shared by a Premium or Business subscriber even if you aren't one yourself.

To add a note to a shared notebook, follow these steps:

1. **Open the Evernote app.**

2. **Tap the Notebook icon.**

   An area opens to show all notebooks that you're sharing.

3. **Tap the shared notebook you'd like to work on.**

   Shared notebooks have a silhouette icon below the notebook name, as shown in Figure 15-11.

Figure 15-11:
This icon
signifies
a shared
notebook.

Shared notebook icon

4. **Tap the plus (+) sign in the top-right corner to create a new note in the shared notebook.**

Gaining offline access

Offline access is also possible for Premium subscribers using an Android device. Whenever you open a notebook in your Evernote app, Evernote asks you whether you'd like to open the notebook offline.

Offline access is outstanding because you no longer have to rely on a signal to work on your notebooks. You can continue working, including making changes and adding new notes, and when you're back online, your account is synchronized automatically.

Finding notes with autotitles

At times, you need to remember something on the go, so you take a snapshot or create a voice memo. But how do you find those notes later? Evernote for Android creates a title based on the content of the note and the time that the note was created, making it much easier to find it later. An example autotitle is `Snapshot @ San Francisco, California`. You can always retitle notes later, if you prefer.

Saving anytime

If you tap the Save button in the note, a version is saved to your device's memory. You don't need to exit the note. When you're finished, tap Done, and the note syncs. This feature is especially useful if you compose lengthy notes on your Android phone or tablet.

Sharing via social media, e-mail, or text

Evernote makes sure that you can always share your notes through social media on your Android device. Whether you want to update Facebook, write a tweet, or send an e-mail, it's all possible with a few taps on your Android screen. You don't have to be a Premium subscriber to share notes to social media.

If you're a typical Evernote user, you more than likely have a Facebook or Twitter account (or both). And what better way to get everything in one location than to post to Facebook from your Android device? (See Chapter 10 for details on connecting your Facebook and Evernote accounts.) You can also e-mail your note.

Here's how to share a note on social media:

1. **Open the Evernote app.**

2. **Tap and hold the note you want to post.**

   A new menu appears, with an option to post to Facebook.

3. **Tap Share.**

   A new menu appears. The options in this menu enable you to send an e-mail or even text with a couple of extra steps.

4. **Do one of the following:**

   - To post a note to Facebook, tap Post to Facebook, add any text you want, and tap the Share button.

   - To share a note over Twitter, tap Twitter, add any text you want, and tap the Share button.

   - To e-mail your note, tap Email, enter the recipient's address, add any text you want, and tap Send.

   - To text the note, tap Share, select the recipient, and tap Send.

Searching notebooks when you're on the go

Evernote makes searching on the go especially easy on Android devices. You can even narrow down the number of notes you have to comb through if you know which notebook to search. You can always run a search from the All Notes screen if you aren't sure where to begin your search.

Here's how to search a single notebook:

1. **Open the Evernote app.**

2. **Tap the notebook you want to search.**

3. **Tap the magnifying glass in the top-right corner.**

   A new screen opens.

4. **Type the text that you want to search for.**

   The notes that contain the text appear below the search box.

5. **Scroll through the notes to find the one you need.**

Editing saved searches

In addition to running searches on your Android device, you can modify your saved searches. Although you can't create new saved searches on your Android phone (yet), after you've created a saved search on a desktop or laptop computer, you can execute it on your Android phone.

To modify a saved search, follow these steps:

1. **Tap the magnifying-glass icon at the top of the Evernote home screen.**

   This opens a list of all of your saved searches beneath the search box. (See the previous section if you want to run a new search.)

2. **Tap and hold the saved search you want to modify.**

   You're asked whether you want to edit the query before searching.

3. **Tap the text to edit the search.**

   The search information appears in the search box at the top of the screen.

4. **Modify the search as needed.**

5. **Tap the magnifying-glass icon to execute the search.**

6. **Select the note you're looking for in the search results.**

Taking advantage of maps and GPS support

Smartphones and tablets enable you to track your location with GPS coordinates. Evernote uses this feature to add location information to your notes. The location tag of a note gives you one more thing to search on and allows for easy retrieval of notes by location. This feature is incredibly handy when, for example, you want to locate that adorable table you found at a store on Route 4 in Paramus but can't remember the name of the store.

To enable the GPS function, follow these steps:

1. **With the Evernote app open, press the Android device's Menu button.**

   Menu is a physical button just below the screen.

2. **Tap Settings.**

   A window opens, displaying your saved settings.

3. **Scroll down to Use GPS Satellites, and make sure that its check box is selected.**

After you enable GPS on your Android device, you can use it with your notes. To take advantage of GPS, follow these steps:

1. **Tap the magnifying-glass icon on the Evernote home screen.**

2. **Tap the pinpoint bubble in the top-left corner of the screen.**

   A map of all your notes appears, with GPS information recorded.

3. **Press the Menu button on your device, select Note Info, and Location button (which is shown in the margin) to plot the note's location on a map.**

   You can do a few things on this map, so just play around until you feel comfortable with the feature.

You can also set up future locations on your phone to make trip planning much easier. Press the Menu button, tap Map > Set Location, and drop a pin at each map location where you plan to go. You can add notes to each pin on the map so that you know what you're interested in seeing. You can even enter opening and closing times to the note so that you have all the information you need in one place.

Editing styled notes

Working with styled fonts, including check boxes and bulleted lists, is a fantastic way to track information and emphasize key phrases.

The formatting bar contains all the icons that you need to style your notes. Follow these steps:

1. **Start a new note.**

2. **Scroll the style menu until you reach the check-box icon (see Figure 15-12).**

The check-box icon

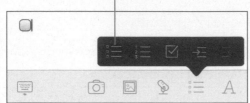

Figure 15-12:
The Style
menu.

3. **Tap the check-box icon.**

   Your phone automatically makes every new row part of a checklist.

Tap the delete button if you want to end the checklist and start a row of regular text.

Creating a notebook

Creating a notebook isn't limited to your desktop or laptop computer; you can also create a notebook on your Android device.

Follow these steps to create a notebook on your Android device:

1. **In the Evernote app, tap the Notebooks icon.**

2. **Press the Android Menu button.**

   This button is a physical button located just below the screen.

3. **Tap New Notebook on the menu that appears.**

   A window appears where you can give the notebook a name.

4. **Name the new notebook, and tap OK.**

   You can't leave the notebook nameless; you have to enter a name before Evernote creates the notebook.

   After a few seconds, your new notebook appears in alphabetical order in a list of your notebooks.

Working with Evernote on BlackBerry Devices

Nowadays, working with Evernote on a BlackBerry is very similar to using it on an iOS device. That's good news. Early versions of Evernote for the BlackBerry were — I can't be delicate — unusable. For one thing, notes took forever to load, find, and upload. Fortunately, all those issues have been fixed. Evernote fully supports BlackBerry 10 (see Figure 15-13).

Figure 15-13: Evernote for Black-Berry 10.

Before you do anything else, make sure that you have the latest version of Evernote installed by navigating to `http://appworld.blackberry.com/webstore/content/1700`.

You can download the app from BlackBerry World on your BlackBerry or your desktop computer, which may be faster. (It was for me, even with a Wi-Fi connection to the BlackBerry.) If you choose the computer route, you may be prompted to install an add-on the first time you use the app. After you've downloaded the app to your computer, the next time you sync your BlackBerry with it, the app is installed on your BlackBerry.

Working with notes

Releases beginning with version 3.3 support offline notes. Sync and loading are much faster. Evernote for BlackBerry lets you create new notes with text, audio, and photos. These notes are pinned to the top of your note list in a pending state until you get on a network, at which point they sync to your account. You can even edit the pending notes, if you need to.

Whenever you create or view a note, it's stored locally on your device. You don't need a network connection to view the note later. If the note has an attached file, such as a PDF, you need to view the file while you have a network connection before it becomes available offline.

You can save to a note, and retrieve from a note, any file stored on the device or on an SD card (as long as it falls within the size restrictions). Also, support for SD cards (where Evernote for BlackBerry stores the local copy of your notes) has been improved so that space is used more efficiently and retrieval is faster.

The basic Evernote functions supported are

- ✔ View headers (All Notes)
- ✔ Create a note (Text Note)
- ✔ Take a photo and add it as a note (Snapshot)
- ✔ Record (Audio Note)
- ✔ Create a new note and upload any file (Upload File)
- ✔ Search anything in Evernote (Search)

Taking advantage of Evernote updates

Improvements to Evernote for BlackBerry include the following useful features:

- ✔ The home screen has been revamped to make it easier to see which items are selected. The screen has better colors, an easy-to-see grid, and clear text labels.
- ✔ You can filter the Notes screen to show your notes by notebook. This improvement is great for quick browsing. To switch among notebooks, tap the green bar along the top of the list, and choose a notebook. All the notes filter instantly.

✔ When you're appending text to complex notes, you can see the content of the note just below the text that you're adding so that you can easily reference the content of your note in what you're appending.

✔ Synchronization is significantly faster, and text throughout the app is easier to read.

✔ The newly redesigned List view shows many more notes on a single screen than in the past.

✔ The PIN Lock security code keeps your Evernote account secure on your device.

✔ The Universal search feature lets you search all your notes and notebooks quickly.

✔ You can download one or more notebooks for offline access.

Locking Evernote

A passcode or PIN lock is another reason to be a Premium or Business subscriber; it enables you to lock Evernote so that people who don't have the code can't access your notes. If you don't want the hassle of always locking your phone just to lock Evernote information, now you can lock just the app.

On both Android and iOS devices, you get five attempts to enter your password before you're locked out. At this point you will be signed out of Evernote and be taken back to the log in screen. After you re-enter your Evernote password, you will be logged back into your account, and the passcode lock feature will be turned off.

Locking on an iOS device

To set Evernote's lock feature on an iOS device, follow these steps:

1. **In the Evernote app, tap Settings in the top-left corner.**

   The Evernote Settings window appears.

2. **Tap Premium.**

   Another window opens, displaying your saved settings.

3. **Tap Passcode Lock > Turn Passcode On.**

4. **When you're prompted to do so, enter and then reenter a four-digit passcode.**

5. **(Optional) Set the length of time your Evernote account can be idle before the app locks.**

   The choices are immediately, and after 1 minute, 5 minutes, 15 minutes, 1 hour, and 4 hours.

Locking on an Android device

To set Evernote's lock feature on an Android device, follow these steps:

1. **In the Evernote app, tap Menu on the home screen and select Settings.**

   This opens up the Settings menu.

2. **Tap Setup PIN Lock**

3. **In the resulting screen, enter and then reenter a four-digit PIN lock.**

Chapter 16

Using Evernote Web

*J*ust like hardware and operating-system platforms, different browsers have various capabilities. In this chapter, I go over universal aspects of using Evernote in web browsers. Then I present some of the differences that make working with browsers unique.

Working with Evernote Web

Evernote Web, like all Internet applications, is constrained by the limitations of Hypertext Markup Language (HTML), the web's universal markup language; inherent nonpersistence (meaning that something is rendered and then forgotten); and the need for fast page rendering without massive downloading.

What offsets these limitations is the fact that as long as you have Internet connectivity, Evernote Web is there for you and is the most consistent way of working with the application.

Another benefit is that using Evernote Web means that you never have to sync because you always make your changes directly on the server.

Having said all that, I confess that I rarely use Evernote Web on my own devices, especially as synchronization is now so fast, frequent, and virtually automatic.

Signing in to Evernote Web

To access Evernote on the web, navigate to `https://evernote.com` and click Sign In in the top-right corner of the screen. If necessary, enter your Evernote account name and password, as discussed in Chapter 2. Evernote Web opens in your browser (see Figure 16-1). Like Evernote on other platforms, the left-most pane of Evernote Web lists your shortcuts (if you created any) and your notebooks.

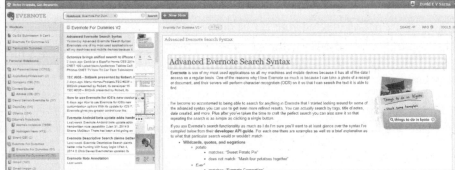

Figure 16-1: Evernote Web home screen, showing shortcuts, notebooks, snippets, and current note.

Working with notes

To work with notes in Evernote Web, follow these steps:

1. **Click any notebook to open its notes in Snippets view.**

2. **Right-click (Windows) or Ctrl-click (Mac) the empty note in the list to open a contextual menu of note actions (see Figure 16-2).**

Figure 16-2: Note actions menu.

Open note in a separate window

Print...

Edit

Delete...

Add Shortcut

3. **Choose a note action.**

You can choose to open the note in a separate window, print it, edit it, delete it, or add a shortcut. Choosing the Edit option displays the Formatting toolbar in the right pane (see Figure 16-3).

Formatting toolbar

Figure 16-3:
Formatting
toolbar
in web
browser.

Attaching files

Attaching files to notes is a very handy feature. If you have a file that you saved on your desktop computer and want to open it on a laptop computer or on one of your mobile devices, attaching it to a note is a quick way to do it.

To attach a file to a note in Evernote, follow these steps:

1. **Log in to Evernote.**

2. **Create a new note or open the note to which you want to attach the file.**

3. **Do one of the following:**

    • Drag the file into the note.

    • Click anywhere in the note to make the Formatting toolbar visible, and then click the paper-clip icon.

4. **Repeat Steps 2 and 3 to attach more files, if you want.**

    You can attach up to ten files to a single note. (For information on dragging and dropping multiple files, see "Moving multiple notes and notebooks" later in this chapter.)

The easiest way to attach a file in Chrome is to simply drag it into the note. (On my machine, I have to drag s-l-o-w-l-y for this method to work reliably, even with my blazing-fast Internet connection.) You can also click the familiar paper-clip icon to attach the file, which is what I do if I'm using Evernote Web (generally on a borrowed computer). Figure 16-4 shows the dialog box that appears when you click that icon, allowing you to browse to the file location.

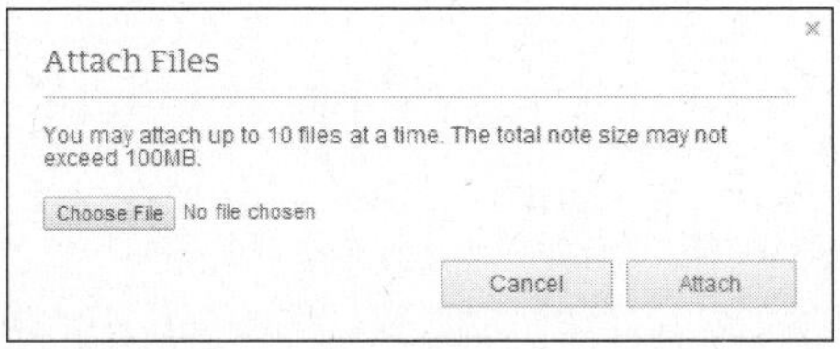

Figure 16-4:
The Attach
Files dialog
box.

Attach Files ✕

You may attach up to 10 files at a time. The total note size may not exceed 100MB.

Choose File No file chosen

Cancel   Attach

Searching

To search, click the Search button. The menu shown in Figure 16-5 opens.

Search button

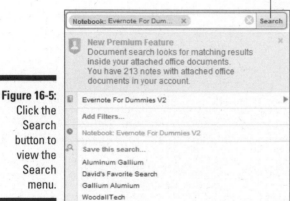

Figure 16-5:
Click the
Search
button to
view the
Search
menu.

Search works the same way on all platforms (the search takes place on the server) and is discussed in Chapter 8.

Moving multiple notes and notebooks

You don't have to click and drag one note at a time. You can move multiple notes, or even notebooks, at the same time. Here's how:

1. **Log in to Evernote online.**

2. **Highlight the notes you want to move.**

   To select more than one note, hold down the Ctrl (Windows) or ⌘ (Mac) key, and then click all the notes you want to move.

3. **Drag the notes into the appropriate notebook, or choose the notebook you want from the Move to Notebook drop-down menu (see Figure 16-6).**

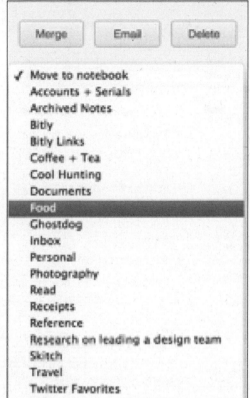

Figure 16-6:
Select a
notebook to
move notes
to.

Comparing Web Browsers

Evernote has worked hard to minimize the differences in Evernote Web on different browsers; however, there are still minute differences in some functionality. For example, the Web Clipper add-on (see Chapter 4) for Evernote Web functions slightly differently in Internet Explorer depending on whether you are using a Mac or a PC. For the most part, however, you will have no problem utilizing all of the robust features that Evernote Web brings to the table, regardless of what web browser you are using.

Google Chrome

Google Chrome is the first browser to get Evernote updates automatically. It provides native support for drag and drop and for HTML5, which (among other features) allows for the display of presentations and video without plug-ins, offline storage, and real-time communication.

KanMeet

KanMeet is a free Chrome extension for Google Calendar that works with most platforms and devices that support the Chrome browser. It's so good at keeping your life in sync that you'll have far fewer excuses for missing birthdays, anniversaries, and appointments.

To use KanMeet with Evernote, follow these steps:

1. **Navigate to** `http://www.kandasoft.com/home/kanda-apps/kanmeet.html`.

2. **Click the green Download Now button in the center of the screen; then click the blue Free button on the right side of the next screen.**

3. **In the pop-up box that appears, click the Add button.**

   A black-and-white pushpin icon is added to your web browser's extension bar.

4. **Click the pushpin icon, and then click the green Authorize button to allow the extension to access your Evernote account.**

The black-and-white pushpin icon turns to color to show that the extension has been activated.

5. **Click the pushpin icon again.**

6. **Select the notebook you want the events to be posted to, and click Apply.**

7. **Start a new Google calendar appointment or edit an existing one.**

   You see a Post to Evernote check box below the time and date settings for the event.

8. **Select Post to Evernote.**

   Google Calendar confirms that the event was saved and posted to Evernote. The process may take a little while.

This feature may not work with some versions of Chrome. As the book went to press, KanMeet version 1.6.0.0 worked with Google Chrome versions 22.0.x through 31.0.x.

Google Chrome is a popular choice among software developers due to its open development tools. New Evernote features are often implemented first in Chrome. For more information, see `http://google.com/chrome/intl/en/more/index.html`.

Mozilla Firefox

In August 2011, Firefox went through some extensive and extremely useful changes, including support for HTML5. The most notable change for Evernote users is support for web clipping (see Chapter 4).

I found no discernable differences between Evernote Web in Firefox and in Chrome.

Internet Explorer

I found no differences between Evernote Web in Internet Explorer and in Chrome.

Internet Explorer also enables you to format your text. It even uses the same shortcut keys as Chrome (Ctrl+C and Ctrl+V) to allow for faster copy/paste work. When you want to add a date stamp to a note, simply press Ctrl-; (semicolon).

Apple Safari

Evernote for Safari has been updated and is now nearly identical to the Chrome version. Be sure you have the latest version of Evernote to get the most from using it on your Mac devices and high-powered desktop machines.

Safari 5.1 significantly changed its support for browser plug-ins, making the Evernote Safari Web Clipper plug-in incompatible with older browsers. At the time this book was written, a new, improved Web Clipper 5.9.1 was available as a beta version. I recommend that you switch to the new extension for the best Evernote experience in Safari. See Chapter 4 for more information about the Web Clipper.

Dolphin

The Dolphin browser is free for Android and iOS devices. It has achieved popularity for being lightweight and faster at rendering pages (at this writing) than any of its competitors.

Dolphin makes it easy to clip web content to Evernote, Twitter, Box accounts (a Dolphin add-on), Facebook, and e-mail. I discuss Dolphin in more detail in Chapter 15.

Part V
Expanding Your Skills

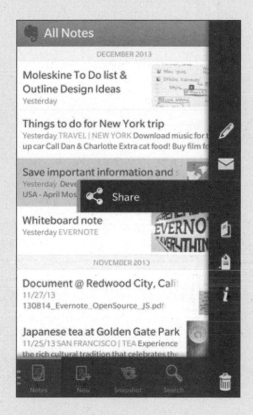

In this part . . .

- ✔ Enhancing Evernote with third-party applications
- ✔ Using Skitch to annotate and draw
- ✔ Scanning and managing business cards
- ✔ Sharing your notes with social media
- ✔ Using Evernote for collaborative decision-making and brainstorming
- ✔ Interfacing with digital cameras, scanners, and smart pens

Chapter 17

Enhancing Evernote with Third-Party Applications

....

In This Chapter

▶ Using apps to enhance your experience

▶ Transcribing voice notes

▶ Integrating Evernote with social media

....

*B*ecause of its open, published interfaces, Evernote has attracted a host of third-party developers whose products can greatly enrich your Evernote experience. In fact, anyone can create an Evernote add-on or interface existing software to work well with Evernote.

There's not enough space in this book to describe all available apps. Also, any compilation would be dated immediately. In this chapter, I highlight the add-ons that I've found to be the most useful. Make sure to browse the App Center for finds I may have missed.

Introducing the Evernote App Center

The Evernote App Center (formerly called the Trunk) offers hundreds of add-ons that enhance your use of Evernote. You can reach it directly at `https://appcenter.evernote.com`. These apps are grouped into seven categories, which Evernote calls collections:

- ✔ **Business:** This collection emphasizes collaboration and business uses.

- ✔ **Drawing & Handwriting:** Apps in this collection are related to drawing, sketching, and handwriting.

- ✔ **Paperless:** These apps facilitate e-faxing and e-scanning into Evernote. Some of these apps even allow e-signing.

- ✔ **Evernote at Work:** Use the apps in this collection for tracking expenses; sharing meeting notes; and searching across Evernote, cloud services, and your local files.

✔ **Productivity:** This collection offers apps for scanners, tablets, and specialized devices that interface with Evernote, as well as specialized tools for grabbing content and sending it to Evernote.

✔ **Lifestyle:** Lifestyle apps let you perform useful tasks such as creating a blog from an Evernote notebook and automatically saving things such as text messages, voice mails, e-mails, receipts, and health information in your Evernote account.

✔ **Education:** These apps turn Evernote notes into flash cards, help you manage book collections, and more.

Unlike Evernote itself, which works well on many platforms, many App Center applications work only on specific platforms. Make sure that the app you want works with your devices.

At this writing, there's no actual commerce in the App Center; you just browse it to see what add-ons you can purchase or download elsewhere by following the links.

Sketching, Annotating, and Drawing

Android, iOS, Mac OS X, and Windows

Skitch, a free app owned by Evernote, has built-in features for taking a photograph or working with an existing one. Its drawing tools are more extensive than those built into Evernote.

Recently, many of its annotation tools have been integrated into newer versions of Evernote, and the company has stated its intention to integrate features of Skitch into all its versions.

To download Skitch, navigate to `http://evernote.com/skitch`.

Converting Voice Notes to Text

With Evernote, no matter what device you're using, you can easily record your thoughts and save them as voice notes. But how do you retrieve those thoughts when you want to hear them again? You need a way to turn the recorded voice into machine-readable text that can be indexed.

Third-party vendors have developed several approaches, described in the following sections.

Dial2Do

All phones (mobile and landlines)

Dial2Do (www.voice2note.dial2do.com) enables you to do exactly what the name suggests: turn a voice recording into a note. This service for Evernote users automatically converts any new audio notes in your Evernote account to searchable, taggable text.

After you've registered for the service, you can create voice notes by using any of Evernote's clients, or simply call Dial2Do at 213-325-2615 to record your note from any phone — mobile or landline — as long as you've registered the number and have Caller ID enabled. Either way, Dial2Do transcribes the first 30 seconds of your note and inserts the text into your note, where Evernote indexes it automatically.

When you call the Dial2Do number, you can record for up to 20 or 30 seconds (depending on the plan you use). Dial2Do always transcribes only the first 30 seconds of your audio note, however, so it's most useful if you first dictate a summary of key points and then the message. In my experience, that amount of time is usually enough to find the note when you do a search.

You can even tag the notes by saying "Tag with" at the end.

Use Dial2Do to capture great ideas that come to mind, keep track of tasks that you need to get done, and save bits of information that you want to remember, all without typing a word.

You can register for the service on the Dial2Do website. Free and paid options are available. Currently, the Basic version is free, and a Pro version is offered for monthly or annual subscription. I suggest that you try the free basic plan before you pay for a Pro subscription. The Pro subscription extends recording time from 20 to 30 seconds and enables you to do the following things:

✔ Send SMS messages by voice

✔ Send, listen to, and replay e-mail by voice

✔ Listen to and post tweets by voice

✔ Post audio notes to Evernote by voice

At this writing, Dial2Do is available in English only. Check out the FAQs for more information on availability (www.voice2note.dial2do.com/faq).

Quicktate

Android, BlackBerry, iOS, Mac OS X, Windows Phone, WebOS, and Windows

Quicktate (www.quicktate.com) is a general transcription service. You can create audio files by dictating notes into your Evernote app, e-mailing your audio files to transcribe@quicktate.com, or calling 888-222-NOTE. Quicktate accurately converts your audio to simple, searchable text and automatically submits the transcript to Evernote.

Quicktate is not a machine-translation service. It uses human typists, who are under strict confidentiality agreements. You pay by the week (for a set number of words) or by the word. Special transcription services, such as legal and medical, are more costly than other services. The average page contains about 250 words, and Quicktate transcriptions typically cost $3 to $5 per page.

Quicktate may be especially cost-effective for dictating short notes, as there is no per-note charge — only a per-word charge.

Total Recall

Android

Total Recall (www.killermobile.com), available for $10 from Google Play, is a call recorder and dictating utility for Android mobile devices. You can automatically or manually record calls and then send them to Evernote via e-mail or upload. When the call is in Evernote, you can use Dial2Do or Quicktate (see the two preceding sections) to transcribe it, if you want.

Total Recall Bluetooth (TRB) is a hardware add-on for non-Android devices that records calls on any mobile phone with Bluetooth capability. For more information, see https://www.killermobile.com/applications/killer-merchandise/trb-mobile-call-recording-device.html.

Managing Business Cards and Scanning Documents

If you network a lot and meet many people, you may have a hard time managing all the business cards you collect. No more! Using one of several third-party apps, you can scan and manage all those business cards you receive.

Business Card Manager

iOS

Business Card Manager (www.sourcenext.com/app_en/116430) is an application that enables you to use your iOS devices to store and manage photos of business cards that you've taken with the device's camera.

Business Card Manager can import photos of business cards into your Evernote account and also save new card images to Evernote. You can synchronize the data in your business-card list with a specified Evernote notebook. To exchange business cards with someone else who has the app installed, simply hold out your devices to each other and then exchange the cards via Bluetooth.

Evernote Hello

Android and iOS

Evernote Hello (http://evernote.com/hello) is a free application that enables you to scan business cards into a contact manager or instantly connect to a group of people.

Hello automatically gathers information about the people you meet from your calendar, Evernote account, online networks, and (optionally) a Google search. It can also maintain a history of meetings and information about the people involved.

Hello users can swap contact info via audio tones. A welcome sound serves as a kind of mating call, as a user's phone discovers that another user's phone is nearby.

Evernote is now building most Hello functionality into Evernote, as discussed in the next section.

Evernote Business Card Scanning

iOS

Evernote's new Business Card Scanning feature is available only for iOS devices at this writing, but I expect it to be rolled out to Android users soon. (See http://blog.evernote.com/blog/2013/12/12/evernote-for-iphone-and-ipad-get-business-card-scanning-and-more.) Free account users can test the functionality on five business cards. Premium and Business users get unlimited access.

To access this feature, swipe left on the camera screen. As soon as you take a picture of a business card, it's converted to editable text that becomes a contact note in Evernote. The action takes place on Evernote servers in the cloud, and it takes a little time for them to analyze the photos.

Because the optical-character recognition (OCR) work is done on the servers, I've found the results to be better than those provided by other phone-based OCR software.

If you connect your Evernote account to LinkedIn, for example, the information on the scanned card is cross-referenced with LinkedIn to create a richer note that even includes a photo of the person you've met.

Shoeboxed

Android, BlackBerry, iOS, Mac OS X, WebOS, and Windows

Shoeboxed (www.shoeboxed.com/evernote) gives you a way to scan all your business cards, receipts, handouts, and papers of all kinds. Shoeboxed sends you a prepaid envelope; you put all your papers in it and mail it back. After Shoeboxed receives the envelope, the staff scans everything, organizes it, and makes it available online.

If you connect Shoeboxed to your Evernote account, you can set it to automatically scan items such as business cards and receipts to Evernote.

1DollarScan

Android, HTC Desire series, Samsung Galaxy, iOS, Mac OS X, WebOS, and Windows

1DollarScan (http://1dollarscan.com/cloud/evernote.php/) takes paper scanning to a new level. 1DollarScan will take those hard-copy books that are taking up space on your shelves, scan them in, and send you the PDF file for you to access on any desktop computer or mobile device that can open PDF files. They even have a free e-reader app you can download for your iPhone or iPad.

When you connect your Evernote and 1DollarScan accounts, your digital files will automatically be uploaded to your Evernote account for you to store and access at any time.

Saving RSS Feeds to Evernote

In Chapter 12, I discuss interfacing Evernote with social applications and RSS feeds. The tools that I describe in this section make it easier to save RSS feeds to Evernote.

IFTTT

Android, iOS, Mac OS X, and Windows

IFTTT (https://ifttt.com) is a free service that enables you to connect 84 feeds to your Evernote account, sending information automatically if those feeds trigger certain recipes that you've set up. Confusing? Not really. Here's an example: You create a "recipe" that connects your Evernote account with your RSS and Atom web reader feeds. You want your RSS feed to send any blog post containing the words *Evernote For Dummies* directly to your Evernote account. *Voilà!* That particular information is automatically sent to your Evernote account for you to check out. When you sign up for an account, just activate your Evernote channel and start building your recipes.

BazQux Reader

Android, iOS, Mac OS X

BazQux Reader (https://bazqux.com/) is a fast and highly customizable RSS feed client that enables you to save articles, web pages, and images to Evernote without leaving the app. BazQux Reader lets you tag and star content, making it searchable in the future.

BazQux Reader lets you perform a variety of tasks, including the following:

- ✔ Save RSS feeds, web pages, and images to Evernote
- ✔ Share via Facebook, Twitter, Google+, and e-mail
- ✔ Subscribe to Facebook, Twitter, and Google+ accounts simply by entering the URL

They have a 30-day free trial; after that the minimum donation for the subscription service is $9/year.

Sharing with Social Media

Social media uses web-based and mobile technologies to turn what otherwise might be one-way communication into dialogue. Evernote and social media fit together like a glove fits a hand.

Postach.io

Android, BlackBerry, iOS, Mac OS X, WebOS, and Windows

Postach.io (`http://postach.io`) is an easy way to publish the thoughts you're already capturing in Evernote. If you currently have notes in your Evernote account, you're ready to publish right now.

After completing a simple setup procedure on the Postach.io website, you simply tag notes published in the Evernote app on any web or mobile device. The notes are properly formatted and published on your Postach.io blog. All the content that Evernote supports — including audio, video, text, and photo posts — is supported by Postach.io. See the Postache.io blog (`http://blog.postach.io`) for the latest product information.

HootSuite

Android, iOS, Mac OS X, Windows Phone, and Windows

HootSuite (`https://hootsuite.com`) is a popular way to view and update your social streams on your phone, computer, and the web.

Now that HootSuite has integrated Evernote, you can stop worrying about forgetting all the interesting things that pop up in your Twitter and Facebook streams. Whenever you see something that you'd like to remember, simply send it to Evernote, and you'll have it forever. Evernote-specific support is discussed in `http://socialbusiness.hootsuite.com/evernote-for-hootsuite.html`.

You can use HootSuite to create notes from Twitter and Facebook content; select the Evernote notebook where you want to save the notes; add and edit titles, descriptions, tags, and comments; and share notes from Evernote to your social networks.

Sending tweets automatically to Evernote is supported only on mobile devices, not on the desktop-computer versions of HootSuite.

Mailplane

Mac OS X

Mailplane (www.mailplaneapp.com) enables you to send Gmail messages and attachments to Evernote with just one click. You can automatically convert a message or an attachment to a new Evernote note with an embedded URL that takes you right back to that message in Gmail.

Mailplane also enables you to capture a conversation and archive it in Evernote, with a link to the e-mail message you previously selected. A full copy of the message is saved as a new note, so you can enter a title and tags, as well as edit text.

Use Evernote with Mailplane to organize projects, store important e-mails and documents, and always find exactly what you're looking for in your Gmail inbox.

Making Meetings Productive

A good meeting has a purpose and generates great ideas. You want to record what was said so that you can refer to all the ideas that came up. This section describes some tools that help you use Evernote to make your time spent at meetings as productive as possible.

TimeBridge

iPhone, Mac OS X, and Windows

TimeBridge (www.timebridge.com) connects to your calendar, and the calendars of your co-workers, to figure out when everyone is free for a meeting. Instead of having to work around everyone's schedule, use TimeBridge to discover when a meeting would fit in and schedule it. TimeBridge also allows meeting participants to save all the notes directly to their Evernote accounts and share those notes via a shared notebook or e-mail.

Curio

Mac OS X

Curio (www.zengobi.com/products/curio) enables you to take notes, manage tasks, make photo collages, sketch, and create index cards and tables. In other words, it is designed to promote visual thinking. The app is integrated with Evernote, so you have access to all your Evernote notebooks from within the Curio environment.

Curio includes an Evernote shelf to display the items you've been collecting in your Evernote notebooks. You can drag notes from the shelf directly into Curio. All tags associated with the note and all text scanned from an image by Evernote are also transferred to Curio via the shelf, so you can search for those items later in Curio.

Managing Your Expenses

For me, perhaps the most hateful job of all is managing expenses. Keeping track of purchases and receipts is a real headache, so apps that help are always welcome. Apps with Evernote support are remarkably helpful, especially at tax time.

Expensify

Android, BlackBerry, iOS, Windows Phone

Expensify (www.expensify.com) is an expense-management tool for individuals and businesses. The tool makes it easy to import your expenses, scan receipts, and create reports so that you can be reimbursed. Simply add receipt images to the Expensify notebook in your Evernote account. The images are automatically copied to Expensify, where you can create and submit expense reports. When a report has been approved, you can export it to Evernote as a searchable PDF for future reference.

Expensify is free for individuals and $6 per submitter per month for companies.

Scanner Pro

iPad and iPhone

Scanner Pro (http://readdle.com/products/scannerpro) is an inexpensive app that converts hard-copy documents to digital form for easy sharing and sending. Scanner Pro detects borders in real time as you take the picture and shows you the result visually so you can choose the best positioning for the scan.

You can use Scanner Pro to scan receipts, convert paper notes and sketches to digital copies, sign and return contracts via e-mail, and save interesting articles to read later.

Uploaded scans can be saved as PDF files, stored in Dropbox and Google Docs, or e-mailed.

Receipts

iOS

Receipts (www.tidalpool.ca/receipts) is a free app that lets you track your receipts, expenses, and mileage, and creates graphs to help you keep track of your income and spending. An autofill feature speeds data entry. You can take pictures, add drawings, and record voice memos, so you have multiple ways to keep track of your expenses. When you're ready, you can send your reports to Evernote.

Collaborating with Others

When collaborating with co-workers, the big ideas and solutions the group comes up with don't always happen when everyone is seated at a table in front of a whiteboard. Ideas can get lost in the shuffle, greatly affecting productivity. Evernote is a place to keep track of all of those ideas so they're available to everyone, regardless of where they are seated.

StreamWork

Android, BlackBerry, iOS, Mac OS X, WebOS, and Windows

StreamWork (www.sapstreamwork.com) is a collaborative decision-making application with both free and premium versions. A Linux-based enterprise edition is also available.

You can use Evernote to take notes, record audio memos, clip web pages, and snap photos, and then easily share them via StreamWork.

Evernote Business for Salesforce

Android, BlackBerry, iOS, Mac OS X, WebOS, Windows Phone, and Windows

Evernote Business for Salesforce (http://evernote.com/business/uses/salesforce) lets you capture and share the information you and your team need, as well as manage your relationships to meet the needs of your customers. It's a no-charge add-on for licensees of Salesforce and Evernote for Business.

As an old enterprise-software guy, I love it when the great divide between personal-use software and big corporate systems is bridged. Ideally, many other enterprise vendors will interface their systems with Evernote.

AutoCAD 360

Android and iOS

AutoCAD 360 (https://www.autocad360.com) is a drawing and drafting app used by architects, designers, and engineers worldwide. Now it's integrated with Evernote. You can export design files to Evernote, including team members' comments, for easy sharing and organizing.

The app allows you to view, edit, and share drawings; perform on-site redlining; prepare as-built documentation; and perform design review and approval. Pro and ProPlus versions are available, with additional capabilities.

Associating Objects with Notes

The Internet of Things and wearable computing are some of the most-talked-about emerging technologies. A few Evernote-aware apps involving things, not just documents, have started to appear.

Tapmynote

Android

Tapmynote (www.tapmynote.com) lets you associate objects with your Evernote notes. Assign Near Field Communication (NFC) tags to your Evernote notes and then open a note by touching its tag on an NFC-enabled mobile phone.

NFC is a contactless technology that made the mobile wallet possible. It's supported by companies such as Google, Nokia, PayPal, Microsoft, MasterCard, Visa, and American Express.

You can buy tags that support the app at http://touchanote.myshopify.com and www.tagstand.com.

ENPower

iOS

ENPower (http://apptreme.com) allows you to create access shortcuts for your Evernote on iOS devices. You can use it to create shortcuts that link to a notebook, tag, or individual notes; create QR (Quick Response) codes that can be saved to the Camera Roll or e-mailed; and use the built-in QR code scanner to view a note either in ENPower or Evernote.

Giving applications access to Evernote

Evernote works with third-party developers to make Evernote functionality available from within the apps made by those developers. Many of these apps (but by no means all) are featured in the Evernote App Center (http://appcenter.evernote.com).

When you use a third-party application and want to connect to Evernote through it, you're prompted to verify that it's okay for the application to interact with Evernote. After you've granted permission, the application is authorized to interface with your Evernote account. You can revoke access at any time.

To see what access you've authorized and to revoke access, navigate to https://www.evernote.com/Authorized Services.action.

Chapter 18

Interfacing with Digital Cameras, Scanners, and Smart Pens

In This Chapter

▶ Working with digital cameras

▶ Using scanners

▶ Getting the most out of smart pens

*E*vernote does amazing things for you on a computer or smartphone. Add some specialized hardware or software, and you can really turbocharge your Evernote experience.

This chapter gives you an inside look at some of the possibilities for extending the power of Evernote with hardware and software.

TIP Not all hardware supported by Evernote is listed in the Evernote Market (`https://www.evernote.com/market`). The Evernote Blog (`http://blog.evernote.com`) usually carries announcements of new supported devices that Evernote has seen.

Getting the Most Out of Scanners

An Evernote-supported scanner is the hardware I use most, other than a computer, when I'm sitting at my desk. (As a writer, that's a good part of my day.) I scan all my paper: business cards, bank statements, bills, pay stubs, receipts, lab tests, handwritten notes, whatever. When I scan my paper items directly into Evernote, those items become searchable and findable on all my devices, wherever I happen to be.

In Chapter 6, I discuss interfacing scanners with Evernote. In this section, I cover specific features of the most popular Evernote-supported scanners. The leading scanner makers have made sure that their Evernote support is up to snuff. Even when they haven't, Evernote's TWAIN support ropes in nearly all scanners, even when the vendor didn't specifically have Evernote in mind.

Canon imageFormula

The Canon imageFormula P-150 is a powerful yet compact personal and portable duplex scanner that can scan up to 15 pages per minute and can be optimized for Evernote. After you install the software that comes with the scanner, just press the scan button on the scanner, and your document is scanned directly into Evernote.

The imageFormula DR-C125 is a newer, slightly larger, and faster scanner suitable for computers or even mobile workstations. It comes bundled with the new Canon CaptureOnTouch software, which can route scanned images to Evernote and other cloud services. Images are scanned in PDF/A format, which Evernote servers can read and index.

Fujitsu ScanSnap

The Fujitsu ScanSnap one-button color scanner feeds documents through automatically and converts both sides to a digital file with just one pass. After you've installed the manufacturer-supplied software, one push of a button makes your documents available on Evernote and searchable on just about any computer or mobile device you utilize the Evernote application on.

A few ScanSnap models are available, including the tiny ScanSnap S1100 Color Mobile Scanner; the somewhat larger S1300; and the speedy desktop S1500 (my personal workhorse), which lets you insert up to 50 pages at a time into the automatic document feeder and scan 20 pages per minute.

Evernote sells its own branded version of the Fujitsu ScanSnap desktop scanner, jointly developed with Fujitsu's PFU subsidiary, through the Evernote Market (`https://www.evernote.com/market/feature/ scanner?sku=SCAN00101`) as the ScanSnap Evernote Edition Scanner. It is Wi-Fi enabled, so you don't need a physical connection. The ScanSnap Evernote Edition recognizes the differences between scanned items like documents and business cards and auto-files them into the appropriate notebook to make searching quick and easy. It works with Mac OS and Windows. When you buy a ScanSnap Evernote Edition scanner, you get a one-year subscription to Evernote Premium.

Lexmark's SmartSolutions Suite

Lexmark International's web-connected inkjet printers with touchscreen interface printers include the Lexmark Genesis S615, Interact S605, and Pinnacle Pro901 and Pro915. These multifunction devices can print, scan, fax, copy, and support one-touch scanning into Evernote without requiring you to turn on your computer.

Visioneer OneTouch

The Visioneer OneTouch scanning utility for Visioneer's RoadWarrior 3g enables you to send scans directly to Evernote's cloud-based service with just one touch, just like the other scanners described in this section, but with an extra feature: It works even if the computer you're using doesn't have Evernote for Windows installed.

Ricoh App2Me

Ricoh's App2Me solution enables you to create personalized workflows that you can use on any App2Me-enabled multifunction product. Simply download the widget to your desktop and enter your Evernote account information, and your Scan to Evernote widget is ready to use on all your App2Me-enabled products.

HoverCam

The HoverCam combines a document scanner and a document camera, and enables you to take a high-resolution image scan in less than a second. Using the HoverCam Flex software, you can send your scans to your Evernote account with a single click.

Sending and Receiving Faxes

Although most messages today are electronic, facsimile (fax) is alive and well. Strictly speaking, e-fax solutions are software products linked to cloud-based services.

In an e-fax solution, the vendor gives you a unique incoming fax number. Faxes sent to that number are actually delivered to you as e-mail, so they can be set up to be delivered to your Evernote e-mail address as well. Usually, incoming faxes can be delivered to multiple addresses. Mine go to my main e-mail inbox as well as to my Evernote e-mail address.

Outgoing faxes are sent out as e-mails, often with files attached. You can register your Evernote e-mail address as an acceptable input source for an e-fax account, which means you can find any note in Evernote, right-click the note, choose Share from the contextual menu, and then choose the Send to E-Mail option. In the window that opens, type *your fax number@your efax provider* as an e-mail address. The note is faxed right out to its destination. This process is not only simple, but also provides a much cleaner fax because it's electronic all the way.

The e-fax solutions listed in Table 18-1 work pretty much alike. I used eFax.com for many years, but in the past few years, I've switched to RingCentral, which I find to be less expensive based on my use pattern.

Table 18-1	Popular E-Fax Solutions	
Vendor	*Monthly Cost*	*Pages per Month*
HelloFax.com	$9.99–$39.99	300–1,000
fax.com	$9.99	300
eFax.com	$16.95–$19.95	150 (send), 150 (receive) 200 (send), 200 (receive)
myfax.com	$10–$40	100 (send), 200 (receive) 400 (send), 400 (receive)
Rapidfax.com	$9.95	300
RingCentral.com	$7.99–$49.99	500–unlimited
send2fax.com	$8.95–$12.95	150–350

Most services have a free or no-commitment test period. Here's the rub: You often can't keep your existing fax number and move it (*port it,* in telephone lingo) to an e-fax service. eFax.com does allow you to port or connect your existing number to its service. RingCentral also allows this service.

If the company supplies the number to you, the company owns that number. There's usually no way for you to take it with you if you change services. The moral of the story is that you shouldn't publish the number until you're sure you're happy with the service.

Working with Smart Pens and Tablets

Let's be honest: In a room with many people, the tap, tap, tap of your keyboard can be a distraction to others. Smart pens and tablets provide a way to capture your thoughts or the spoken word electronically without keying. Everything you capture with a smart pen or tablet can be moved to Evernote for searching, editing, and forwarding.

Livescribe smart pen

Livescribe makes a family of smart pens that record what you hear and write, so you'll never miss a word. One example is the Livescribe Sky Wi-Fi smart pen. This comes with a built-in microphone, speaker, memory storage (up to 8GB, depending on the model), a USB connector to transfer the recording, and (most important) a note recorder that records your scribbles as you write. You can play back lectures or meetings with a simple tap of your notes. After the recorded information makes it to your computer, you can also share to Evernote, Facebook, OneNote, Google Docs, and e-mail.

When notes are in Evernote, they're searchable and available wherever you have Evernote installed. Viewing your handwritten notes is as easy as simply clicking the note as you normally would while using Evernote. If there is any audio that goes along with it, clicking the page image loads the Livescribe Player. Through this player you can watch your notes being rewritten right in front of you while you listen to the corresponding audio. You can also click anywhere on the digital page to skip ahead to that part of the recording. With the purchase of a Sky smart pen, you get a one-year subscription to Evernote Premium.

In order to share your notes and audio sessions with your Evernote account, you must use the Livescribe Desktop software to convert the default audio file format (ACC) to a WAV format that Evernote can import. The conversion is easy and you'll be on your way to accessing your saved notes and recordings in no time.

You cannot auto-sync your notes to Evernote using only the Livescribe desktop program. The best way for you to back up your data within the app is to use a cloud service such as iCloud, which can be used for Macs or PCs. However, you can easily open/save any document to Evernote from the share menu as long as you have the Evernote installed. You can read more about this issue at `https://support.livescribe.com/entries/22916515-Intregration-with-Evernote`.

Sending notes and audio to other people is as easy as scribbling on some paper. These interactive digital documents are called *pencasts,* and they let you see and hear these notes exactly as they were recorded. All you have to do is transfer your recording to a computer that is running the Livescribe software.

If you want to send your pencasts to Evernote as well as to other recipients, you can use Livescribe Connect, a web-based service that makes the connection between Livescribe and Evernote as easy as writing the word *Send* on a piece of paper!

Wacom Bamboo pen tablet

Wacom pen tablets were introduced in 1984. Early models were very expensive and were mostly used in high-end design shops. Today, these pen tablets have come down in price. They enable you to create digital ink notes and annotate images in Evernote. In many ways, I find them similar to Livescribe, which I describe in the preceding section, except that Livescribe does a better job of relating ink and audio.

If you use Evernote for Windows, you can create ink notes right inside Evernote. On both Windows and Mac computers, you can use Wacom pen tablets to annotate images in your favorite image editor and then bring those annotated images into Evernote.

Getting Creative with Whiteboards

When Abraham Lincoln and I were growing up (I was in elementary school in the mid-1960s), teachers used blackboards and chalk in classrooms. The ubiquitous whiteboard was invented by Martin Heit, a photographer and Korean War veteran. It was erasable and chalk-free. Whiteboards began to appear in classrooms in the 1960s (my school was not an early adopter of this technology), and by the 1990s, whiteboards had been widely adopted.

As people figured out great ideas by using whiteboards, the need to capture those memorable thoughts grew. Whiteboard sessions are meant to be collaborative, so it feels counterproductive when the team spends as much time feverishly re-creating the whiteboard sketches in their notebooks as participating in the creative discussions. The advent of the digital camera did much to encourage memory retention of solutions crafted on whiteboard, by capturing the whiteboard images as snapshots. Evernote does much more. Evernote's image-recognition technology processes all those snapshots and makes the handwritten text searchable so you can find all those great ideas.

I frequently use the FaceTime camera built into my Apple MacBook Air laptop to capture whiteboard drawings as notes in Evernote. This technique requires no special equipment.

This section covers a few whiteboard products you can use with Evernote.

Panasonic Panaboard

Education institutions love the Panasonic line of pricey but interactive whiteboards. The Panaboard lets you display the contents of a computer screen directly onto the board. It enables three people to write simultaneously on the board and is sensitive to finger touch and electronic pen. With Panaboard, you get built-in speakers, two USB hubs to connect to a printer and document camera, and an optional wireless kit. You can use Wi-Fi to transfer the digital images to Evernote.

IdeaPaint

IdeaPaint is a special kind of paint that can turn anything into a dry-erase writing surface. After a productive brainstorming session with IdeaPaint, snap a photo of your notes with your digital camera or smartphone. Bring the image into Evernote to make all the text searchable so that you can find your great ideas whenever you want from any device you use. Use Evernote's sharing features to share those images with your class, team, or colleagues.

Skitch

Skitch (www.skitch.com), now owned by Evernote, is free and is being fully integrated into Evernote. At this writing, versions for the Windows, Mac, Android, and iOS platforms are available. The product works similarly on all platforms.

Skitch greatly eases what you do with interactive whiteboards. You can annotate, edit, and crop sketches, and then share your creation publicly or only to whom you have chosen. Under the covers, it has a vector engine, so the lines and shapes you draw are smooth.

With Skitch you can

- ✔ **Take screen shots of anything.** Capture a shot of a document, a webpage, something that inspires you, or just about anything else, and save it to Evernote.

- ✔ **Drag files into Evernote.** Hold down the Drag Me tab and pull the file into Evernote.

- ✔ **Annotate images.** Annotating an image is easy. Just click any of the annotation tools on the toolbar, select a color, and start annotating.

- ✔ **Rotate images.** Rotate arrows, text, and shapes by simply tapping the object, pressing with two fingers, and rotating. You can also rotate multiple objects by tapping them individually to select them and then doing the two-finger rotate. Save the result as a note in Evernote.

✔ **Save files in different formats.** Choose your preferred file format from a pull-down menu next to the Drag Me tab, or tap the elephant icon to save in Evernote.

✔ **Resize and crop an image.** Tools let you change an image's size (shrink or stretch it) simply by clicking on the different sized dots. Tap the Crop toolbar icon and select the portion of the image you'd like to crop out and keep as a note in Evernote.

A Skitch overview of all platforms is available at `https://evernote.com/skitch/guide/mac/#9`. A video guide to using Skitch for Mac is available at `https://evernote.com/skitch/guide/mac`.

Getting Images to Evernote with the Eye-Fi Camera Interface

The digital camera on your computer or mobile device usually takes pretty good pictures. After you have pictures, getting them into Evernote is easy (see Chapter 6).

For really important occasions, however, pretty good pictures aren't enough. For great pictures, you need to use a high-quality digital camera. What do you do to get those photos into Evernote? Making those high-quality images findable anywhere can be a challenge.

Until now, you needed to perform many steps: store the images on a memory card; get them into a computer (usually by inserting the memory card into a computer); and upload them to the Internet for further processing, storage, or posting to social media.

I've found that Wi-Fi memory cards, such as the Eye-Fi X2, make backing up and sharing photos right from your camera as easy as working with the low-resolution cameras built into smartphones. The Eye-Fi card works in your camera and connects your camera to an in-range Wi-Fi network. Hotspots, such as those provided in public places like coffee shops and hotels, are also supported.

The Eye-Fi X2 creates its own Wi-Fi connection, so wherever you are, you can use direct mode on your Eye-Fi X2 card to transfer photos and videos from your camera to your iOS or Android device.

Evernote does all the work of organizing and backing up photos for you. After you take a photo, Eye-Fi wirelessly sends the photo to its own servers and from there to Evernote, where Evernote processes it and makes the text searchable. Then you can find those photos any time by using Evernote on your computer or mobile device. (Read more about Eye-Fi in Chapter 6.)

A good comparative review of Eye-Fi and Transcend wireless cards is available at www.dpreview.com/articles/4616822206/battle-of-the-wi-fi-cards-eye-fi-vs-transcend.

Part VI
Adding Professional Power

Check out our video library. It's full of tutorials, demos, tips and tricks, great partners, and more.

TUTORIALS   STORIES AND TIPS   PRODUCTS WE LOVE

Evernote: Remember Everything Play video	Evernote Web Clipper for Chrome Play video	How to create a table of contents Play video	Evernote Reminders Play video
Using Search in Evernote Play video	The Evernote Smart Notebook by Moleskine Play video	Evernote Food for Android Tutorial Play video	Evernote Hello 2.0 Play video
Hello Connect Tutorial Play video	Hello Business Card Scanning Tutorial Play video	Penultimate 4.0 with Evernote Play video	Tutorial of Evernote 5 for Mac Play video
The New Skitch Play video	Tutorial of Skitch for iPhone and iPod Touch Play video	Evernote Food 2.0 Play video	Tutorial of Evernote Food Play video
Evernote Business Play video	Evernote Food: New Features Play video	Evernote Hello: An Introduction Play video	Introducing Evernote Food Play video
Introducing Skitch Play video	Introducing Evernote Peek Play video	Introducing Evernote Clearly Play video	Sending Tweets to Evernote Play video
File Drag and Drop on Evernote Web Play video	Evernote and the Wacom Bamboo Pen tablet Play video	Cooking with Evernote and Laurine Wickett Play video	Premium feature: PDF Search Play video
The Live Update Feature Play video	Encrypting and Decrypting text Play video	Evernote to the Rescue! Play video	Evernote Introduction Play video
Evernote Elevator Pitch Play video	We Work With Evernote Play video		

To read more about working with Evernote using the command-line interface, visit www.dummies.com/webextras/evernote.

In this part . . .

- ✔ Using AppleScript with Evernote
- ✔ Using command-line scripting in Windows
- ✔ Getting tips and staying up to date with Evernote

Chapter 19

Saving Time with Evernote's Open Scripting

*O*pen Scripting Architecture (OSA) is an optional way to leverage the power of the applications on your computer to perform new tricks. When you write a script, you're creating a recipe. The computer is the faithful cook who follows your recipe precisely. The ingredients are the applications on your computer. Create a recipe for wholesome and tasty bread. Produce ten tasty loaves, all prepared precisely in accordance with your recipe.

In this chapter, I give you a taste of how Evernote works with OSA on the Mac and with Evernote's proprietary scripting language for the Windows platform. I encourage you to overcome the fear factor and to get your imagination working so that you can create recipes that will make you more productive, and also dazzle and amaze your friends.

Thousands of developers worldwide are leveraging the power of Evernote with their own applications. The whole is greater and stronger than the sum of the parts.

Getting the Inside Scoop on Scripting

Scripting is a form of programming that lets you control what happens more precisely than by just selecting menu commands. Scripting is useful because it makes things much easier by giving you much greater control. Even more exciting, after you have a script that does what you want, you can run it over and over (*execute* it, in technicalese), and with a little more work, you can make it do the same thing to lots of different data.

A simple script may just run a set of commands, saving you from the tedium of doing the same thing repetitively. The real power comes from introducing a little logic to control the flow of commands. Techies call this *conditional logic,* and it sounds scary, but conditional logic is just a way of stating and controlling the rules for what you want to happen.

OSA is scripting on steroids. It means that you use somebody else's scripting logic but can also define your own. Your new logic fits in so smoothly and naturally that it's as though your logic were part of the original design.

The beauty and power of OSA are that you don't need to do it all yourself, and you aren't limited to prewritten logic in any one application. You stand on many tall shoulders. You can harness the functions of many applications, including Evernote, on your computer and get them all to dance to your flute in a beautifully choreographed dance symphony. The functionality of many programs is at your beck and call.

 Scripting languages are like loyal and subservient valets. They do exactly, and unquestioningly, what you tell them to. They don't "think" independently, and if you tell them to do foolish things, they aren't going to come back and challenge you. Therefore, always test a script thoroughly on a practice notebook.

Being Efficient with Mac Scripting

Mac scripting has always been the most user-friendly software around for extending what you can do with computers and for automating repetitious tasks. Mac scripting makes it easy to interact with the components of the Mac.

Using AppleScript and the AppleScript Editor

AppleScript is the scripting language for the Mac, and the AppleScript Editor is a tool for editing scripts written in AppleScript.

You can create scripts in three ways:

- ✔ Start a new script, turn on the recorder, and just do your thing. Your actions are recorded as a script. After you save the script, if you play it back, it repeats your actions.
- ✔ Type the script directly in AppleScript.
- ✔ Record a script and then edit it in AppleScript (often, to generalize it).

All programs that support AppleScript make their major functions available to be controlled by AppleScript. Making functions available for controlling by scripts is called *exposing* the functionality, because the functions are visible in the AppleScript dictionary and you can use AppleScript commands to command them to perform their tricks. (When you open the Script Editor, you can open the dictionary by choosing File⇨Open Dictionary.) In other words, they agree to respond to AppleScript commands in ways that are defined in the AppleScript dictionary entry for that application. As with all dictionary entries, if you want to know the meaning of the commands, you can look them up.

When you open the dictionary, you get a listing of the available applications that have dictionaries. If Evernote is installed, select Evernote and click Open to view the dictionary entries.

For more information about AppleScript, I recommend *AppleScript For Dummies,* 2nd Edition, by Tom Trinko, or, for a more in-depth treatment, *AppleScript (Developer Reference),* by Mark Conway Munro (both from John Wiley & Sons, Inc.). In addition, AppleScript documentation is available at `http://developer.apple.com/documentation/AppleScript/Conceptual/AppleScriptLangGuide/index.html`.

Exploring Evernote support for AppleScript

Evernote's interaction with AppleScript is natural, robust, and simple. You can use AppleScript to open a notebook, create a note, perform a search, and accomplish other Evernote tasks. One really useful thing you can do is create a search, as complicated as you like, and have the search executed whenever you want on your most up-to-date notebooks. So if you clip and save news about your company, you can save the search and run a script any time to see the accumulated notes.

This book provides general information about controlling Evernote's functionality through AppleScript. The Evernote dictionary entries for AppleScript assume that you already know Evernote's basic concepts. Don't try to use scripting until you've created and used notes in the Evernote application.

To get information on specific functionality, follow these steps:

1. **Choose Applications⇨Utilities⇨AppleScript Editor.**

2. **Choose File⇨Open Dictionary.**

3. **Select Evernote.**

Creating notes from AppleScript

You can create notes from AppleScript in several ways. Here's one way:

1. **In the AppleScript Editor, enter the following lines to create a new notebook called** `MyAppleScriptNotebook`**:**

```
-- create notebook AppleScriptNotebook1
tell application "Evernote"
if (not (notebook named "AppleScriptNotebook1" exists)) then
-- NOTE also check out the "create notebook" command
make notebook with properties {name:"AppleScriptNotebook1"}
end if
```

Except for specific titles, such as in `AppleScriptNotebook1`, you virtually never have to type caps. You do need to pay close attention to the punctuation, however.

2. **To create a new HTML note in the notebook** `MyAppleScriptNotebook`**, type the following:**

```
tell application "Evernote"
create note title "Note 2" with html "<strong> Here is my new HTML
         note</strong>"
Notebook "MyAppleScriptNotebook"
end tell
```

Replacing notes in AppleScript

Here's a sample AppleScript to illustrate how you can replace the contents of a note:

```
set new_Text to text returned of (display dialog "Enter New Text"
default answer "")
tell application "Evernote"
set the_Note to selection
set HTML content of item 1 of the_Note to new_Text
end tell
```

Converting a note to plain text in AppleScript

Here's a script for stripping the formatting from a note and converting it to text:

```
on getTextInNotebook(NbName)
tell application "Evernote"
activate
tell notebook NbName
set totalNotes to (count notes)
set totalWords to 0
set allWords to ""
repeat with n from 1 to totalNotes
set hc to HTML content of note n
set w to (count words of hc)
set totalWords to totalWords + w
log (title of note n) & " - " & w
```

```
set allWords to allWords & " " & hc
end repeat
end tell

set totalCharacters to (count characters in allWords)
log totalCharacters

-- eliminate stuff between < and > markers
set c to ""
set i to 0
set allText to ""
repeat while i < totalCharacters
set i to i + 1
set c to character i of allWords
if c = "<" then
repeat until c = ">"
set i to i + 1
set c to character i of allWords
end repeat
else
try
set allText to allText & c
end try
end if
end repeat

log allText
log "Size of allText    " & (count characters of allText)
end tell

return allText
end getTextInNotebook
```

More AppleScript/Evernote resources

A useful AppleScript script to export one or more notes from Evernote to Rich Text Format (RTF) is available at `http://veritrope.com/tech/evernote-rtf-export`. A whole collection of useful scripts is available at `http://veritrope.com/tech/evernote-applescript-resources-and-accessories`.

Visit `http://dev.evernote.com/doc/start/ios.php` for other ways to create notes. You can also get some basics on working with tags and new notebooks. The Evernote dictionary entries in AppleScript show the full set of commands that Evernote responds to.

Compiling and saving scripts

You can save your script as a compiled script that runs when you double-click it in the Finder. To compile and save a script, follow these steps:

1. **Choose File⇨Save to open the Save dialog.**

2. **Choose a location to save your file.**

3. **Choose Script from the File Format pop-up menu.**

4. **Enter a name for the script.**

   `.scptd` is the file extension.

5. **(Optional) To save the script in a form that can't be changed or edited, select the Run Only check box.**

   If you select Run Only, you can't edit the script again. If you want to be able to change the script in the future, save the original script in the standard editable format and then save the run-only version with a different name.

6. **Click Save.**

Scripting in Windows

Windows, unlike Mac OS X, doesn't have a built-in scripting language, so Evernote provided its own, which is based on the command line that has been around since the earliest days of Windows.

Using Automator

Apple's Automator (`http://support.apple.com/kb/ht2488`) lets you use a simple drag-and-drop process to create and run scripts that perform simple or complex tasks on demand. These scripts can work with many services that expose their functionality to work with scripting, including Calendar, Contacts, Mail, and Evernote. You can run a script to send e-mails from Mail.app directly to Evernote by using an Automator action, for example. See `https://www.evernote.com/shard/s7/sh/6c72cc9b-eca0-4c22-9771-79fc7e3e847b/3a465f9b0fdb9cb94e061840f53a4997` for details.

Useful published scripts for interfacing Evernote with other applications are available at `http://veritrope.com/code_type/evernote`.

Finally, a useful script for using Mac OS X services to import files into Evernote is available at `www.nineboxes.net/2009/09/using-mac-os-x-services-to-import-files-into-evernote`.

There are no official Automator actions from Evernote (yet). Some of the actions contained in the links I've provided, which work at this writing, could stop working in the future, as they are unofficial.

Command-line scripting

In Windows, you can drive Evernote by invoking it from the command line. Table 19-1 shows you the commands you can use.

Table 19-1	Scripting Commands in Windows
Command	*What It Does*
`[filename]`	Creates a new note if you pass the full path to a file. If you pass a `.txt`, `.htm`, or `.html` file, the file contents are used as the new note's content. If you pass an `.enex` file, the Evernote notes that it contains are imported. If you pass a `.url` file, the hyperlink is used as the new note's content. If you pass any other file type, that file is attached to the new note.
`/NewNote`	Opens a new window with a new, empty note. This command is equivalent to right-clicking the Evernote icon on the taskbar and choosing New Note from the contextual menu.
`/NewInkNote`	Opens a new window with a new, empty ink note.
`/NewWebCamNote`	Opens a new window that enables you to capture a new webcam note.
`/Task:ClipScreen`	Invokes Evernote's screen-shot clipper, which enables you to take a screen shot of the desired portion of the screen and save it in a new note. This command is equivalent to right-clicking the Evernote icon on the taskbar and choosing Clip Screenshot from the contextual menu.
`/Task:PasteClipboard`	Creates a new note containing the contents of the clipboard. This command is equivalent to right-clicking the Evernote icon on the taskbar and choosing Paste Clipboard from the contextual menu. If the clipboard contains a `.txt`, `.htm`, or `.html` file, that file is used as the new note's content. If the clipboard contains an `.enex` file, the Evernote notes that it contains are imported. If the clipboard contains a `.url` file, the hyperlink is used as the new note's content. If the clipboard contains any other type of file, that file is attached to the new note.
`/Task:SyncDatabase`	Causes Evernote for Windows to synchronize with the Evernote service. This command is equivalent to right-clicking the Evernote icon on the taskbar and choosing Sync from the contextual menu.

You can't combine individual commands. If Evernote is already running, your command is passed to the existing instance.

ENScript.exe scripting

When you install Evernote for Windows, one of the programs that is installed is a scripting program called ENScript.exe, which is installed in the same path (directory) as Evernote. Although it's not nearly as convenient as scripting on a Mac with AppleScript, ENScript.exe lets you accomplish the same things to control Evernote, if a little less elegantly.

I initially had some trouble getting ENScript.exe to work because I didn't pay sufficient attention to the following caveat: To invoke one of the executables, you must make sure that Evernote's program directory is in your shell path, or you must give the full path to the executable when you invoke the command.

Table 19-2 lists the main verbs you can use with ENScript.exe.

Table 19-2	ENScript.exe Main Verbs
Main Verb	**What It Does**
createNote	Creates a new note
importNotes	Imports one or more notes from an Evernote Export (.enex) file
showNotes	Sets the current note list to view the results of a query
printNotes	Prints a set of notes
exportNotes	Exports a set of notes to an .enex file
listNotebooks	Lists your existing notebooks
syncDatabase	Synchronizes your Windows desktop with the Evernote service

To create a new notebook with ENScript.exe, for example, assuming that the path is correct, you'd type the following:

```
ENScript.exe createNotebook /n "New Notebook"
```

These commands are documented at http://dev.evernote.com/doc/articles/enscript.php.

Chapter 20

Connecting with the Evernote Community

....

In This Chapter

▶ Exploring the user forums

▶ Meeting up with other Evernote users

▶ Keeping current on Evernote developments

....

*E*vernote has an awesome community, and other users have ideas and techniques that they'd love to share with you. This chapter describes how you can meet other users and exchange ideas with them.

Getting Tips from the Evernote User Forum

The Evernote User Forum (`http://discussion.evernote.com`) is the online place for users to meet and help one another.

The forum is organized in major subgroups, such as Evernote Products, Learn & Share, and General Discussions. Major forums you might be interested in include the following:

- ✔ Evernote Discussion
- ✔ Evernote for Windows
- ✔ Evernote for Mac
- ✔ Evernote for the Web
- ✔ Evernote Mobile
- ✔ Third Party Application Discussions
- ✔ Evernote for Developers

You can also find forums in Japanese and Russian, as well as a section on Localization (translating Evernote into languages it doesn't currently support) and a section for Skitch users.

Anyone can read the posts, but active participation in the forum requires registration, which is free.

Business-account holders have their own forum at `http://discussion.evernote.com/forum/134-evernote-business`.

Registering for the forum

To register, go to `http://discussion.evernote.com`. You're asked to agree to the terms of use, which essentially request that you not post any abusive, obscene, vulgar, slanderous, hateful, threatening, or sexually sugges-tive content, or any other material that may violate any laws.

Finding forum topics

After you've registered, you can follow a topic and reply to posts on it. You can search for a forum by typing your search terms in the search box in the top-right corner of the main forum page.

The forums are indexed by Google, so when you need to search the forums, you may find it easier to type **Evernote** followed by your query in Google.

Popular topics aren't just product-specific. Some very popular topics include Get Organized and Increase Your Productivity with Evernote, Large Amount to Get into Evernote, and Wrangling Recipes.

Another hot topic related to using Evernote, for example, is GTD (short for *Getting Things Done*), the work–life management system developed by David Allen (`www.davidco.com/about-gtd`). Many people use Evernote as the basis for their own GTD systems, so it's not surprising that GTD is one of the most popular forums, with thousands of page views.

Following forum topics

If you find a topic that interests you and want to be notified of new posts, follow these steps:

1. **Click Follow This Forum in the top-right corner.**

   The window shown in Figure 20-1 opens.

Figure 20-1:
Set notifica-
tion options
here.

2. **Choose the frequency of notifications.**

   Your options are Instantly, Only When Not Online, Daily, and Weekly.

3. **Clear or check the Follow Anonymously check box.**

   This option is selected by default.

4. **Click Follow This Forum.**

If you change your mind later about following a forum, you can unfollow it by visiting the forum and clicking Unfollow This Forum in the top-right corner of the page. When the confirmation window opens, click the Unfollow This Forum button.

Being Social with Meetups

Evernote meetups are great ways to meet fellow Evernote users, swap stories, share ideas, have a great time, and build your network. You can locate Evernote gatherings through Meetup (www.meetup.com/Evernote), which claims to be the world's largest network of groups.

Meetup recognizes where you are (based on your IP address) and shows you nearby meetups on a zoomable map of the world (see Figure 20-2). Details on nearby meetings are shown below the map, followed by a list of the largest Evernote communities. Evernote meetups are also hosted by their specially selected Ambassadors. See the "Evernote ambassadors" section later in this chapter on more information about who they are and what they do.

At this writing, there are 716 Evernote communities in 696 cities, but not all meet regularly.

If you live in or near a large city, you may find more than one meetup. Austin, Texas, is home to the largest community, with 289 Evernoters; Paris has 125 Evernoters, London 102, New York 98, Los Angeles 96, and Tokyo 93. These numbers are increasing all the time, so regularly check to see if new ones popped up nearby!

Figure 20-2:
Map show-
ing Evernote
meetups.

In addition to in-person events, Evernote also hosts virtual events such as Google Hangouts, webinars, and Twitter chats. Be sure to check the events tab on the Facebook page (`https://www.facebook.com/evernote/events`) and follow the Twitter account (`https://twitter.com/evernote`) for the most up-to-date information on upcoming events.

If you plan to hold a meetup, post details on the Evernote User Forum (discussed earlier in this chapter), which gets lots of views. You can e-mail `meetups@evernote.com` with question about meetups.

You can get notified of meetings by signing up at `https://secure.meetup.com/quick_reg`.

Keeping Up to Date with Evernote

Evernote is constantly — and I mean constantly — improving. Each of the versions for the various platforms is being improved on an ongoing basis, and new things happen on a weekly basis. It's also a very substantial product with many possibilities. Therefore, you may want to stay up to date on the latest improvements and stay in touch with other users, who are always finding innovative things to do with Evernote and work-arounds for limitations that you may encounter.

Evernote Blog

The Evernote Blog (`http://blog.evernote.com`) provides the latest in what Evernote dubs "noteworthy news." You can visit this blog to get the latest on all things Evernote. Check out tips, news, and cool ways people are making their world more notable. You can subscribe to the feed at `http://blog.evernote.com/feed`. Just enter this URL into a RSS reader such as Feedly (`http://feedly.com/`). There is also a Techblog for developers at `http://blog.evernote.com/tech`.

The Evernote Blog includes a series of "Quick Tip" posts. To find them, search for *"Quick Tip"* on the home page. These posts are short snippets of helpful information for the beginner Evernote user. They are perfect for learning a new trick in just a few seconds! Here are some topics:

- How to Organize Your Notebooks in Evernote
- Travel Smarter with Evernote Offline Notebooks
- How to Search for Text Inside an Image
- Collect the Web

One section of the blog that I find to be the most useful is the News section. This area of the Evernote Blog is devoted to product updates as well as corporate news. You can click the News tab on the blog home page or access the updates directly at `http://blog.evernote.com/blog/category/news/`.

Evernote ambassadors

Evernote has appointed *ambassadors* — experts and fellow users who help you get the most out of Evernote. Each ambassador has a Twitter feed and maintains a discussion forum. At this writing, there are 65. You can meet the ambassadors at `http://evernote.com/community`. Each ambassador specializes in a particular area, including the following:

- Organization
- Teaching
- Paperless living
- Lifestyle
- Crafts
- Productivity
- Blogging and public speaking
- Design

You can connect to Evernote ambassadors around the world. In addition to English, some speak Spanish, Portuguese, French, German, Italian, Indonesian, Japanese, Korean, Dutch, Turkish, Russian, and various Chinese dialects.

To contact an ambassador, click his or her name. You see links to the ambassador's forum, website, and Twitter account, and you may also see links to his or her published tips.

Case studies

Another interesting part of the Evernote Blog is the case studies, which you can find on the Tips & Stories tab (`http://blog.evernote.com/blog/category/tips-stories`). They're also among my favorite parts of the blog. Try reading the case studies to get ideas about cool things you can do with Evernote.

Community posts are at `http://blog.evernote.com/blog/tag/community-tag/`. Interesting posts include topics such as these:

- ✔ How American Figure Skater David Pelletier Uses Evernote and Skitch
- ✔ Capture Images from the Public Domain in Evernote
- ✔ 3 Ways to Manage a Sales Team

Other online resources

If you haven't found what you're looking for using the resources covered thus far, a couple of other tools can help you stay current with Evernote happenings:

- ✔ **Social media:** Evernote has a Facebook page (`www.facebook.com/evernote`) and a Twitter account (`https://twitter.com/evernote`).

- ✔ **Webinars and conferences:** Evernote periodically offers free webinars, which usually are geared toward users of Evernote Business. In addition, Evernote hosts an annual conference where guest speakers talk about how to become a pro at using Evernote (`http://evernote.com/ec/`). They livestream the event so you don't even have to be there in person to gain all of the knowledge presented by the industry experts.

  Webinars and conferences are prominently announced on the Evernote Blog (`http://blog.evernote.com`). You can also subscribe to the Evernote RSS feed (`http://blog.evernote.com/feed`) to ensure that you see new blog posts as they become available. Just enter the feed URL into a feed reader such as Feedly (`http://feedly.com/index.html#discover`).

- ✔ **Chat (English only):** Premium subscribers can chat with Evernote staff Monday through Friday between 9 a.m. and 5 p.m. U.S. Pacific Time. Access this service by clicking Chat with Evernote on the support page (`http://evernote.com/contact/support`).

Part VII
The Part of Tens

Want more ideas for ways to use Evernote? Visit www.dummies.com/webextras/evernote to read "10 Ways Evernote Can Enhance Your Productivity."

In this part. . .

✔ Discovering ten ways to use Evernote for home-improvement projects

✔ Understanding ways Evernote can help you manage your education

✔ Finding out ten ways to use Evernote to be productive at work

Chapter 21

Ten Home Improvements

*E*vernote is extremely useful for doing nearly anything necessary for organizing and maintaining your home life. Personal organization is always a matter of preference. Whether you need ten notebooks to get yourself in order or just one in which notes are properly tagged and titled, Evernote can help you do just about anything around the house. Here are ten ideas to transform your desk from messy to fantastically organized.

Managing a Successful Home Decorating Project

Without a doubt, Evernote makes home decorating simple. If you're planning to go to as many stores as possible to make sure that you get the best price, tracking all the prices, styles, and thoughts on each option will be difficult. With Evernote, all you have to do is create a notebook, take pictures, and add notes about each item from your phone or tablet. You can compare the places you've been and colors you're interested in while you take a lunch break or at the end of the day. All your information will be neatly organized when you're ready to make your final home-decorating decisions.

The pictures you snap with your smartphone can go to Evernote automatically so everything is available in one place. Tagging the photos ensures that your Evernote account stays organized.

Voting Smarter

You may not think that Evernote can be a big help on election day, but you can use it to keep yourself organized and aware of everything you need to know when you head to the polls.

During the weeks or months leading up to the vote, start clipping all your research and news articles into an election notebook. Create a checklist of qualities you want in candidates and how they rate, or post all the latest news on bills and propositions of concern to you. Don't forget to get the statistics and charts that help summarize information.

If you go through everything in your notebook in the days leading up to the election, you can create a list of how you want to vote. When the time comes, you'll have all your voting notes right there on your mobile device, making the process much quicker.

Monitoring Your Home Finances

Using Evernote for your daily finances is a fantastic way to keep track of everything you do without having messy countertops. Evernote can help you organize everything from all the receipts you accumulate during vacation to your regular bills. It's safe, too, because all your notes are securely stored on Evernote's servers.

You can use Evernote to track all your receipts so that you no longer have to worry about entering information from scraps of paper. Simply take a picture of the receipt on your phone. If you're shopping at a place that offers to e-mail the receipt to you, all you have to do is forward the e-mailed receipt to Evernote (a process that can be automated with IFTTT or Zapier; see Chapter 10) to be stored in a receipts notebook. At the end of the day, all purchases are in one notebook so that they're easy to follow. At tax time (ugh). this notebook can save countless hours of prep time, and if — heaven forbid — you're unlucky enough to be audited, the substantiation (as the Internal Revenue Service calls receipts) is readily at hand in one electronic place.

Your notes are safe and available even if your phone is stolen or if lose your tablet. Encryption really helps protect you in case of theft or loss. Check out Chapter 11 to set up encryption.

You can also e-mail sales information (such as coupons or special sales events) to your financial notebook or create a separate Sales and Bargains notebook so that you have it on hand when the time comes. This organization is especially helpful if you get information that you won't remember weeks later. You can also keep notes on gift ideas between holidays.

Creating a Memorable Baby Book

On its own, Evernote is a powerful tool for saving all cherished memories, but with Lil'Grams (`http://lilgrams.com`), it becomes a way to create a memorable baby book so that you never miss a shot or important "first" of your baby. Lil'Grams makes creating and electronically sharing baby albums fast and easy. The website offers numerous packages, starting at $19 a year for 1GB of storage. Check out `http://lilgrams.com/guides/evernote` to set up and link your accounts.

After you link your Lil'Grams and Evernote accounts, all you have to do is let Lil'Grams know which tags and notebooks to associate with your account, and it automatically pulls them into your Lil'Grams account. Then all you have to do is add notes to your baby book to let people know what's going on in the picture.

You set your own privacy settings and decide who has access. Lil'Grams and Evernote ensure that your information stays secure. Linking the two accounts makes sharing the latest on your baby much easier than scrapbooking or even e-mailing.

Creating a Notebook for School Information

The amount of information that schools send home with students is staggering. Evernote gives you a couple of ways to keep your student's information easy to access, depending on whether you prefer to scan or take pictures. For any paperwork that comes home, whether in the mail or in your child's backpack, scan it as soon as it arrives, and move it into a school-specific notebook.

You can also scan homework assignments (assigned and completed). No longer will the dog eat the homework.

I strongly recommend putting any forms or other items that need your signature in a location where they're easy to access or tagging them for easy retrieval. Use reminders to stay on top of due dates.

You can also track events with Evernote and Google Calendar. To keep up with school events, connect your Evernote account with Google Calendar or use KanMeet (see Chapter 16), and you'll have all school appointments, notes, and forms in one place.

See Chapter 22 for more ways to use Evernote for school-related notes.

Managing Your Shopping Lists

If you're like me, you've spent several days diligently writing down what you need at the store on a single piece of paper, only to forget the list when you actually head to the store. Thanks to Evernote, you don't have to worry about forgetting your list because you can write your list right on your mobile device and take it with you.

Evernote's check boxes are especially helpful for creating task lists and marking items off as completed. You might create a list of regular shopping items and simply check those that you need to buy on the next grocery run.

 If you prefer to continue keeping a physical list so that other people can jot down things you need, just remember to take a picture periodically and update the note with the latest additions. This simple technique ensures that you have most, if not all, of your shopping list every time you go to the store.

Maintaining a Home Inventory

A special combination of Evernote and storage totes can make your home, garage, and closets so neat that you look like you're the most organized person in town. Here's what to do:

1. **Pack a storage box with the items you want to keep out of sight but nicely organized.**

2. **Place a label on the outside for tracking.**

3. **Take a picture of the contents.**

   Try to include the exterior label in the picture.

4. **Add text to Evernote detailing what's in the box.**

   Don't forget to note the box's location in your home (a specific closet or the garage, for example).

Now when you need to find items, it's so simple and quick that you'll wonder how you used to find stuff. It's also useful for providing the information to the insurance company. Getting it on file will help you if the unthinkable happens and you need a list of what you lost.

Having twice suffered substantial storm damage accompanied by long-lasting power outages, I can attest that having a detailed inventory in Evernote makes filing claims infinitely easier, quicker, and less stressful.

Keeping a Light-Bulb Database

Tracking your light-bulb use through a database in Evernote really illuminates the application's abilities. Track how long light bulbs are lasting, which lamps or sockets seem to be defective, or which bulbs seem to work best for your home. All you have to do is start a note with the types of bulbs you have and which rooms and lamps have which light bulbs. Take pictures so you can match bulbs easily at the store. You'll not only save money, but also see which bulbs work best in different parts of the house. You can also create a bulb checklist and check off what you need to shop for. As manufacturers are mandated to phase out incandescent bulbs, and we're all slowly moving to alternatives such as LED, fluorescent, and halogen bulbs, keeping a light-bulb database in Evernote is very helpful.

Listing Your Packing Information

Packing for a trip is challenging enough without having to keep track of a paper copy of your packing list. Evernote makes dealing with lists much easier and even gives you a way of checking things off on your mobile device. Whether you're packing your suitcase or doing some last-minute shopping, your packing list is always right there with you.

Create a checklist of things you need to pack, and mark them off as you load them into your suitcase. You can add things to the list over time so that you no longer have to rely on your memory while you dash about to gather everything together.

You can even create a list of all your traveling items with pictures of what's in them and what the cases or bags look like so that you'll know exactly what goes missing if you leave a bag behind or if something gets lost on the way to your destination.

Planning Your Next Vacation

There's much more to vacationing than just packing. With so many places to go and things to do, tracking everything can be overwhelming unless you have Evernote to organize and plan your vacation.

From the start, you can do the research and create comparison notes to help you decide where you (and maybe your family) want to go. After you decide where you want to go, you need to figure out what you want to do. Create a schedule or clip pages that tell you the opening times for theme parks, hotels, restaurants, or anywhere else you want to go. Add all your travel plans for planes, trains, and automobiles, with pictures of reservations and restaurant reviews for good measure.

Before long, you'll want to plan all holidays and vacations with Evernote. If you're the type who plans in detail, you can map out your schedule down to the minute, barring the unexpected. If you prefer to keep your options open, you'll have a way to find out which things of interest are open on any particular day. It's your notebook; have it all your way.

Chapter 22

Ten School Shortcuts

This chapter is for students. Evernote may not be able to help you clean out your locker, but with a little bit of time and effort, it can work marvels on the organization of your book bag and binders, and even help you remember your gym clothes or the campus bus schedule.

Taking Notes in Class

Do you have a teacher who likes to show slide shows or write all over the chalkboard? Nowadays, homework is often posted on the Internet, but some old-school teachers may still expect you to jot down assignments from the board. Fortunately, no matter which method you use, Evernote offers you a couple of ways to record your notes and assignments in one place. Also, the built-in annotation features let you mark up the pictures while the information is still fresh.

If you have a laptop and love typing your notes, Evernote gives you a single place to get everything into one application; you don't have to try to remember where you stored the information. Simply type a quick blurb in Evernote, give it a time/date stamp, and then attach whatever file you were working on (such as a spreadsheet, a graphic, or even a web page) to that note. The process takes you an additional 2 minutes and saves you 20 minutes of searching for everything later.

You can also scan or photograph class handouts so that everything is in one place for ease of review before test time.

Evernote does an amazing job with scanned handwritten notes, too. Check out Chapter 6 to find out how to scan into Evernote. See the next section for details on how Evernote recognizes your handwriting.

For me, keeping everything in one note —audio, text, images, and even my chicken-scratched handwriting — adds significant power to finding what I need.

Recognizing and Accessing Your Handwritten Notes

Maybe you don't have a laptop, and your cellphone's battery is dead. Occasionally, you may have to resort to handwritten notes, but Evernote has them covered too.

As always, your scanner or smartphone (so long as you keep it charged) is going to save your bacon and get your handwritten notes into Evernote. And you won't lose your ability to search for these notes because Evernote reads your handwriting and interprets all but the worst handwriting (although for the sake of your own reading, you should probably aim to keep the writing clear). You no longer have to worry about someone "borrowing" your notes or having them get drenched in the rain. Now they're backed up and ready to go whenever you need them.

Going Paperless

Binders can become obsolete if you get organized in Evernote. On the first day of school, keeping up with all the teachers' handouts used to mean a messy backpack at the end of the day. How on earth are you supposed to track it all, keep up with your new schedule, and get to the next class on time with this increasing mountain of paperwork? Easy. Evernote to the rescue.

Before you even go to class, use a scanner or your smartphone to capture your schedule so that all you need is your phone (make sure the battery stays charged) or other mobile device to get around. (See Chapter 18 for more on how to scan notes.)

When you get to class, you can take an extra couple of minutes to take pictures. Are you afraid that you won't have time to take pictures and still dash across campus in the next 15 minutes? Place all your syllabi in your book bag and scan them in when you get home. Use reminders to track your due dates.

You can also use to-do lists to track what you need to do each week for school. Make sure to enter that information the first evening so that you can make the most of it right from the start of the semester. An Evernote to-do list helps you track each class's important assignments (such as research assignments, midterms, and finals) right off the syllabus.

Lugging Textbooks No More!

Back pain has historically been an issue for students — it's almost a rite of passage — but with Evernote, you can work your brain without punishing your back. For large books, either scan the pages into Evernote or use your camera phone to collect pictures of the pages you need to study. The process is fast, easy, and painless. Your back thanks you in advance.

Managing Your Life

With so many things to track in college, keeping up with everything is a real juggling act, especially with the many applications (calendars, e-mail, alarms, Facebook, Twitter, and on and on) required to schedule your day. Although this tracking is excellent practice for what life will be like after college, you may wish for a way to make organization and socializing easier. Enter Evernote. Check out Chapter 16 to see how to connect Google Calendar or KanMeet to Evernote. See Chapter 17 for several apps that make keeping track of appointments, study sessions, club meetings, and fun activities effortless. Chapter 6 tells you how to use social media and e-mail with Evernote.

You can create tags and notebooks to track various events, such as sporting events, student-government meetings, and clubs you want to visit. Store everything in one place, and you'll know what you have going on every day and night of the week.

Remembering Your Numbers

When school starts, tracking all the random numbers thrown at you can be an insurmountable task. Classroom numbers, class times, phone numbers, important dates, and personal information take a lot of effort to track if you don't have a handy tool like Evernote. With Evernote, you can easily store all this information and access details when you need them. Keep up with everything from your student ID to your locker combination to addresses to classroom numbers without having to dig through a packed book bag.

Remember to encrypt sensitive information. It takes only a second more. Encryption is discussed in Chapter 11.

Shopping and Window Shopping

It's Monday, and you've found the perfect school-spirit shirt and hat, but you don't have the money to buy them right now. You get paid Friday and want to come back. The only problem is that you're in a different part of town, and you don't know the name of the place. Take a quick picture of the clothing and the name of the shop, and you're good to go. You can come back any time to pick up your stuff (as long as the store doesn't sell out first).

Another excellent time to use Evernote for shopping is when it's time to buy school textbooks. You can go to the school bookstore to take pictures of the books that you need for class and then access the pictures from home to compare prices on the Internet. If you can find the book online for less money, even with shipping, you have no reason to pay more money as long as you can wait until the book arrives. And now you may be able to go back and buy that shirt and hat you were looking at a couple of stores ago!

Making Documents Smarter

Often, you can find books and information you need online as PDF files. In addition, many college libraries offer short stories and books as PDFs, and some college instructors even choose to forgo traditional textbooks in favor of PDFs so they can control the information contained therein. Evernote is a great place to store them all so you can access them anywhere at any time.

You also have document search to take advantage of. Any attached document, PDF, presentation, or spreadsheet created with Microsoft Office or iWork will show up in your search results across almost every Evernote platform.

Organizing Your Research

Researching today is nothing like it was even a decade ago. The Internet has so much information of varying quality that finding reliable sources that won't disappear can lead to long nights. Also, you may still be required to use hardcopy sources, such as newspapers and magazines, for some of your work.

The good news is that Evernote can store all your research, regardless of the source. Clip pertinent information from the Internet or save entire web pages (see Chapter 4), scan or use your cellphone to take pictures of hard-copy text in the library (see Chapters 7 and 18), and share information for group projects through a shared notebook (see Chapter 10).

Recording Important Lectures

Typing isn't always practical in class, especially if you aren't a terribly efficient typist. With a mobile device, particularly a cellphone, you can make an audio recording of everything that your teacher says and that the class discusses.

You don't want to be distracted by taking notes; it's better to concentrate on listening to and thinking about the discussion. Also, starting and stopping your recorder can be a big distraction. So record the entire discussion so that you can listen the first time through and get reinforced on the lecture or conversation later. The Evernote size limits are generous, and the new apps for smartphones make recording a note as easy as tapping. On my iPhone, I found the recorded quality to be excellent.

Be sure to follow the rules when it comes to recording lectures. Some teachers and schools have no problem with it, but others forbid it. If a teacher doesn't allow class recordings, he or she typically adds that notice to the class syllabus or mentions it early in the semester. If you're unsure, always ask ahead of time.

If you have a larger budget, products like Livescribe (described in Chapter 18) let you capture thousands of handwritten notes and 200 hours of audio while carrying nothing more weighty than a pen.

Chapter 23

Ten Best Business Uses

*E*vernote can be useful for every aspect of your life, both personal and business. Evernote Business (http://evernote.com/business) has powerful sharing and collaboration features for teams. It's a good way for team members to collaborate while giving them their own personal Evernote accounts and private notes. Whether you're a small-business owner or an executive, you may never completely separate your business and personal lives. Evernote can help you organize even the most stressful aspects of your life. Making your business streamlined and more efficient has never been easier. This chapter shows you ten ways you can take a load off your mind by using Evernote as your loyal assistant.

Generating and Capturing Ideas

Inspiration is one of the hardest things to create, let along capture. Waking up in the middle of the night to find a full writing pad or no pencil means that your brilliant ideas may be gone by daybreak. Odds are that you have your smartphone close by. After all, smartphones have become alarms, e-mail conduits, and work devices for many people. When you have a middle-of-the-night brainstorm, use Evernote on your mobile device to record the idea.

Why not make your smartphone useful in another positive way? When you see something interesting on the Internet, clip it to an ideas notebook. When inspiration strikes, jot down notes or take pictures, and expand your thoughts later. With Evernote, it's always easy to capture ideas and save them for later.

Doing Your Research

As all business owners know, research isn't just for students; it's also a requirement for every successful business.

If you have a project that involves research, create a new notebook, and start clipping your research into it. With most of the Web Clipper implementations, saving a page is as quick as highlighting and clicking or tapping. If your research leads you to the library or to an off-site location, make sure to have your camera or smartphone fully charged; then take snapshots of the pages, storefronts, or other items you need. If you need information from numerous pages in a book, you can use a scanner to get what you need so that you don't fill your phone with individual pictures. When the time comes to pull all the research together, you have a single notebook that covers everything.

Many scanners can be set up to scan directly into Evernote, such as ScanSnap Evernote Edition (see Chapter 18), which is what I use.

Saving Material to Read Later

If you find a great article in a magazine while you're at the dentist's office and know you won't have time to read it until later, use your phone to capture the article in a note that you can view when you have more time. If you're surfing the web while you're waiting in a ticket line and come across a breaking-news story, clip it to Evernote for later perusal. Check out Chapter 7 for details on using your smartphone to take pictures in Evernote or to clip websites. Web clipping is covered in Chapter 4.

No matter where you are or what you're doing, you can capture text to read when you have time. All you need are your mobile device and Evernote.

Planning Your Day More Effectively

You know what they say about the best-laid plans of mice and men, but Evernote helps consolidate your lists and activities to maximize your efficiency, barring the unexpected, and update them when the unexpected happens. Use Evernote to create a list of all your daily activities, from opening a shop to setting up your morning workload. Make sure to put your highest priorities at the top of the list.

Mynd Calendar (`http://myndcalendar.com`) is a mobile calendar for iOS devices. It's an on-the-go virtual assistant, keeping track of both your personal and professional responsibilities. It works by learning about you, your activities, and your needs and then delivering relevant information to help you get things done. The more you use it, the more you train it, so the information it presents to you becomes more relevant, further simplifying and organizing your life.

If you have a Google Calendar account, you can access it from Evernote, and vice versa, by using KanMeet (see Chapter 16).

Calculating Expenses the Easy Way

Depending on your preference, you can scan or take pictures of your notes and receipts and then save them in an expenses notebook.

To track bills and expenses separately without having to store them in different notebooks, you can keep a single spreadsheet. At the end of the day, mark expenses as entered so that you won't have to wonder whether you've already recorded them; then flip over to another tab and do the same for bills.

Plenty of apps and other accessories can help you get and stay organized if you want a more advanced method of handling your expenses. The Evernote App Center (`http://appcenter.evernote.com`) is the best place to find reliable apps that are known to work well with Evernote.

For expense reporting, consider Expensify (see Chapter 17), a web-based expense management tool that makes it easy to import expenses and scan receipts. Simply add receipt images to the Expensify notebook in your Evernote account.

Collaborating and Whiteboarding

Most collaborative sessions end up being more about trying to record everything that's being discussed than they are about generating ideas. At your next collaborative effort, whether it involves storyboarding or whiteboarding, bring Evernote to record ideas.

After you have an idea fully developed on the screen or board, snap a picture, save it to a new note, erase the board, and keep brainstorming. Just make sure to save the note with each addition you make. You can save up to ten pictures from each session and add other notes if you need more. When you want to review the notes later, you can. Evernote has developed recognition software just for reading images, enabling you to run searches on the text in photos. Check out Chapter 8 to find out more about running searches on images.

Premium and Business subscribers have a distinct advantage, because all team members can write in shared notebooks. Distributing ideas through a single medium is a vast improvement over e-mail and shared locations that can't be accessed from everywhere. Now you can collaborate without losing focus on what's important, and you won't have to worry about forgetting brilliant ideas, which can be fleeting.

Creating Mood Boards

A storyboarding or whiteboarding session (see the preceding section) helps develop established ideas, and mood boards get everyone thinking along the same lines. Generally used for design projects, *mood boards* are collages of ideas, illustrations, and colors that help establish the base of the project and the direction. A mood board is the perfect type of project for organization with Evernote.

Mood boards are about visual presentation, but you have to do your research first. Starting with a new notebook, clip images and graphics into the notebook. You can use as many notes as you like. When you feel that you have enough to start putting together the collage, create a new note, and put your collection of notes together in an aesthetically pleasing display. Not sure that the first version works for you? Make a second note, and try again.

Archiving and Retrieving Articles and Blogs

You've probably found websites that you loved or words of wisdom that made you feel better but couldn't find them later. You never know when websites will just disappear, of course. With Evernote, it doesn't matter whether those pages, blogs, or articles are unceremoniously yanked from Internet existence. By simply clipping them into Evernote as you find them, you create an archive so that you can always retrieve them when you want them.

The best way to make sure that you can find items later is to tag them. (Chapter 8 provides details on tagging.) Make sure to use a tag that's descriptive but not too specific. You don't want to make such a specific tag that you can't remember it later. Tags make it easy to locate your notes in the All

Notes or All Notebooks area without having to remember where you saved them. You can also use Postach.io (see Chapter 17) to make a blog out of an Evernote notebook.

Planning for Year-End Taxes

As a business owner, you know that the amount of paperwork associated with taxes makes tax season just about unbearable. Completing taxes is always a chore, but Evernote can help streamline the process.

As you collect tax-related information throughout the year, scan or photograph the items into notes and save them in a tax notebook. This step makes sure that all your tax information is in a central location instead of being spread over many locations. Add your statements, receipts, charitable donations, and basic business information (such as ID and address) to the notebook. Save your tax form from last year in the folder to speed up filling out this year's form. When it's time to pull everything together, you have everything you need in one notebook.

After the painful process is over for the current year, don't forget to save your completed tax information so that it's available for next year.

You can also use FileThis Fetch for Evernote (https://filethis.com) to import online account statements and send them to your Evernote account each month. Documents are delivered as searchable PDF files and organized in account-specific notebooks in a single Evernote notebook stack. FileThis fetches all the past documents that are available online, so you have access to all your statements anywhere you have access to Evernote.

Tracking Customer Relationships

Businesses thrive by relating to their customers and managing these relationships. In Evernote Business for Salesforce, Evernote has teamed with Salesforce to make it easy to store your proposals and any supporting documents in notes and then share those notes directly with customers. You can share items such as proposals, research, reports, spreadsheets, and other documents.

The benefit of this partnership is that Evernote Business lets you consolidate all paperwork, including signed contracts. Paper contracts can be scanned into Evernote, and signed PDFs you've received via e-mail can be forwarded directly to Evernote Business. Find out more about Evernote for Salesforce at http://evernote.com/business/uses/salesforce.

Appendix

Evernote for Developers

● ●

More than 8,000 developers are working on apps and customizations for Evernote, and that number is growing by leaps and bounds. This chapter is geared to developers who want to build Evernote support into their own applications and to those who want to extend Evernote's capabilities.

Before starting to develop applications for Evernote, I suggest that you gain some experience using scripting, which is covered in Chapter 19. In this appendix, I assume that you're familiar with the information in that chapter.

Getting Started with the Evernote API

The website for Evernote developers is `http://dev.evernote.com`. Evernote's application programming interface (API) lets your applications access the Evernote service by using the same protocols that are used under the covers by Evernote's own client software.

The most powerful way to integrate with Evernote is to develop based on directives sent to the Evernote web-service API. The API enables you to access a user's account in the cloud, whether or not that user has an Evernote client installed on the machine (so long as he or she has an Evernote account and Internet connectivity). With the API, you can create, search, read, update, and delete notes, notebooks, and tags. This ability to access the user's account on the web eliminates concerns about whether the local version of Evernote has been synchronized. Of course, anything not synced to the server from your client before invoking the script will not be seen by the server and is not reflected in the results when the script is executed.

Another way to develop an app that works with Evernote is to develop for one of Evernote's mobile client applications on a user's desktop computer or mobile device. Use the following links to find out more about the platform that you're interested in developing for:

Using dynamic interfaces

You can view the Evernote mobile-web application by using plain or dynamic interfaces. The plain interface targets a larger variety of mobile devices and has a simple and flat navigational design. The dynamic interface targets higher-end devices with browsers that support JavaScript and touch navigation. Evernote attempts to deduce which type of interface to use based on the incoming HTTP requests. A perfect match isn't guaranteed, however.

✔ **Android:** Android apps can work with the Evernote web-service API and with intents (see the next paragraph). See `https://dev.evernote.com/doc/start/android.php`.

Three of the core components of an Android application — activities, services, and broadcast receivers — are activated through messages, called *intents.*

✔ **iOS (iPhone, iPad, and iPod touch):** The great popularity of iOS devices, the simplicity of development with Objective-C Cocoa, and the quality of Evernote support have made iOS the most popular development platform for Evernote. See `http://dev.evernote.com/doc/start/ios.php`.

✔ **Mac:** Evernote for Mac has great support for AppleScript, as discussed in Chapter 19. See `http://dev.evernote.com/doc/articles/applescript.php`.

✔ **Windows:** Applications integrate with Evernote for Windows by passing command-line options to the `Evernote.exe` and `ENScript.exe` executables. Interface notes are provided at `http://dev.evernote.com/doc/articles/enscript.php`.

Note: Evernote scripting isn't supported for the BlackBerry operating system at this time. Evernote has considered creating a JME code generator for Thrift to produce Java mobile stubs for the API that would work on BlackBerry and other JME-based devices.

Registering for an API key

To get the Evernote API and all the goodies it provides, you need to request a free API key. Follow these steps:

1. **Navigate to** `http://dev.evernote.com/doc/articles/permissions.php`**.**

2. **Click Get an API Key.**

3. **Complete the online form (see Figure A-1).**

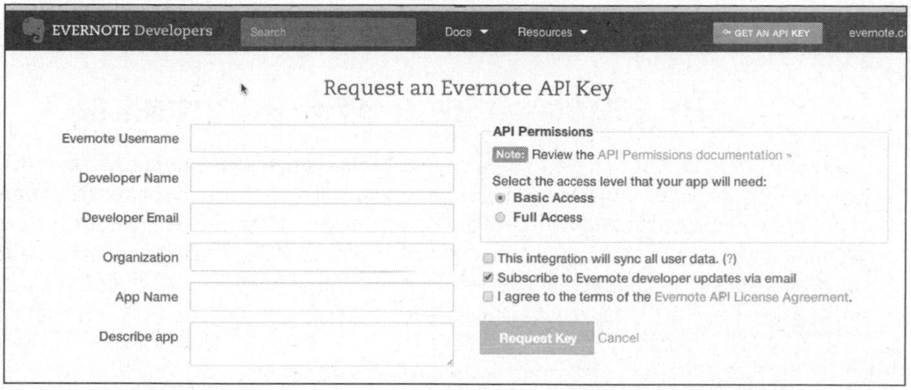

EVERNOTE Developers   Search   Docs ▾   Resources ▾   ☞ GET AN API KEY   evernote.c

Request an Evernote API Key

Evernote Username

Developer Name

Developer Email

Organization

App Name

Describe app

API Permissions

Note: Review the API Permissions documentation »

Select the access level that your app will need:
- Basic Access
- Full Access

☐ This integration will sync all user data. (?)
☑ Subscribe to Evernote developer updates via email
☐ I agree to the terms of the Evernote API License Agreement.

[Request Key] Cancel

Figure A-1:
Complete
this form to
request an
API key.

4. **Choose the access permissions that your application will need:**

   - *Basic access:* For apps that create new content in Evernote but don't read or update existing content

   - *Full access:* For apps that create, read, and update notes, notebooks, and tags

   Details on the permissions granted for each type of access are available at http://dev.evernote.com/doc/articles/permissions.php. If you request a full-access API key, you need to justify the permissions when you request activation of your API key on the production service. If your application doesn't require permission to read existing notes or update existing notes, notebooks, or tags, Evernote removes the unused permissions during the activation process and works with you to retest your application.

5. **If your app needs to sync Evernote, select the check box titled This Integration Will Sync All User Data.**

6. **(Optional) If you want, select the check box titled Subscribe to Evernote Developer Updates via Email.**

7. **Select the check box titled I Agree to the terms of the Evernote API License Agreement.**

8. **Click Request Key.**

   The key is sent to you by e-mail.

Registering for a web-service key

Client keys require a username and password for authentication, and can be used by desktop and mobile client applications that allow one user to log in per session. You need this type of key if your application accesses Evernote as a single user at a time. It's delivered as described in the preceding section.

If you want to develop a server application that is Evernote-aware and that many users can connect to, you need a web-service key.

Evernote's web-service API is provided under the terms of the Evernote API license agreement, which is available at http://dev. evernote.com/doc/reference/api_ license.php.

Testing your application

When you receive your key, you can test your application. The test server's host name is http://sandbox.evernote.com. Initially, the API key works against http://sandbox.evernote.com but not against www.evernote. com. Evernote can activate the API key on the production system after you let it know that you're ready to go live. Also, you need to let Evernote know by e-mail if you want to change any detail of the service configuration, such as organization name and session duration. Details are provided when you apply for the key, which is free.

For web-service keys, users authorize your application to access their account for up to 24 hours for a testing period, with full permission to read and modify their accounts. Contact Evernote if you'd like to change the access duration or user permissions.

Keep an eye on the developer forum at http://discussion.evernote. com/forum/61-evernote-for-developers to stay on top of any changes that can affect developers.

Authorizing an application for authentication

Evernote users entrust Evernote with important information, so security and authentication are important considerations to ensure that data can't be hacked. For this reason, Evernote needs to know who you are and to ensure that your code is authorized to access the user's information. The account and authentication information for every user is bundled into a logical component called the UserStore. According to Evernote, a user's notebooks and all of the contents (notes, tags, resources, saved searches, and so on) are maintained within the NoteStore component of the Evernote service. The NoteStore is responsible for maintaining the correct data model for each notebook in a persistent transactional database.

For local (desktop or mobile) client applications, the primary function of the UserStore is to authenticate a user to create an authentication token. An authentication token is required for any requests to access private data via the NoteStore API. You ask for and then get a token, and you're granted access to the NoteStore for a short time.

Here are considerations for using UserStore:

- **Local access:** Local (single-user) applications can take a username and password from an Evernote user. The user's login information isn't transferred to any third parties; it's used only for direct authentication to Evernote's servers (over SSL).

- **OAuth:** OAuth (`http://oauth.net`) is an open protocol for publishing and interacting with protected data. It's also a safe, secure way of granting access to secure data. The idea is that if you're storing protected data on your users' behalf, they shouldn't be spreading their passwords around the web to get access to it. OAuth gives your users access to their data while protecting their account credentials. Therefore, web applications that need to access data from multiple Evernote accounts shouldn't retrieve an authentication token via a username and password; instead, they should use OAuth to receive authorization via the OAuth protocol.

  Evernote has implemented an OAuth service provider that complies with a profile (subset) of the OAuth 1.0 Protocol as defined in RFC 5849, available at `http://tools.ietf.org/html/rfc5849`.

- **XML:** Evernote uses Extensible Markup Language (XML), a set of rules for encoding documents in machine-readable form. XHTML (Extensible Hypertext Markup Language) is a general name for a family of standards-based markup languages that mirror or extend versions of the widely used Hypertext Markup Language (HTML). The current version of HTML is HTML5, which is still being refined. See `http://dev.w3.org/html5/html4-differences/#refsHTML` for more information about HTML5.

- **EDAM and ENML:** Evernote's accessibility is based on an API called Evernote Data Access and Management (EDAM) protocol. The related Evernote Markup Language (ENML) is a flavor of XHTML designed to provide secure, portable document representation that can be rendered on various clients and platforms. The service validates the note content against the document type definition (DTD) before accepting any call to `NoteStore.createNote()` or `NoteStore.updateNote()`.

Gaining Secure Programmatic Access to Evernote

Evernote's API provides secure access for your trusted local or web-based applications, using the same network communications that are used by Evernote's own client software. In the following sections, I discuss secure access to Evernote via programmatic interfaces.

EDAM

Evernote Data Access and Management (EDAM) allows secure access to account data via standard web protocols. This API is used internally by all of Evernote's own client applications, and Evernote has made this protocol available at no charge for third-party developers to integrate into their applications.

EDAM is designed to support both *thick* applications and *thin* applications. Thick applications remember how they left off even if the user moves to another application. These are known as *stateful* and include most desktop clients that maintain a full local copy of user data. *Thin* applications need to access only a small amount of current information at a given time, as with web services. They do not maintain a full local copy of user data. Thin applications vary a bit in how they securely authenticate users, but they use a common set of interfaces when authentication is complete.

Thrift

Thrift (`http://thrift.apache.org`) is a software framework for development of cross-language services. It's maintained by the Apache Software Foundation, which supports about 100 open-source projects, including Open Office.

Thrift enables you to define your own data types and service interfaces, called declarations, using a standardized and simple definition file. The Thrift compiler uses that file as input. Then the compiler generates code that developers can use, using the Remote Procedure Call (RPC) protocol to build RPC clients and servers for a variety of programming languages.

You can find the Evernote Thrift declarations at `https://github.com/evernote/evernote-sdk-js`. Also, a white paper describing Thrift is available at `http://thrift.apache.org/static/files/thrift-20070401.pdf`.

Keeping up with Evernote developers

The Developer Forum (`http://discussion.evernote.com/forum/61-evernote-for-developers`) is Evernote developers' private space, where technical development issues of interest to third-party developers can be discussed separately from end-user discussions.

Another resource is Techblog (`http://blog.evernote.com/tech`), which contains a lot of information on Evernote's inner workings. In addition, developers can find details on the Evernote API and on security and architecture, and peruse questions posed and answered by other developers.

API Software Development Kits

To get started using the API Software Development Kits, download them at `http://dev.evernote.com/doc`. These files contain documentation, Thrift declarations, and many useful sample codes that can help you understand the Evernote API and use it in your programming language of choice.

Exploring Open-Source Projects

If you want to develop an application to support and work with Evernote, it helps to see some examples of applications that other developers have created. Open-source projects are great ways to find out how to build an application that works with Evernote. Following are some of the open-source projects and applications that the Evernote developer community has produced:

- **Apple Aperture 3 to Evernote (AppleScript):** This simple program posts image thumbnails from Aperture right into Evernote.

- **Delicious bookmarks importer (Perl):** This code takes an export file from Delicious and imports the bookmarks into Evernote.

- **Emacs Evernote mode (Ruby):** Emacs Evernote mode is a collection of code that offers functions for viewing and editing Evernote notes directly from Emacs, which is an extensible open-source text editor.

- **en4j (Java):** This code is a Java replacement for Evernote desktop client applications.

- **Everboard (PHP):** This online idea board, which is integrated with the Evernote API, takes its inspiration from a traditional corkboard or wall with lots of photos, images, and sketches pasted to it to form a collective theme. It enables you to visualize your notebooks in a unique way and to share your inspiration with your collaborators in real time.

- **CFEvernote (ColdFusion):** This project is a ColdFusion implementation of the Evernote API. ColdFusion is a server-side scripting language.

- **Evernote RubyGem (Ruby):** This project is a high-level wrapper around Evernote's Thrift-generated Ruby code that enables you to create some simple wrapper classes for using Evernote in your Ruby applications.

- **Journler to Evernote (AppleScript):** This project converts Journler entries to Evernote notes.

- **NeverNote (Java):** This open-source clone of Evernote is designed to run on Linux.

- **NoteScraper (AppleScript):** This script exports your Kindle notes and highlights to Evernote.

- **Veritrope (AppleScript):** The Evernote page at `http://veritrope.com/tech/evernote-applescript-resources-and-accessories` enables you to share your bits of AppleScript with others or find snippets of code you can reuse in your own AppleScript projects.

Other resources

GitHub is the main repository for open-source code. For Evernote-related code, navigate to `https://github.com/evernote`.

Complete Evernote developer documentation is available at `http://dev.evernote.com/doc`. There, you can obtain quick-start guides for your favorite supported development platforms, including Android, JavaScript, Python, Ruby, and iOS.

Evernote SDKs are available for these platforms:

- ActionScript 3
- Android
- C++
- C#
- iOS
- Java
- JavaScript
- Mac OS X
- Perl
- PHP
- Python
- Ruby

Index

• F •

About the Author

David E. Y. Sarna is a writer and a technologist. He has more than 43 years of experience as a management consultant and as an executive of high-technology companies. He has been a director of publicly traded companies specializing in computer technology and has served as chairman of audit and compensation committees, as well as in an advisory position to the boards of directors of public, private, and not-for-profit organizations. He also served on the advisory board of Hudson Venture Partners. As an entrepreneur, David attracted investments from first-tier venture capital firms, and he has taken two companies public on the NASDAQ through underwritten offerings.

David has authored or co-authored six books, holds several patents, and has published 120 articles in professional magazines and in major publications such as *The Washington Post* and *The Jerusalem Post*. His books include *Evernote For Dummies* (John Wiley & Sons, Inc., 2012), *PC Magazine Windows Rapid Application Development* (Ziff-Davis Press, 1994; translated into several languages), and *Implementing and Developing Cloud Computing Applications* (CRC Press, 2010). He is currently working on a book about the Talmud and is finishing his first novel.

David is married and has three grown children. He makes his home in northern New Jersey.

Dedication

This book, which helps you remember everything, is lovingly dedicated to my favorite dear aunt, Edith Maagan, who recently celebrated her 92nd birthday, and who (unlike me) still has instant command and recall of all her memories.

Author's Acknowledgments

Charlotte Kughen is a great, sensitive, and thoughtful editor; this book has benefited greatly from her efforts, as well as from the support of all of the other hardworking folks at Wiley.

Amy Fandrei, acquisitions editor, admirably picked up where her predecessor, Bob Woerner, left off, running with the ball to score a touchdown.

Kelly Ewing, Kathy Simpson, and Michelle Krasniak helped make the first and second editions of this book look and feel like all the great books in the Wiley *For Dummies* series. Vanessa Richie also assisted greatly in writing the first edition.

My literary agent Bill Gladstone and his colleague Carole Jelen at Waterside Productions saw the potential of this book and prodded me to get it done, despite many distractions.

Phil Libin, CEO of Evernote, enthusiastically supported this project, and all of the folks at Evernote, especially Andrew Sinkov and Mie Yaginuma, contributed freely of their prodigious expertise in all matters Evernote — and beyond.

I would be remiss if I did not thank Dr. Fabian Bitan, Dr. Todd Albert, Dr. Neil Lyman, Dr. Lyle Dennis, and Dr. Yair Litvin, who helped me through some difficult medical issues while the first edition of this book was being written, and who continue doing the Lord's work in managing my care.

As always, my family has been helpful in ways small and large.

Publisher's Acknowledgments

Acquisitions Editor: Amy Fandrei

Project Editor: Charlotte Kughen

Copy Editor: Kathy Simpson

Technical Editors: Michelle Krasniak and Mie Yaginuma

Editorial Assistant: Annie Sullivan

Sr. Editorial Assistant: Cherie Case

Project Coordinator: Melissa Cossell

Cover Image: Background © iStockphoto.com/ JacobH; tablet PC © iStockphoto.com/ hohos; smartphone © iStockphoto.com/ pictafolio; laptop © iStockphoto.com/ppart; screen images © iStockphoto.com/hddigital; icons © iStockphoto.com/katnipjones

Apple & Mac

iPad For Dummies,
5th Edition
978-1-118-49823-1

iPhone 5 For Dummies,
6th Edition
978-1-118-35201-4

MacBook For Dummies,
4th Edition
978-1-118-20920-2

OS X Mountain Lion
For Dummies
978-1-118-39418-2

Blogging & Social Media

Facebook For Dummies,
4th Edition
978-1-118-09562-1

Mom Blogging
For Dummies
978-1-118-03843-7

Pinterest For Dummies
978-1-118-32800-2

WordPress For Dummies,
5th Edition
978-1-118-38318-6

Business

Commodities For Dummies,
2nd Edition
978-1-118-01687-9

Investing For Dummies,
6th Edition
978-0-470-90545-6

Personal Finance
For Dummies,
7th Edition
978-1-118-11785-9

QuickBooks 2013
For Dummies
978-1-118-35641-8

Small Business Marketing Kit
For Dummies,
3rd Edition
978-1-118-31183-7

Careers

Job Interviews
For Dummies,
4th Edition
978-1-118-11290-8

Job Searching with
Social Media
For Dummies
978-0-470-93072-4

Personal Branding
For Dummies
978-1-118-11792-7

Resumes For Dummies,
6th Edition
978-0-470-87361-8

Success as a Mediator
For Dummies
978-1-118-07862-4

Diet & Nutrition

Belly Fat Diet For Dummies
978-1-118-34585-6

Eating Clean For Dummies
978-1-118-00013-7

Nutrition For Dummies,
5th Edition
978-0-470-93231-5

Digital Photography

Digital Photography
For Dummies,
7th Edition
978-1-118-09203-3

Digital SLR Cameras &
Photography For Dummies,
4th Edition
978-1-118-14489-3

Photoshop Elements 11
For Dummies
978-1-118-40821-6

Gardening

Herb Gardening
For Dummies,
2nd Edition
978-0-470-61778-6

Vegetable Gardening
For Dummies,
2nd Edition
978-0-470-49870-5

Health

Anti-Inflammation Diet
For Dummies
978-1-118-02381-5

Diabetes For Dummies,
3rd Edition
978-0-470-27086-8

Living Paleo For Dummies
978-1-118-29405-5

Hobbies

Beekeeping
For Dummies
978-0-470-43065-1

eBay For Dummies,
7th Edition
978-1-118-09806-6

Raising Chickens
For Dummies
978-0-470-46544-8

Wine For Dummies,
5th Edition
978-1-118-28872-6

Writing Young Adult Fiction
For Dummies
978-0-470-94954-2

Language &
Foreign Language

500 Spanish Verbs
For Dummies
978-1-118-02382-2

English Grammar
For Dummies,
2nd Edition
978-0-470-54664-2

French All in One
For Dummies
978-1-118-22815-9

German Essentials
For Dummies
978-1-118-18422-6

Italian For Dummies,
2nd Edition
978-1-118-00465-4

 Available in print and e-book formats.

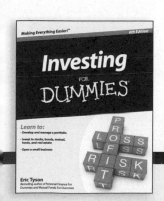

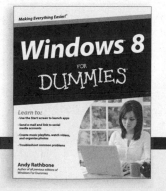

Math & Science

Algebra I For Dummies,
2nd Edition
978-0-470-55964-2

Anatomy and Physiology
For Dummies,
2nd Edition
978-0-470-92326-9

Astronomy For Dummies,
3rd Edition
978-1-118-37697-3

Biology For Dummies,
2nd Edition
978-0-470-59875-7

Chemistry For Dummies,
2nd Edition
978-1-1180-0730-3

Pre-Algebra Essentials
For Dummies
978-0-470-61838-7

Microsoft Office

Excel 2013 For Dummies
978-1-118-51012-4

Office 2013 All-in-One
For Dummies
978-1-118-51636-2

PowerPoint 2013
For Dummies
978-1-118-50253-2

Word 2013 For Dummies
978-1-118-49123-2

Music

Blues Harmonica
For Dummies
978-1-118-25269-7

Guitar For Dummies,
3rd Edition
978-1-118-11554-1

iPod & iTunes
For Dummies,
10th Edition
978-1-118-50864-0

Programming

Android Application
Development For
Dummies, 2nd Edition
978-1-118-38710-8

iOS 6 Application
Development For Dummies
978-1-118-50880-0

Java For Dummies,
5th Edition
978-0-470-37173-2

Religion & Inspiration

The Bible For Dummies
978-0-7645-5296-0

Buddhism For Dummies,
2nd Edition
978-1-118-02379-2

Catholicism For Dummies,
2nd Edition
978-1-118-07778-8

Self-Help & Relationships

Bipolar Disorder
For Dummies,
2nd Edition
978-1-118-33882-7

Meditation For Dummies,
3rd Edition
978-1-118-29144-3

Seniors

Computers For Seniors
For Dummies,
3rd Edition
978-1-118-11553-4

iPad For Seniors
For Dummies,
5th Edition
978-1-118-49708-1

Social Security
For Dummies
978-1-118-20573-0

Smartphones & Tablets

Android Phones
For Dummies
978-1-118-16952-0

Kindle Fire HD
For Dummies
978-1-118-42223-6

NOOK HD For Dummies,
Portable Edition
978-1-118-39498-4

Surface For Dummies
978-1-118-49634-3

Test Prep

ACT For Dummies,
5th Edition
978-1-118-01259-8

ASVAB For Dummies,
3rd Edition
978-0-470-63760-9

GRE For Dummies,
7th Edition
978-0-470-88921-3

Officer Candidate Tests,
For Dummies
978-0-470-59876-4

Physician's Assistant Exam
For Dummies
978-1-118-11556-5

Series 7 Exam
For Dummies
978-0-470-09932-2

Windows 8

Windows 8 For Dummies
978-1-118-13461-0

Windows 8 For Dummies,
Book + DVD Bundle
978-1-118-27167-4

Windows 8 All-in-One
For Dummies
978-1-118-11920-4

 Available in print and e-book formats.

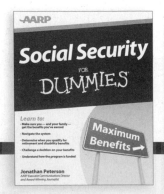

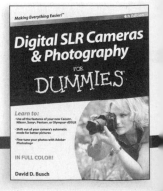

Take Dummies with you everywhere you go!

Whether you're excited about e-books, want more from the web, must have your mobile apps, or swept up in social media, Dummies makes everything easier .

Dummies products make life easier!

- DIY
- Consumer Electronics
- Crafts
- Software
- Cookware
- Hobbies
- Videos
- Music
- Games
- and More!

For more information, go to **Dummies.com®** and search the store by category.

A Wiley Brand